Philosophy and Politics - Critical Explorations

Volume 13

Series Editors
David M. Rasmussen, Boston College, Chestnut Hill, MA, USA
Alessandro Ferrara, Dipartimento di Storia, University of Rome 'Tor Vergata', Rome, Italy
Abdullah An-Na'im, Charles Howard Candler Professor of Law, Emory University, Atlanta, USA
Bruce Ackerman, Sterling Professor of Law, Yale University, New Haven, CT, USA
Robert Audi, O'Brien Professor of Philosophy at the University of Notre Dame, Notre Dame, IN, USA
Seyla Benhabib, Eugene Meyer Professor for Political Science and Philosophy, Yale University, New Haven, CT, USA
Samuel Freeman, Avalon Professor in the Humanities, University of Pennsylvania, Philadelphia, PA, USA
Jürgen Habermas, Professor Emeritus, Goethe-University, Frankfurt am Main, Frankfurt, Bayern, Germany
Axel Honneth, Goethe-University, Frankfurt am Main, Germany and Columbia University, New York, USA
Frankfurt am Main, New York, Germany
Erin Kelly, Professor of Philosophy, Tufts University, Medford, MA, USA
Charles Larmore, W. Duncan MacMillan Family Professor in the Humanities, Brown University, Providence, RI, USA
Frank Michelman, Professor Emeritus, Harvard University, Cambridge, MA, USA
Tong Shijun, Professor of Philosophy, East China Normal University, Shanghai, China
Charles Taylor, Professor Emeritus, McGill University, Montreal, Montreal, QC, Canada
Michael Walzer, Professor Emeritus, Institute of Advanced Study, Princeton, Princeton, NJ, USA

The purpose of Philosophy and Politics - Critical Explorations is to publish high quality volumes that reflect original research pursued at the juncture of philosophy and politics. Over the past 20 years new important areas of inquiry at the crossroads of philosophy and politics have undergone impressive developments or have emerged anew. Among these, new approaches to human rights, transitional justice, religion and politics and especially the challenges of a post-secular society, global justice, public reason, global constitutionalism, multiple democracies, political liberalism and deliberative democracy can be included. Philosophy and Politics - Critical Explorations addresses each and any of these interrelated yet distinct fields as valuable manuscripts and proposal become available, with the aim of both being the forum where single breakthrough studies in one specific subject can be published and at the same time the areas of overlap and the intersecting themes across the various areas can be composed in the coherent image of a highly dynamic disciplinary continent. Some of the studies published are bold theoretical explorations of one specific theme, and thus primarily addressed to specialists, whereas others are suitable for a broader readership and possibly for wide adoption in graduate courses. The series includes monographs focusing on a specific topic, as well as collections of articles covering a theme or collections of articles by one author. Contributions to this series come from scholars on every continent and from a variety of scholarly orientations.

More information about this series at http://www.springer.com/series/13508

Volker Kaul

Identity and the Difficulty of Emancipation

Volker Kaul
Department of Political Science
LUISS 'Guido Carli' University
Rome, Italy

ISSN 2352-8370   ISSN 2352-8389   (electronic)
Philosophy and Politics - Critical Explorations
ISBN 978-3-030-52374-9   ISBN 978-3-030-52375-6   (eBook)
https://doi.org/10.1007/978-3-030-52375-6

© The Editor(s) (if applicable) and The Author(s), under exclusive license to Springer Nature Switzerland AG 2020
This work is subject to copyright. All rights are solely and exclusively licensed by the Publisher, whether the whole or part of the material is concerned, specifically the rights of translation, reprinting, reuse of illustrations, recitation, broadcasting, reproduction on microfilms or in any other physical way, and transmission or information storage and retrieval, electronic adaptation, computer software, or by similar or dissimilar methodology now known or hereafter developed.
The use of general descriptive names, registered names, trademarks, service marks, etc. in this publication does not imply, even in the absence of a specific statement, that such names are exempt from the relevant protective laws and regulations and therefore free for general use.
The publisher, the authors, and the editors are safe to assume that the advice and information in this book are believed to be true and accurate at the date of publication. Neither the publisher nor the authors or the editors give a warranty, expressed or implied, with respect to the material contained herein or for any errors or omissions that may have been made. The publisher remains neutral with regard to jurisdictional claims in published maps and institutional affiliations.

This Springer imprint is published by the registered company Springer Nature Switzerland AG.
The registered company address is: Gewerbestrasse 11, 6330 Cham, Switzerland

Preface and Acknowledgements

From a certain point of view, this work has its origin in the early days of my childhood. We moved from Romania to Germany in 1987. As part of the German minority in Romania, we were so-called "ethnic Germans," and the German state not only granted us permission to take up residence in Germany but also granted us German citizenship practically upon arrival in the reception camp for emigrants set up at the time in Nuremberg. Although those blood-based immigration policies ended in 1994, a great part of ethnic Germans living in Central and Eastern Europe did access German citizenship this way, even if many of them neither speak German nor had any relationship to German culture other than a family tree demonstrating that they have "German blood." At the same time, my Turkish classmates and friends at high school in Bayreuth, to where we eventually moved, did not have the right to access German citizenship, though they were born in Germany, spoke fluent German, had a German education, and were part of German popular culture. To me this always seemed like a gross injustice. What had ethnic and blood ties to do with citizenship and politics? How could we ethnic Germans justify our "moral luck" to our Turkish friends? How could a secular state be grounded in cultural and ethnic identities?

The more-than-six-century lasting experience of the so-called Saxons in Romania made me rather wary of ethnic nationalism and multiculturalism. German settlers upon arrival in Romania were granted royal privileges and self-government rights with an autonomous territorial-administrative entity that lasted until the incorporation of Transylvania into the Romanian state after the end of World War I. In order to retain those privileges and rights, Germans had of course to persist as a distinguishable, visible community over time. As a result, German-Romanians largely maintained folkloristic traditions and medieval language from their territory of origin that was the vaster area around the Rhine (the area located today between Germany, Belgium, and the Netherlands), so that today's Saxon dialect corresponds in large parts to Luxembourgish. Yet at the same time, the community turned highly conservative and repressive in order to avoid mixed marriages with the residing Romanian and Hungarian population that could put into question the distinguished character of the German-Romanian community. Accordingly, the

German-Romanian community took on a very exclusive shape with attitudes highly condescending of the other communities.

At the same time, while skeptical of the normativity of identity, I was also suspicious of people who in the name of certain standards of emancipation related to modernity and consumption levels started to question and disregard the identity of persons, considering it obstacle to progress. My grandparents were among the very small fraction of German-Romanians that resisted and partly rejected the call of the sirens from the Golden West. Instead of migrating to a country that after all they knew only from the media and family stories, they preferred remaining in Romania, the land in which they grew up, and conclude their life in an environment and context that from the point of view of living standard were clearly indefinitely poorer, but provided a meaning and familiarity that contemporary Germany did not have for them. Not moving to Germany, they deprived themselves of Western comforts and a welfare system that would certainly have relieved some of the pain of aging and prolonged their lives. I always defended their choice within our family and considered it a powerful expression of dignity and personal autonomy. After all, what could be more worthy than living up to one's own values and attachments?

These two intuitions stand in opposition with each other. If I value the expression of identitarian attachments, why do I reject so wholeheartedly communitarianism? To some extent, this book is trying to strike a balance exactly in between these two positions and provides theoretical grounds that explain why normativity is wrong, but identity nevertheless has its foundation.

The theoretical groundwork of the book was laid while studying political and social sciences at Freie Universität Berlin and Sciences Po Paris. Ulrich K. Preuß in Berlin introduced me to a radical political conception of citizenship that originates in Rousseau's equation of the rulers with the ruled. According to Preuß's constitutional theory, individuals cannot be excluded from the democratic process and political life, if the laws of a polity are considered binding and obligate them. Citizenship is a *moral* right that individuals have qua moral beings with a practical will. The question that remains nevertheless open in Preuß's Rousseauian conception, and to which the second part of this book is providing an answer, is if citizenship has to be unitary and one and the same for every citizen or if it can be differentiated along community lines as multicultural theory proposes. Preuß, as a Habermasian, is, according to my conclusions in the second part, rightly skeptical about multicultural arrangements. His argument is that identity politics risks contribute to a potentially unlimited fragmentation of democratic politics.

It was Jean-François Bayart at Sciences Po Paris who introduced me to the theoretical foundations of my other, opposite intuition, namely that identity is related to the dignity of a person. Sciences Po Paris is rather known for its elitist-institutional approach, but in his lectures on *Espace mondial*, Bayart provided students with the exact opposite perspective, the politics from below or, as he called it, "the politics of the belly." Bayart, famous for his studies on the African state and politics, categorically refutes the developmentalist perspective on Sub-Saharan Africa, so prevalent in the Global North and the direct result of the modernist heritage of both liberalism and Marxism. Both theories, with all their differences, are based upon certain standards, a *telos*, to which African societies do *not yet* live up and which we from the North need to help them to achieve through development aid and strategies.

Together with Achille Mbembé, Bayart dismisses those positions as forms of "Afropessimism" and shows through his anthropological studies of African politics the great dignity, honor, and beauty of African cultures and traditions despite the context of generalized poverty. After the fall of the Berlin wall and with the imposition of the Washington Consensus by international financial institutions (IMF and World Bank), practically a whole continent descended into civil wars centered around the capture of natural resources such as in particular diamonds and coltan,[1] and only recently, due to increasing trade and exchanges with China, African societies emerged from an immense political instability and volatility. And still, however harsh and violent the conditions were, Bayart would insist on the agency of individuals engaged in civil wars, claiming that their autonomy makes it impossible to see and treat them as victims (see "Communalism in Sub-Saharan Africa: The Reintegration of Child Soldiers" in this volume). In my master's thesis, I argued for a very similar thesis showing that the civil war in Congo/Zaire has its origin in civil society and not in the interventions of the neighboring states and the exploitation of natural resources by multinational companies.[2]

Theoretically, Bayart relies for his thesis on Foucault's late conception of governmentality[3] that he defines as "the encounter between the technologies of domination of others and those of the self."[4] Foucault increasingly became interested in the technologies of the self, the first-person point of view, that he describes as "those intentional and voluntary actions by which men not only set themselves rules of conduct, but also seek to transform themselves, to change themselves in their singular being, and to make their life into an *oeuvre* that carries certain aesthetic values and meets certain stylistic criteria."[5]

Foucault claims that in order that rules introduced by discourses of truth and political power give actually rise to society, individuals have to relate themselves, in one sense or another, *intentionally* to the rules. They have to follow the rules. Probably the best account of what Foucault has in mind with regard to governmentality is found in the second volume of *History of Sexuality: The Use of Pleasure*. Here he maintains that the history of sexuality is not only about "the establishment

---

[1] See Milo Rau's extraordinary documentary *The Congo Tribunal* (2017) in which he stages a civil tribunal in Eastern Congo that gathers victims, perpetrators, witnesses, and analysts of the Congo War. For the first time in history of this war, three exemplary cases were heard, exposing an unveiled portrait of one of the biggest and bloodiest economic wars in the history of mankind.

[2] Volker Kaul (2007), "Diamantenhandel und der Krieg in Kongo/Zaire," in *Afrika Spectrum* 42(1), pp. 49–71.

[3] See Jean-François Bayart (2005), "Foucault au Congo," in M.-C. Granjon (ed.), *Penser avec Michel Foucault*, Paris, Karthala, pp.183–222.

[4] Michel Foucault (1997), "Technologies of the Self," in M. Foucault, *Ethics: Subjectivity and Truth. Essential Works of Foucault 1954–1984 (Vol. 1)* (ed. by Paul Rabinow), New York, The New Press, p. 225.

[5] Michel Foucault (1990), *History of Sexuality (Vol. 2): The Use of Pleasure*, New York, Vintage Books, pp. 10–11.

of a set of rules and norms which found support in religious, judicial, pedagogical, and medical institutions," but concerns also "changes in the way individuals were led to assign meaning and value to their conduct, their duties, their pleasures, their feelings and sensations, their dreams."[6] As a result, in order to give an account of the history of sexuality, "it was a matter of seeing how an 'experience' came to be constituted in modern Western societies, an experience that caused individuals to recognize themselves as subjects of a 'sexuality,' which was accessible to very diverse fields of knowledge and linked to a system of rules and constraints."[7]

Here below I quote a longer passage from Foucault that shows to what extent we individuals *actively* constitute ourselves and our identity through the political, economic, and social context given to us. This context provides the material through which we shape ourselves, through which we construct our point of view of the world, through which we make ourselves who we are. Therefore, it is so offensive to people when their experiences are not recognized as having value and their lives are measured up to some external ideal. In Foucault's perspective, victimization is a violation of a person's dignity and autonomy.

> "In short, for an action to be 'moral,'" moral in the sense Foucault understands the government of self, "it must not be reducible to an act or a series of acts conforming to a rule, a law, or a value," the government of others. "Of course all moral action involves a relationship with the reality in which it is carried out, and a relationship with the self. The latter is not simply 'self-awareness' but self-formation as an 'ethical subject,' a process in which the individual delimits that part of himself that will form the object of his moral practice, defines his position relative to the precept he will follow, and decides on a certain mode of being that will serve as his moral goal. And this requires him to act upon himself, to monitor, test, improve, and transform himself. There is no specific moral action that does not refer to a unified moral conduct; no moral conduct that does not call for the forming of oneself as an ethical subject; and no forming of the ethical subject without 'modes of subjectivation' and an 'ascetics' or 'practices of the self' that support them. Moral action is indissociable from these forms of self-activity, and they do not differ any less from one morality to another than do the systems of values, rules, and interdictions."[8]

At LUISS "Guido Carli" University during my PhD studies in political theory in Rome, I learned to be somewhat more careful with Foucault's position on identity and dignity. I received formal training in Rawlsian, Habermasian, and analytic political philosophy by the faculty at LUISS University consisted of the director Sebastiano Maffettone as well as Alessandro Ferrara, David Rasmussen, Akeel Bilgrami, and Ingrid Salvatore, among others, teachers with whom until today I remained in a lively exchange. It was in particular my supervisor Ingrid Salvatore, an unorthodox Rawlsian and socialist thinker,[9] who pointed out the political dangers of Foucault's position.

---

[6] Foucault (1990), *History of Sexuality (Vol. 2): The Use of Pleasure*, pp. 3–4.
[7] Foucault (1990), *History of Sexuality (Vol. 2): The Use of Pleasure*, p. 4.
[8] Foucault (1990), *History of Sexuality (Vol. 2): The Use of Pleasure*, p. 28.
[9] A good starting point for discovering her position is Ingrid Salvatore, "Sharing a Conception of Justice, Sharing a Conception of the Good. Liberalism as a Pluralist Theory vs. Pluralism as a Non-

Salvatore, together with Maffettone, pressed the point that Foucault's theory of governmentality would undermine any attempts and efforts by the international civil society to denounce human rights abuses, severe poverty and forms of deprivation, child labor, gender injustices, social inequalities, labor exploitation, racism, and so on. After all what counts and what provides dignity is the very fact that individuals construct their agency; the external material given by an individual's context and that provides the *content* of agency is irrelevant for bringing about the very *form* of agency. All content gives *equally* rise to forms of agency; it is not the case that a content that we consider closer to justice constitutes more coherent and viable forms of agency than a content that arises out of contexts of violence. At least this is what Foucault's position seems to imply and what Bayart claims to be the case when he attacks "Afropessimism" and denounces the normativity of liberalism and Marxism. To put in a nutshell, the problem of Foucault's theory is its implicit relativism that undercuts any possibility to formulate a critique of the existing living conditions and life forms and eventually runs counter to any theory of justice.

In the first part of this book, I take Salvatore's and Maffettone's challenge very seriously and argue that it would be quite weird for Foucault, the philosopher with the exceptional sense for the latency of power, insisting on the contingency and arbitrariness in the "order of things," to suddenly justify in his theory of governmentality whatever kind of political power. In fact, Gayatri Chakrovarty Spivak is famously criticizing Foucault for giving back the voice to the subaltern, reproaching him that a "politics of the oppressed 'speaking for themselves' restore[s] the category of the sovereign subject within the theory that seems most to question it,"[10] a subject that is "self-proximate, if not self-identical."[11] Richard Rorty maintains equally that Foucault "sought to define autonomy in purely human terms, without the Kantian notion of a universal law," claiming that "Foucault tells us that liberal democracies might work better if they stopped trying to give universalistic self-justifications."[12]

Gilles Deleuze, on the other hand, sustains just the opposite. He writes that "to imagine that Foucault rediscovered, came back to the subjectivity he'd initially rejected, is as fundamental a misunderstanding as the one about 'the death of man'."[13] "A process of subjectification, that is, the production of a way of existing, can't be equated with a subject, unless we divest the subject of any interiority and

---

Liberal Theory," in Volker Kaul & Ingrid Salvatore (eds.) (2020), *What Is Pluralism?*, New York/London, Routledge.

[10] Gayatri Chakravorty Spivak (1994), "Can the Subaltern Speak", in Patrick Williams & Laura Chrisman (eds.), *Colonial Discourse and Post-Colonial Theory*, New York, Columbia University Press, p. 73.

[11] Spivak, "Can the Subaltern Speak," p. 73.

[12] Richard Rorty (1991), "Moral Identity and Private Autonomy: The Case of Foucault," in R. Rorty, *Essays on Heidegger and Others. Philosophical Papers. Volume 2,* Cambridge, Cambridge University Press, p.193.

[13] Gilles Deleuze (1995), *Negotiations*, (transl. by Martin Joughin) New York, Columbia University Press, p. 93.

even any identity. Subjectification isn't even anything to do with a 'person'. It's a mode of intensity, not a personal subject."[14] "It's to do, rather, with an electric or magnetic field, an individuation taking place through intensities (weak as well as strong ones), it's to do with individuated fields, not persons or identities."[15]

My thesis in the first part of the book is that Spivak and Rorty are right and that Foucault in his late work on the hermeneutics of the subject, the technologies of the self, the government of self, and the care and culture of the self, as much as other desire-based theories[16] or reason-based theories[17] that presuppose *practical* identities, introduce a conception of the self-conscious individual that is not so distant from the Kantian autonomous person (see "Identity, Difference and Anti-Essentialism," "Freedom and Identity" and "Psychology, Autonomy and Liberalism," in this volume). It is through the will that people come to endorse a conception of themselves that stands in accordance with social rules. Yet, although in this way we save all the intuitions about justice and emancipation through a conception of morality that is inherent to human reason, we are unable to recognize and respect the dignity of a life that is lived in accordance with norms and rules that have come to constitute it. But it also shows that Foucault's thesis on subjugated knowledge, and the continuity between the government of others and the government of self as source of a profound concern for individuals and their dignity, has to be brought in accordance with our sense of justice through a route that stays away from transcendentalism. Throughout the book, I propose a strategy that is based upon a psychological, empirical conception of identity.

If the content of the book is the result of an early concern with identity that in general is central to the experience of migration,[18] the form and course the research documented in this book has taken was largely determined by my role as scientific coordinator of the Istanbul seminars and today's Venice seminars, a position that I hold for the foundation Reset-Dialogues on Civilizations since 2008. Istanbul seminars were held yearly at Istanbul Bilgi University and meant to promote an East-West dialogue, "Encounters Across all Divides" in which "Philosophers Cross the Bosphorus," a topic that after 9/11 and the subsequent Islamic terrorism has been very high on the political agenda over the last two decades. The dialogues were initiated by the two founders of Reset-Dialogues, Giancarlo Bosetti and Nina zu

---

[14] Deleuze (1995), *Negotiations*, pp. 98–99.

[15] Deleuze (1995), *Negotiations*, p. 93. See also Gilles Deleuze (1991), *Empiricism and Subjectivity*, (transl. by Constantin Boundas) New York, Columbia University Press.

[16] Harry Frankfurt (1988), *The Importance of What We Care About*, Cambridge, Cambridge University Press and H. Frankfurt (2006), *The Reasons of Love*, Princeton (NJ), Princeton University Press. See also for the vast discussion on Frankfurt's theory of autonomy Sarah Buss & Lee Overton (2002), *Contours of Agency. Essays on Themes from Harry Frankfurt*, Cambridge (Mass.), MIT Press – A Bradford Book; see in particular Gary Watson (1975), "Free Agency," in *The Journal of Philosophy* 72(8), pp. 205–220.

[17] Christine Korsgaard (1996), *The Sources of Normativity*, Cambridge, Cambridge University Press.

[18] Andreea Deciu Ritivoi (2002), *Yesterday's Self: Nostalgia and the Immigrant Identity*, Lanham (MD), Rowman & Littlefield.

Fürstenberg, and supported by an Executive Committee consisted of Asaf Savaş Akat, Seyla Benhabib, Murat Borovali, Alessandro Ferrara, Abdou Filali-Ansary, Nilüfer Göle, Ferda Keskin, David Rasmussen, and Nadia Urbinati, whose work I coordinated. Over the years, we treated different issues related to identity and the proceedings were published by the journal *Philosophy & Social Criticism* and edited by Alessandro Ferrara, David Rasmussen, and myself.[19] In 2016, Seyla Benhabib and I published a selection of the debate in *Toward New Democratic Imaginaries: Istanbul Seminars on Islam, Culture and Politics* for Springer.

As coordinator of the seminars and editor of the proceedings, the seminars with its lectures and graduate workshops attended by many students and young scholars from the countries of the Middle East, North Africa, and South Asia other than Europe and the US provided the perfect setting for going about with my research on identity with respect to salient political questions, that in the Global South take on a rather urgent character and are accompanied by high levels of conflict. At the beginning of the seminars toward the end of the first decade of the new millennium, with Turkey and Erdogan's AK Party embodying a role model of a possible reformist-liberal political Islam questions concerning the role of religion in the public sphere, postsecularism and the challenge of pluralism were at the center of our research and discussions. Chapters 8 and 12 in this book were written at those occasions and previously published as "Multiculturalism and the Challenge of Pluralism," in *Philosophy & Social Criticism* 37(4) 2011: 505–516 and "Jürgen Habermas, Tariq Ramadan and Michael Walzer in a Dialogue on Politics and Religion," in *Philosophy & Social Criticism* 36 (3–4) 2010: 505–516.

After the dramatic failure of the Arab Spring in the MENA region, the increasingly authoritarian stance that Erdogan took in the aftermath of the Gezi Park protests and the rise of Islamic terrorism in Europe and Turkey questions about the nature of Islam and its relation with politics became more central. Chapters 3, 7, and 9 here were written as response to those events and were published as "Freedom and Identity," in *Philosophy & Social Criticism* 39(4–5) 2013: 487–498, "'Can Muslims be Suicide Bombers?' An Essay on the Troubles of Multiculturalism," in *Philosophy & Social Criticism* 38(4–5) 2012: 389–398, and "Foreword: Islam and Democracy," in Seyla Benhabib & Volker Kaul (eds.) (2016), *Toward New Democratic*

---

[19] See *Philosophy & Social Criticism* 46(4) 2020: "Sources of Democracy – Citizenship, Social Cohesion and Ethical Values;" of *Philosophy & Social Criticism* 45(4) 2019: "Fountainheads of Toleration – Forms of Pluralism in Empires, Republics, Democracies;" *Philosophy & Social Criticism* 44(4) 2018, "The Populist Upsurge and the Decline of Diversity Capital;" *Philosophy & Social Criticism* 43(4–5) 2017, "Religion, Rights and the Public Sphere;" *Philosophy & Social Criticism* 42(4–5) 2016, "Politics Beyond Borders. The Republican Model Challenged by the Internationalization of Economy, Law and Communication;" *Philosophy & Social Criticism* 41(4–5) 2015, "The Sources of Pluralism – Metaphysics, Epistemology, Politics and Law;" *Philosophy & Social Criticism* 40(4–5) 2014, "The Sources of Political Legitimacy;" *Philosophy & Social Criticism* 39(4–5) 2013, "The Promises of Democracy in Troubled Times;" *Philosophy & Social Criticism* 38(4–5) 2012, "Overcoming the Trap of Resentment;" *Philosophy & Social Criticism* 37 (4) 2011, "Realigning Liberalism: Pluralism, Integration, Identities;" *Philosophy & Social Criticism* 36(3–4) 2010 on "Postsecularism and Multicultural Jurisdictions."

Imaginaries, Basel, Springer: 89–96. Chapter 6 is based upon two articles published as "Is Religious Pluralism Simply a Matter of Justice?" in Aurélia Bardon, Maria Birnbaum, Lois Lee, Kristina Stoeckl (eds.) (2015), *Religious Pluralism: A Resource Book*, Fiesole (FI), European University Institute (EUI): 89–93 and "What Makes a Fundamentalist? Metaphysics, Morality and Psychology," in *Philosophy & Social Criticism* 41(4–5) 2015: 409–415.

After the 2016 coup d'état attempt in Turkey and Erdogan's declaration of the state of emergency, it was definitely no longer safe to hold the seminars in Istanbul, in particular since many of the Turkish intellectuals who were regularly speakers at the seminars over the years faced prosecutions after they signed a peace petition in January 2016. The seminars relocated to Venice and with the move from Istanbul to Venice the focus turned from intercultural dialogue and discourse ethics to questions about populism and nationalism that became prevalent after the crisis of liberal globalism. Chapters 2 and 11 tackle those challenges and were published as "Populism, Liberalism and Nationalism" in Volker Kaul and Ingrid Salvatore (eds.) (2020), *What is Pluralism*? New York/London, Routledge: 225–237 and "How to Deal with Populism" in Volker Kaul and Ananya Vajpeyi (eds.) (2020), *Minorities and Populism: Comparative Perspectives from South Asia and Europe*, Basel, Springer: 29–40.

Since Ca' Foscari University of Venice and its Department of Asian and North African Studies with the sinologists Tiziana Lippiello and Francesca Tarocco became precious new partners of Reset-Dialogues, the seminars will be more radically comparative concentrating on justice in different cultural contexts. This way the seminars will combine questions about the normativity of cultures with issues of autonomy and dignity related to cultural identity. The empiricist perspective of identity proposed in this book is supposed to provide the framework for the research to come and for the construction of new common worlds over and above mere toleration.

Rome, Italy   Volker Kaul

References

Bayart, Jean-François. 2005. Foucault au Congo. In *Penser avec Michel Foucault*, ed. M.-C. Granjon, 183–222. Paris: Karthala.
Buss, Sarah, and Lee Overton. 2002. *Contours of Agency. Essays on Themes from Harry Frankfurt*. Cambridge (Mass.): MIT Press – A Bradford Book.
Deciu Ritivoi, Andreea. 2002. *Yesterday's Self: Nostalgia and the Immigrant Identity*. Lanham: Rowman & Littlefield.
Deleuze, Gilles. 1991. *Empiricism and Subjectivity*. Trans. Constantin Boundas. New York: Columbia University Press.
Deleuze, Gilles. 1995. *Negotiations*. Trans. Martin Joughin. New York: Columbia University Press.
Foucault, Michel. 1990. *History of Sexuality (Vol. 2): The Use of Pleasure*. New York: Vintage Books.

Foucault, Michel. 1997. In *Ethics: Subjectivity and Truth. Essential Works of Foucault 1954–1984 (Vol. 1)*, ed. Paul Rabinow. New York: The New Press.

Frankfurt, Harry. 1988. *The Importance of What We Care About*. Cambridge: Cambridge University Press.

Frankfurt, Harry. 2006. *The Reasons of Love*. Princeton: Princeton University Press.

Kaul, Volker. 2007. Diamantenhandel und der Krieg in Kongo/Zaire. *Afrika Spectrum* 42 (1): 49–71.

Korsgaard, Christine. 1996. *The Sources of Normativity*. Cambridge: Cambridge University Press.

Rorty, Richard. 1991. Moral Identity and Private Autonomy: The Case of Foucault. In *Essays on Heidegger and Others. Philosophical Papers*, ed. R. Rorty, vol. 2. Cambridge: Cambridge University Press.

Salvatore, Ingrid. 2020. Sharing a Conception of Justice, Sharing a Conception of the Good. Liberalism as a Pluralist Theory vs. Pluralism as a Non-Liberal Theory. In *What Is Pluralism?* ed. Volker Kaul and Ingrid Salvatore. New York/London: Routledge.

Spivak, Gayatri Chakravorty. 1994. Can the Subaltern Speak. In *Colonial Discourse and Post-Colonial Theory*, ed. Patrick Williams and Laura Chrisman, 66–111. New York: Columbia University Press.

Watson, Gary. 1975. Free Agency. *The Journal of Philosophy* 72 (8): 205–220.

Contents

1	Identity and the Difficulty of Emancipation........................	1

Part I   Liberalism in Search of Identity

2	Liberal Nationalism	15
3	Freedom and Identity	29
4	Psychology, Autonomy, and Liberalism	43
5	Identity, Difference and Anti-essentialism	55
6	Agency, Psychology and the Self: The Case of Religious Fundamentalism	65

Part II   Identity and the Quest for Multiculturalism

7	Multiculturalism, Islam and Suicide Bombers.....................	79
8	Foundations of Multiculturalism (1): Self-Knowledge	89
9	Foundations of Multiculturalism (2): Recognition	101
10	Islam and Democracy	111

Part III   Identity Politics

11	Populism..	123
12	Postsecularism...	133
13	Postcolonialism	145
14	Communalism in Sub-Saharan Africa: The Reintegration of Child Soldiers	169
15	Conclusion: For the Time Being: *Modus Vivendi* Liberalism or Political Liberalism?	195

Chapter 1
Identity and the Difficulty of Emancipation

Abstract The book addresses the complicated nexus between identity and emancipation in politics. It keeps the two aspects closely connected and examines if there is a political project that manages to integrate both. The expected pay-off is a new form of liberalism that is able to overcome the widespread identitiarian resistance in the Global South and the populist crisis in the West. Recent studies of liberalism and multiculturalism precisely try to ground individual emancipation *within* identities. In particular in what regards liberalism this stands in strong contrast with its characteristic anti-culturalist stance. Accordingly, the first two sections of this introduction are having an extensive discussion to what extent liberal and multicultural theories are successful in keeping the two moments of emancipation and identity firmly united. The third section analyzes current examples of global identity politics and evaluates their effectiveness in bringing about individual emancipation.

Keywords Liberalism · Multiculturalism · Identity politics · Enlightenment · John Rawls · Political liberalism · Postmodernism · Poststructuralism · Hybrid identities · Multiple identities · Transcendentalism · Liberal nationalism · Freedom · Recognition · Religious fundamentalism · Islam · Populism · Postsecularism · Postcolonialism · Communalism

This book addresses the complicated nexus between identity and emancipation in politics. Generally, identity is not analyzed in the light of emancipation and, vice versa, any politics of emancipation rarely focuses on questions of identity. With the consequence, that identity politics tends to be stylized as alternative to the project of modernity and its achievements in terms of individual freedom and well-being, as formidably demonstrated by Foucault's infamous support of the Iranian revolution in 1979[1] and latent nativist tendencies in much of postcolonial thought. ('Postcolonialism', in this volume).

On the other hand, emancipation in the history of political thought and the way it actually unfolded in world politics through colonialism first and modernization later is largely formulated *against* identities, so that today we can observe a worldwide identitarian backlash against liberalism in form of populism and nationalism. The opposition between identity and emancipation runs like a red thread through political modernity. The Turkish Republic as much as the other Middle Eastern and North African Republics emerging from the Ottoman Empire were staunchly antireligious, banning Islam from the public sphere and controlling its practice through government agencies. Kemalism and Nasserism are the ideal types of a modernization directed against religion. Also in Europe modernization went hand in hand with the secularization of societies, although the state played a much more indirect role here. (see also 'Postsecularism', in this volume) Moreover, cultures are often accused to be responsible for the underdevelopment and gender inequalities in the Global South. So are menstrual taboos in South Asia supposed to cause girls to leave school. Belief in evil spirits and witchcraft is said to hinder vaccination campaigns in Sub-Saharan Africa and thereby to increase infant mortality. In short, local customs hold individuals back from doing valuable things.[2]

The project of this book is to keep the two aspects closely connected and to examine if there is a political project that manages to integrate both. The expected pay-off is a new form of liberalism that is able to overcome the widespread identitiarian resistance in the Global South and the populist crisis in the West.[3]

Recent studies of liberalism and multiculturalism precisely try to ground individual emancipation *within* identities.[4] In particular in what regards liberalism this stands in strong contrast with its characteristic anti-culturalist stance.[5] Accordingly, the first two parts of this book are having an extensive discussion to what extent liberal and multicultural theories are successful in keeping the two moments of emancipation and identity firmly united. The third part of the book analyzes current examples of global identity politics and evaluates their effectiveness in bringing about individual emancipation.

---

[1] Afary & Anderson, *Foucault and the Iranian Revolution*.
[2] Khader, *Why are Women Poor?*.
[3] Kaul, *Populism and the Crisis of Liberalism*.
[4] See for example Patten, *Equal Recognition* and Laborde & Bardon, *Religion in Liberal Political Philosophy*.
[5] See in particular Moller Okin, *Is Multiculturalism Bad for Women?* and Barry, *Culture and Equality*.

1.1 Liberalism in Search of Identity

Liberalism is ambivalent with regard to the question of identity. On the one hand, liberalism, originating in Enlightenment and grounded in individual autonomy, is formulated against cultural and religious identities. To some extent, emancipation and identity represent two antipodes, where emancipation stands for modernity and identity is equivalent to tradition and backwardness. This becomes nowhere clearer than in Kant's moral and political philosophy and his definition of Enlightenment: "Enlightenment is man's emergence from his self-incurred immaturity. Immaturity is the inability to use one's understanding without guidance from another. This immaturity is self-imposed when its cause lies not in lack of understanding, but in lack of resolve and courage to use it without guidance from another. Sapere Aude! 'Have courage to use your own understanding!' – that is the motto of enlightenment."[6]

Kant does not use the term 'identity' here, but it is clear that what he refers to, when reproaching his fellow citizens to depend in their reasoning upon others and to not lead lives of their own, are today's collective identities. Kant blames people for being heteronomous and not autonomous, for following socially generated ideas about how people ought to conduct themselves. And we could add, for following social *scripts* or *narratives* about how people of a certain *type* ought to conduct themselves, to introduce the contemporary vocabulary of collective identities.[7]

On the other hand, however, a theory that takes individualism seriously cannot but be concerned with the values that individuals come to embrace, regardless of the fact if they have their source in collective identities or not. Accordingly, there is a second strand in liberalism, that has its origins in Mill, Berlin but also Hegel, that opposes the rationalism of Enlightenment liberalism.[8]

In the wake of globalization and in particular after John Rawls' seminal work on *Political Liberalism* (1993), this alternative tradition of liberalism, going back to Romanticism, has gained the upper hand and contemporary liberal political thought increasingly feels the necessity to accommodate identities rather than to oppose them.[9] The question then is, if a liberal order really can be grounded in identities themselves and this first section is going to provide an answer to it. Before doing so, let me briefly review why Rawls does not have the last word on pluralism, identity and liberalism.

Rawls revises Kant's moral universalism and argues that his monism about reason is wrongheaded. To some extent, reason does not stand in opposition to identity, but embraces at least some of the identities. If reason comes up with practical principles that not everyone shares and are endorsed only by a certain group of people, this does not mean that there occurred some logical error or incoherence. According to Rawls, given the burdens of judgment reason *necessarily* produces

---

[6] Kant, *What is Enlightenment?*, p. 1.
[7] Appiah, *The Ethics of Identity*, pp. 1–35.
[8] Appiah, *The Ethics of Identity*.
[9] Maffettone, *Rawls*.

different results and practical principles.[10] Persons do not reason in a vacuum and reason is not completely independent from "our total experience, which naturally differs."[11] Accordingly, it is not a merely contingent fact that people follow different practical principles in their lives; pluralism is inherent to reason and will persist over time.[12] In principle, reason does not have any problem with national, religious, ethnic or gender identities. They are the ordinary outcome of human reasoning.

Yet, most of the identities emerging from reason might be outspokenly illiberal. Religions are generally anti-individualist, not to speak about nationalism and ethnicity. Why should illiberal comprehensive doctrines agree upon liberal politics?

Rawls thinks that although the different doctrines and identities might profoundly disagree about social, economic and political matters, they nevertheless can come to an overlapping consensus with regard to constitutional essentials. All reasonable identities share despite their deep disagreements and frequent anti-individualism a core of principles, a *thin* sort of liberalism that Rawls labels political conception of justice. Rawls argues that "all those who affirm the political conception start from within their own comprehensive view and draw on the religious, philosophical, and moral grounds it provides."[13]

If Rawls thinks that an overlapping consensus is to some extent a historical achievement,[14] he claims that it is above all a *moral* achievement. We might come to reasonably endorse a principle that runs counter to the liberal tradition, such as the Catholic doctrine of *extra ecclesiam nulla salus*. Yet, we could not reasonably conceive this doctrine as a principle of justice. Here is why: " It proposes to use the public's political power – a power in which citizens have an equal share – to enforce a view bearing on constitutional essentials about which citizens as reasonable persons are bound to differ uncompromisingly. When there is a plurality of reasonable doctrines, it is unreasonable or worse to want to use the sanctions of state power to correct, or to punish, those who disagree with us."[15] But from where does Catholicism derive or take the principle of tolerance, if everything that it holds to be the truth runs against it?

Rawls' argument is not that there is anything liberal in the reasonable comprehensive doctrine of Catholicism as such and as it has been practiced over the course

---

[10] The burdens of judgment are the following: (1) evidence can be conflicting and complex, and thus hard to assess and evaluate; (2) even where we agree abut the considerations that are relevant, we may disagree about their weight; (3) to some extent, all concepts are vague and thus subject to interpretation; (4) the way we assess evidence, and weigh moral and political values, is shaped to some extent by our total experience, which naturally differs; (5) different normative considerations may carry different force, and it is difficult to make an overall assessment; (6) setting priorities and making adjustment among different moral and political values involves hard decisions that may seem to have no clear answer. (Rawls 1993: 57)

[11] Rawls, *Political Liberalism*, p. 57.

[12] See on this point Kaul & Salvatore, *What is Pluralism?*.

[13] Rawls, *Political Liberalism*, p. 147.

[14] Rawls, *Political Liberalism*, p. 163–164.

[15] Rawls, *Political Liberalism*, p. 138.

of history. What he wants to claim is that a Catholic in a pluralist and democratic society, and only under such circumstances, comes to incorporate the political principle of justice within its own comprehensive doctrine, as happened with the Second Vatican Council. Comprehensive doctrines tend to converge on the political conception of justice within the context of pluralism. And they do so because they come to see the justification of other truths. Moreover, the context of pluralism "makes it rational for them to move out of the narrower circle of their own view and to develop political conceptions in terms of which they can explain and justify their preferred policies to a wider public so as to put together a majority."[16] However, the outcome of this is that "citizens have two views, a comprehensive and a political view; and that their overall view can be divided into two parts, suitable related."[17] Citizens might have at the same time liberal and illiberal attitudes.

Rawls clearly seeks to reconcile identity and emancipation, identity and public reason. Identities are no longer conceived in opposition to liberalism. Reason does not longer require us to universalize our practical principles. We can reasonably live according to our identities. However, in Rawls' view reason asks us to agree upon one principle, the political conception of justice, while we can justifiably disagree about all other matters. Reason commands one universal principle, at least within a democratic public culture, namely some form of liberty of conscience and freedom of thought. Reason comes to this result reflecting upon and understanding the very workings of reason itself given the burdens of judgment. Public reason is no less transcendental than in Kant. Yet, in view of this universal principle of tolerance can a Catholic really stick to the doctrine of *extra ecclesiam nulla salus* and Catholicism's most foundational, non-liberal values? If the political conception of justice trumps all other values of a comprehensive doctrine, how long can a person live with this cognitive dissonance before she is going to shed her identity? Rawls' liberalism wants to be much less comprehensive than Kant's, but eventually it risks collapsing into some version of Kantian liberalism, opposing identities.

Given the problems the Rawlsian position runs into with regard to identities, it is important to look for alternative approaches in liberal political thought. We can distinguish here between two liberal approaches based upon identity, one that is grounded in agency and has Kantian roots, and the other that refers to the reality of values, although both address identity through the lenses of individual freedom and choice. In the neo-Kantian interpretation, individuals have the capacity to commit and to endorse specific *practical* identities.[18] In the reading of a specific version of moral realism, individuals need a particular context in order to make meaningful and ethically relevant choices.[19] Accordingly, in both approaches identities are constitutive of freedom.

---

[16] Rawls, *Political Liberalism*, p. 165.

[17] Rawls, *Political Liberalism*, p. 140.

[18] For the concept of practical identity see Korsgaard, *The Sources of Normativity*.

[19] Joseph Raz develops this point in detail in his *The Morality of Freedom* (see also 'Liberal Nationalism,' Chap. 2, in this volume).

We have to mention a third approach to identity, that emerges out of postmodernism and poststructuralism and that liberal thinkers, such as Amartya Sen[20] and Samuel Scheffler,[21] have come to embrace. In postcolonial studies in particular, such as in the work of Homi Bhabha,[22] but also in cultural studies and anthropology more in general, materializes a concept that conceives culture as hybrid and fluid, constantly in flux. Deconstructionism rejects the latent essentialism of communitarianism and makes cultural and religious identities fundamentally compatible with individual freedom.

The essays in this section come to the conclusion that, first, also more empirical foundations of agency, as we find them in Harry Frankfurt's conception of freedom, but also, more surprisingly, poststructural approaches *à la* Derrida do not succeed in avoiding traditional transcendendalism – a theory that locates, in the last instance, the grounds of autonomy and emancipation in the individual and practical reason rather than identity itself. Second, political theories, according to which cultural identities instantiate real values and constitute meaning, risk to collapse into some form of communitarianism, a theory that puts the community rather than the individual first.

It emerges a causal conception of identity and a third paradigm of liberalism from this section, one that is neither rationalist, nor identitarian, but in substance egalitarian. In the theory of liberal egalitarianism, public policies shape identities, rather than taking them into account and searching to accommodate them.

The first chapter on "Liberal Nationalism" reconstructs Joseph Raz's and Will Kymlicka's theories of nationalism according to which national societal cultures constitute the context for meaningful and ethically good individual choices. It argues that liberalism is incompatible with nationalism. If meaning is constitutive of choices, then individual freedom does presuppose an already given national identity. The resulting obligation of national solidarity, however, stands in contrast with fundamental freedoms. The essay concludes with the suggestion that nationalism must be governed and shaped in order to counter the current populist political order.

The second chapter on "Freedom and Identity" shows to what extent a conception of agency and freedom does not depend upon identities that are chosen, as Christine Korsgaard and John Rawls claim, but relies upon identities that are given, as communitarianism maintains. Yet, identities are not culturally fixed, but their shape depends upon our psychological needs. Therefore liberalism can flourish only in contexts where resentment is not a political driving force.

The third chapter on "Agency, Psychology and Liberalism" discusses Harry Frankfurt's and Isaiah Berlin's psychological accounts of agency. The political advantage of Frankfurt's and Berlin's theories with respect to Kantian moral theories is that they ground negative freedom precisely in individual identities and do not have to recur to any arguments of transcendental reason. However, the essay

---

[20] Sen, *Identity and Violence*.
[21] Scheffler, "Immigration and the Significance of Culture".
[22] Bhabha, *The Location of Culture*.

makes clear that psychology cannot be the foundation of agency and that eventually both Frankfurt and Berlin risk to collapse into a Kantian-style theory of agency in their efforts to ground liberalism.

The next chapter "Identity, Difference and Anti-Essentialism" analyzes in detail poststructural theories of difference that question the grand narratives and rationality of Enlightenment liberalism and pay close attention to subjugated knowledges and the diversity of social and cultural contexts. It argues that Foucault ultimately has a Kantian and thus a liberal conception of identity. Derrida, on the contrary, in his theory of *différance*, gives up on the notion of agency and puts the very concept of identity, in the name of difference, radically into question. The article shows, however, that Derrida's deconstructionism, in the last instance, is also grounded in some form of ethical transcendentalism.

The last essay of the section on "Agency, Psychology and the Self: The Case of Religious Fundamentalism" discusses the pros and cons of a reductionist, psychological account of identity examining the case of religious fundamentalism. It first lays out arguments in favor of theories that account for the agency of religious fundamentalists and demonstrates, in the second part, why nonetheless fundamentalists are not motivated by cultural or religious beliefs and reasons. The essay maintains that their intolerance is caused and driven by purely emotional reactions.

1.2 Identity and the Quest for Multiculturalism

Theories of pluralism are divided between those approaches that, as in the first section, argue that cultural and religious identities are compatible with liberalism and those that maintain that the resurgence of identities requires a wholly new political paradigm, namely that of multiculturalism. Multiculturalism holds that identities are not of our own making and do not have their source in the individual, but are essentially collective identities that are given to us through the communities to which we belong.

The Roman Empire and the Ottoman Empire as well as the Mughal Empire in India, to mention just two non-European historical examples, all granted extensive autonomy and rights of self-government to the communities present on their territories in order to defuse possible conflicts.[23] The common law of the empire was *neutral* with respect to the conflicting values of the communities and its sole function was to regulate intercommunitarian affairs and to protect communities from mutual interventions. Historically, this was the standard recipe for social peace and actually lasted with the Habsburg Empire long into European modernity. And until today, multicultural arrangements and communalism remain the predominant

---

[23] Walzer, *On Toleration*, pp. 14–19.

political models in particular in Sub-Saharan Africa and in India.[24] ('Communalism in Sub-Saharan Africa,' in this volume).

The second part of the book discusses the emancipatory potential of multicultural theories. We can distinguish between four approaches, according to which strong communitarianism relies upon modern democratic foundations. First, Hegelian dialectics are supposed to give rise to a philosophy of history.[25] Second, hermeneutics claims that cultural norms are not simply given, but require our interpretations and narrations that necessarily have to take place within a modern historical context.[26] Third, all comprehensive cultural and religious traditions contain arguments for accepting toleration and pluralism,[27] that can be brought forth by way of conjectures.[28] Forth, metaphysical realism holds that cultures have to correspond to truth.[29]

This section engages in particular with the latter three approaches and argues that hermeneutics runs into the problem of relativism, whereas the emphasis on the pluralist traditions of cultures and religions could risk to rely upon essentialist arguments. Last but not least, the section concludes that truth might put at risk multicultural claims. It proposes, as a possible solution, a multicultural theory that is based upon self-knowledge, rather than knowledge *tout court*.

The opening chapter on "Multiculturalism, Islam and Suicide Bombers" addresses the problem multiculturalism is facing head-on, namely the question of cultural and religious authenticity. In a multicultural theory, communities are the ultimate grounds of value. Yet, which precisely is the identity of the community? Discussing the case of Muslim suicide bombers, the essay demonstrates the difficulties the different multicultural approaches have to define the moral identity of Islam and to show that suicide bombing is incompatible with Islam.

The second chapter on "Foundations of Multiculturalism (1): Self-Knowledge" seeks to provide an answer to the challenge above. The essay starts with introducing liberal, postmodern theories (Richard Rorty) and alternative non-cognitive theories (Bernard Williams), that evaluate and judge cultural identities on epistemological grounds. It criticizes these theories for either dismissing our commitments or ridiculing commitments as such. This chapter, on the contrary, proposes that commitments are integral part of who we have become and with which we have to come to

---

[24] See Kaul & Vajpeyi, *Minorities and Populism*.

[25] Bilgrami, *Secularism, Identity, and Enchantment*.

[26] For the *locus classicus* see Taylor, „Interpretation and the Sciences of Man". For interpretation in a democratic context and the concept of democratic iterations see Benhabib, *Another Cosmopolitanism*. For hermeneutics in Islam see Abu Zayd, "The 'Others' in the Qur'an: A Hermeneutical Approach".

[27] On the concept of multiple modernities see Rasmussen, "The Emerging Domain of the Political". For the Islamic context see An-Na'im, *Islam and the Secular State* and March, *Islam and Liberal Citizenship*.

[28] Ferrara, *The Democratic Horizon*.

[29] See in particular Dreyfus & Taylor, *Retrieving Realism*. For the Islamic tradition see El Fadl, "The Epistemology of Truth in Modern Islam".

terms. It therefore defends a conception of identity based upon self-knowledge, according to which the simple awareness and knowledge of our cultural and religious commitments make it possible for us not to impose our values upon other individuals who do not share them, justifying at the same time the multicultural project.

The third chapter on "Foundations of Multiculturalism (2): Recognition" discusses the principal paradigm of multiculturalism, the struggle for recognition. The first part shows to what extent our need for recognition has epistemological grounds. The second part argues that truth cannot be the ground for cultural recognition. If truth is relative to cultures, then the grounds for recognition cease to apply. If truth is a metaphysical concept, then cultures do not provide the basis for judgment and criticism. The essay concludes that we must have an a proper reason for recognition and suggests that in an empirical concept of culture recognition would occur independent of the question of truth.

The closing essay on "Islam and Democracy" provides an overview and analyzes in detail the different contemporary theories that seek to establish the compatibility of Islam and democracy. It distinguishes between epistemological theories that, on the one hand, argue that we cannot but access Islam from the point of view of political modernity (Abu Zayd) and those that, on the other hand, maintain that Islam has to correspond to moral reality (El Fadl). Last but not least, it introduces ethical theories that evoke the freedom and agency of Muslims in the face of their understandable resentment of the West (Bilgrami).

1.3 Identity Politics

Classic liberalism with its emphasis on individual freedom and agency pays little to no attention to the structural discrimination, marginalization and oppression of minority groups and the cultural imperialism of the majority.[30] Identity politics has become from the second half of the twentieth century onwards a powerful tool of stigmatized and exploited social groups to counter injustices and the lack of recognition.

Already Adorno and Horkheimer in *Dialectic of Enlightenment* (2007) criticize reason for its instrumental character. However it is Foucault in his early masterpiece *Madness and Civilization* (1988) who illustrates to what extent the Enlightenment discourse on reason justifies marginalization and exclusion. He shows that what counts as reason is nothing else as a social construct. All points of view are embedded; reason cannot stand apart from our experiences, culture, history etc. But if reason is so closely tied to identity, how can we then achieve emancipation?

The essays in this section cover more contemporary expressions of identity politics, such as populism, postsecularism, postcolonialism, but also communalism in

---

[30] See in particular Young, *Justice and the Politics of Difference*.

Sub-Saharan Africa. This last section shows that identity politics are a problem, rather than a solution to injustice. Foucault is right that identities are social constructions, but as such they incorporate to some extent false consciousness and inauthentic values. It is not clear, how from within the perspective of the different subjugated identities, even with the help of positive redescriptions and consciousness-raising,[31] true emancipation becomes possible without a larger structural transformation of society. Accordingly, the section discusses various solutions to identity politics.

The first chapter on "Populism" rejects the different approaches that take the populists' claims seriously and engage with them (liberalism) or even defend them (radical left). Jan-Werner Müller proposes that one has to deal with populism at the level of ideas and to show that nationalism in itself is not justified, because it does not take into account the pluralism of modern societies. However, Müller and liberals in general do not take into account, that populism could be the result of unsatisfied needs, rather than the product of bad reasoning. Although the radical left sees indeed in a certain form of populism a powerful instrument for realizing social claims, this essay argues that left-wing populism risks to be no less nationalistic than right-wing populism.

The second chapter on "Postsecularism" discusses Jürgen Habermas', Tariq Ramadan's and Michael Walzer's approaches to religion and politics, analyzing in particular the identity politics of the Muslim communities in Europe. All the three thinkers concede religion to play a fundamental role in society and stress the political importance of religion. But how far should religious identity politics go? Habermas and Ramadan, despite their different philosophical backgrounds, fundamentally agree that religious groups, despite their identity claims, have to eventually embrace the principles of liberal democracies from *within* their distinctive religious perspective. Walzer, on the other hand, argues that the state alone can regulate and put a limit on identity politics.

The next chapter on "Postcolonialism" discusses the nature of postcolonial identity politics. Most of contemporary postcolonial philosophers believe postcolonial self-constitution to be 'multiple' or 'hybrid'. Aim of this paper is to refute the postmodern strains in postcolonial studies and to show that, on the contrary, postcolonial self-constitution is centered around strong identities. Analyzing postcolonial self-constitution in terms of identitarian hybridity is wrong, insofar as this incorrectly ignores the fundamental evaluative aspects of agency in self-constitution. It is the confrontation with and the rejection of colonialism that can be considered as the source of postcolonial self-constitution. The essay concludes with the question, if strong postcolonial identity can be considered as a foundation of autonomy.

The last essay in this section on "Communalism in Sub-Saharan Africa: The Reintegration of Child Soldiers" analyzes new forms of communalism in Sub-Saharan Africa, that have been adopted by the international community after the countless civil wars involving child soldiers and devastating the continent on all

---

[31] Appiah & Gutmann, *Color Conscious*.

levels. Communalism is considered to be a highly effective tool in the disarmament, demobilization and reintegration programs of child soldiers. Psychosocial approaches judge the child soldiers' identity as the obstacle to reintegration and propose child soldiers' participation in cultural practices of civil society to redress and 'heal' their identity. This essay argues that psychosocial-oriented programs push child soldiers back to a cultural and social context that constituted the 'root causes' of their becoming soldiers. Children endorse soldiering, insofar as warfare provides them with means of emancipation from poverty and social exclusion as well as some sense of dignity. Therefore, successful reintegration of child soldiers is intrinsically linked to the promotion of their personal autonomy.

1.4 Conclusion

To conclude, there are three ways of how to conceive identity and emancipation in politics. First, identity and emancipation are pursued independently from each other, as social contract theory and *modus vivendi* liberalism is proposing. Emancipation takes place in the public sphere and identity is lived out in the private sphere. Second, emancipation, so as it is formulated in the Enlightenment and recently, though much more prudently, in theories of political liberalism, requires overcoming of at least certain identities and is supposed to stand in opposition to them. Last but not least, emancipation in a great deal of contemporary political and moral theory is envisaged from *within* the different identities.

The book concludes that the efforts made both in the traditions of liberalism and multiculturalism are still provisional and that we are struggling to find a definite reconciliation between emancipation and identity. It proposes that for the time being and until new research consolidates a liberal political theory that takes social practices as its point of departure, the governance approach of liberal egalitarianism, so as it is laid out in Rawls' *A Theory of Justice*, seems to be in the best position to take into account the social constructedness of our identities.

References

Abu Zayd, Nasr. 2016. The 'Others' in the Qur'an: A Hermeneutical Approach. In *Toward New Democratic Imaginaries – Istanbul Seminars on Islam, Culture and Politics*, ed. Seyla Benhabib and Volker Kaul, 97–110. Basel: Springer.
Afary, Janet, and Kevin Anderson. 2005. *Foucault and the Iranian Revolution: Gender and the Seductions of Islamism*. Chicago: Chicago University Press.
An-Na'im, Andullahi. 2009. *Islam and the Secular State*. Cambridge, MA: Harvard University Press.
Appiah, Anthony Kwame, and Amy Gutmann. 1998. *Color Conscious. The Political Morality of Race*. Princeton: Princeton University Press.
Appiah, Kwame Anthony. 2005. *The Ethics of Identity*. Princeton: Princeton University Press.

Barry, Brian. 2000. *Equality and Culture. An Egalitarian Critique of Multiculturalism*. Cambridge: Polity Press.
Benhabib, Seyla. 2008. *Another Cosmopolitanism*. Oxford: Oxford University Press.
Bhabha, Homi. 2004. *The Location of Culture*. London/New York: Routledge.
Bilgrami, Akeel. 2014. *Secularism, Identity, and Enchantment*. Cambridge, MA: Harvard University Press.
Dreyfus, Herbert, and Charles Taylor. 2015. *Retrieving Realism*. Cambridge, MA: Harvard University Press.
El Fadl, Khaled Abou. 2016. The Epistemology of Truth in Modern Islam. In *Toward Democratic New Imaginaries – Istanbul Seminars on Islam, Culture and Politics*, ed. Seyla Benhabib and Volker Kaul, 111–124. Basel: Springer.
Ferrara, Alessandro. 2014. *The Democratic Horizon. Hyperpluralism and the Renewal of Political Liberalism*. Cambridge: Cambridge University Press.
Foucault, Michel. 1988. *Madness and Civilization: A History of Insanity in the Age of Reason*. New York: Vintage Books.
Horkheimer, Max, and Theodor Adorno. 2007. *Dialectic of Enlightenment. Philosophical Fragments*. Palo Alto: Stanford University Press.
Kant, Immanuel. 2009. *An Answer to the Question: 'What is Enlightenment?'*. London: Penguin.
Kaul, Volker. 2018. Populism and the Crisis of Liberalism. *Philosophy & Social Criticism* 44 (4): 346–352. Special issue on "The Populist Upsurge and the Decline of Diversity Capital. Reset DOC Seminars 2017" (eds. Alessandro Ferrara, Volker Kaul und David Rasmussen).
Kaul, Volker, and Ananya Vajpeyi. 2020. *Minorities and Populism – Critical Perspectives from South Asia and Europe*. Basel: Springer.
Khader, Serene. 2019. Why are Women Poor?. In *New York Times*, September 11, 2019.
Korsgaard, Christine. 1996. *The Sources of Normativity*. Cambridge: Cambridge University Press.
Laborde, Cécile, and Aurélie Bardon. 2017. *Religion in Liberal Political Philosophy*. Oxford: Oxford University Press.
Maffettone, Sebastiano. 2010. *Rawls. An Introduction*. Cambridge: Polity Press.
March, Andrew. 2009. *Islam and Liberal Citizenship. The Search for an Overlapping Consensus*. Oxford: Oxford University Press.
Moller Okin, Susan. 1999. *Is Multiculturalism Bad for Women?* Princeton: Princeton University Press.
Patten, Alan. 2014. *Equal Recognition. The Moral Foundations of Minority Rights*. Princeton: Princeton University Press.
Rasmussen, David. 2016. The Emerging Domain of the Political. In *Toward New Democratic Imaginaries – Istanbul Seminars on Islam, Culture and Politics*, ed. Seyla Benhabib and Volker Kaul, 253–264. Basel: Springer.
Rawls, John. 1993. *Political Liberalism*. New York: Columbia University Press.
———. 1971. *A Theory of Justice*. Cambridge, MA: Belknap Press.
Raz, Joseph. 1986. *The Morality of Freedom*. Oxford: Oxford University Press.
Sen, Amartya. 2007. *Identity and Violence: The Illusion of Destiny*. New York: W. W. Norton.
Scheffler, Samuel. 2007. Immigration and the Significance of Culture. *Philosophy and Public Affairs* 35 (2): 93–125.
Charles, Taylor. 1985. Interpretation and the Sciences of Man. In *Philosophy and the Human Sciences. Philosophical Papers*, ed. C. Taylor, vol. 2, 15–57. Cambridge: Cambridge University Press.
Young, Iris Marion. 1990. *Justice and the Politics of Difference*. Princeton: Princeton University Press.
Walzer, Michael. 1997. *On Toleration*. New Haven/London: Yale University Press.

Part I
Liberalism in Search of Identity

Chapter 2
Liberal Nationalism

Abstract Populism puts the nation first and defends nationalism on the basis of a moral obligation that has its origin in national identity. The moral framework of populism is similar to that of communitarianism, even though the latter denounces the xenophobia, chauvinism and aggressiveness of the populists. Meanwhile, also many liberals believe that the current political crisis can only be explained by the neglect of the idea of the nation in recent decades. Therefore, they are in favor of nationalism. They emphasize, however, that liberal nationalism should not be confused with populist nationalism. Where populism has formed in opposition to liberalism, liberal nationalism is based on individual freedom. This essay deals with the question of whether nationalism can be justified from a liberal point of view. It argues that liberalism is incompatible with nationalism. Nationalism cannot justify either positive or negative freedom. First, every form of nationalism is morally relativistic, in the sense that it cannot be said whether the nation realizes moral values or not. Second, only personal identity and not individual freedom can be the source of nationalism. The resulting obligation of national solidarity, however, stands in contrast with fundamental freedoms. The essay concludes with the suggestion that nationalism must be governed and shaped in order to counter populism.

Keywords Populism · Liberalism · Nationalism · Communitarianism · Autonomy · Identity · Meaning · Raz · Kymlicka · Appiah

The first analyses after the surprising successes of populism with Brexit and Trump's election as President of the United States were still conducted in the light of liberalism, which dominated the international political scene in recent decades, especially after the fall of the Berlin Wall. For Jan-Werner Müller (2016), there is no question that the nationalist anti-pluralism, that he reproaches to populism, is illegitimate.[1]

---

[1] Galston (2018) makes very similar claims.

As a strategy for dealing with populism, he can therefore point to John Rawls' *Political Liberalism* (1993), whose moral pillar is precisely pluralism. Interestingly, Müller does not even see himself constrained to deal with questions and problems related to nationalism. The only alternative approaches he critically discusses are those that, like class struggle and social-psychological theories, try to explain populism and reduce it to other factors without taking the populists' claims really seriously.

This is no longer so clearly the case in recent research on populism. Although there are still weighty voices that blame social injustice and inequality (Rodrik 2018, Eichengreen 2018, Bilgrami 2018) and the democratic deficit (Azmanova 2018, Müller 2016: 174–185) for the rise of populism, the question of the nation and its importance has clearly taken over. Even more so, it is the very pluralism that liberalism endorses and Müller proposes as solution, that is said to have prepared the ground for the political success of populism.

Michael Sandel accuses the Democratic Party in the United States to have dropped, under the pretext of pluralism, existential questions that concern Americans as a *nation* rather than just as individuals. According to Sandel, pluralism presupposes the neutrality of the state with regard to the various life plans, with the consequence that ethical questions about the good life are excluded from the public sphere. Where the state, according to the liberal principle of avoidance, is more likely to play an administrative role, the market takes increasingly charge of the accommodation of the various interests. The result is that politics, despite a constant reference to equal opportunity, is relatively powerless in the face of increasing wealth and power inequalities as well as social inequality. Politics can no longer address and make issues of self-esteem and social prestige part of the public discussion. The populist achievements are based on this sense of humiliation, deprivation and powerlessness, which then manifests itself in the ugliest forms of xenophobia.

For Sandel, national identity, that lies at the heart of the populist discourse, is the solution to the problem: "What is the moral significance, if any, of national borders? Do we owe more to our fellow citizens than we owe citizens of other countries? In a global age, should we cultivate national identities or aspire to a cosmopolitan ethic of universal human concern?" (Sandel 2018: 357)

The criticism of the liberal understanding of community has always been at the center of Sandel's communitarianism. On the other hand, it is more surprising that even liberals break with pluralism in the wake of populism. In one of the key analyses of the defeat of the Democratic Party in the presidential elections in 2016, Mark Lilla accuses the left-wing establishment to have got lost in divisive identity politics, that puts cultural, religious, sexual and ethnic diversity over national unity. Democrats have failed to make sense of the idea of the common good and of a common American future, "losing a sense of what we share as citizens and what binds us as a nation." (Lilla 2017: 13) Accordingly, Democrats should reassert common realities, address a sense of shared commitment among Americans, and help to rebuild it: "There can be no liberal politics without a sense of we – of what we are as citizens and what we owe each other." (Lilla 2017: 19f.)

Yascha Mounk also sees a rebellion against pluralism to take place in Western democracies. He relates it to the fact that "the residents of various European countries were much more attached to their national cultures, and much more resistant to thinking of themselves primarily as Europeans, than I had wanted to believe." (Mounk 2018: 275) As a political solution, he therefore suggests a form of inclusive patriotism.

Lilla's and Mounk's analyses show how difficult it is for pluralistic approaches to shape individual-transcendent policies for the whole community. This void of liberalism in what concerns community issues has been exploited by populism and I agree with Lilla and Mounk that insisting once again on the value of pluralism cannot be the solution. (Kaul 2018b) The question however remains, whether liberals therefore need to take national issues more into account. (Kaul 2018a)

According to current liberal patriots, the nation faces two challenges. On the one hand, it is internally weakened by identity politics and multiculturalism. (Lilla 2017) On the other hand, the nation is externally eroded by supranational institutions and globalization. (Mounk 2018: 216–236) Liberal patriots believe that populism has its roots in this decline of national identity. Therefore, they believe that in order to rein in populism, the national idea needs to be reinvigorated.

Liberal patriots face the question of what idea of the nation should be defended. Communitarians and populists basically agree upon one point, even though the former, of course, do not share the xenophobia, racism, and aggressiveness of the populists: For them, the nation always comes first. That is, because of our national affiliation, we have moral obligations towards members of our nation.[2] This brings with it that we must prioritize their interests above everything else. If, for example, the welfare of certain workers is at stake through immigration, offshoring and free trade agreements, we have the moral obligation to protect them and, if necessary, to close the borders. Sandel makes this very clear, when he asks about the moral value of national borders above, but also in the passages on "Buy American" and US citizens' voluntary guarding of the border with Mexico in his book *Justice: What's the Right Thing to Do?* (2010: 230–234).

However, liberals cannot derive obligations from national identity to which individuals do not have consented in some way. Nor can they defend a policy that limits the basic liberties of their own citizens. That is why liberal patriots have a different, more reduced understanding of the nation than communitarians.[3] They agree with communitarians that the good and meaningful life can be realized only within the

---

[2] So-called left-wing populists would question this point and clearly distinguish themselves from the communitarian understanding of the nation of right-wing populists. Right-wing populists presuppose the nation as *given*. Left-wing populists make it their task to *construct* the people (see in particular Laclau 2005). Similar to Müller (2016: 98f.), I believe, however, that the concept of nation of left-wing populism is indistinguishable from that of right-wing populism. (Kaul 2020)

[3] Liberals define the nation as "societal culture": "A culture which provides its members with meaningful ways of life across the full range of human activities, including social, educational religious, recreational and economic life, encompassing both public and private spheres... [it involves] not just shared memories or values but also common institutions and practices." (Kymlicka 1995: 76)

nation, and that the nation offers individuals ethically good life plans that promote their personal autonomy. Yet, liberals do not believe that this creates special obligations that go beyond the preservation of the nation. Although liberal patriots agree with restrictions on immigration, they cannot ignore the freedom of their own citizens when it comes to economic policy. (Kymlicka 2001)

Will Kymlicka makes a distinction between internal and external restrictions. "The first kind is intended to protect the group from the destabilizing impact of internal dissent (e.g., the decision of individual members not to follow traditional practices or customs), whereas the second is intended to protect the group from the impact of external decisions (e.g., the economic or political decisions of the larger society)." (Kymlicka 1995: 35) Only the latter are justified from a liberal point of view.

For communitarians, the comprehensive moral obligation to put the nation first is grounded in the embeddedness of the self. The nation constitutes the practical identity of individuals. It not only provides individuals with principles according to which they have to act, but also forms the basis for the special obligations they have with regard to each other. Liberals do not deny that individuals can actually have a national identity. However, they claim that this can only be the result of an active and voluntary identification on the part of the individuals. (Appiah 2005: 65–71, Christine Korsgaard (1996)) National identity is not simply given to individuals, but it is freely chosen. Since individual freedom is the foundation of national identity, the nation can never abolish certain freedoms. Given their understanding of identity in terms of identification, for liberal patriots freedom always comes before the nation.

With regard to populism, liberal patriots have a very attractive understanding of the nation. They take full advantage of the liberal model and yet are able to put the nation at the center of their politics. More radical populists may complain about the weakened concept of the nation, yet given the fact that the majority of citizens of Western nations prefer the liberal-democratic system, liberal nationalism seems to constitute a successful compromise.

I would like to defend the thesis that liberal nationalism cannot maintain the tension between freedom and the nation, and ultimately is indistinguishable from traditional nationalism, as represented by populism. Liberal patriots can neither show that the nation embodies the good life and thus guarantees positive freedom. Nor are they able to question the embeddedness of the self and to understand identity as an expression of our freedom.

In the first part, I focus on Joseph Raz's theory of freedom, which forms the basis of liberal nationalism. In the second part, I refute step by step the connection between autonomy and nation as well as between freedom and identity. In the conclusion, I make some suggestions about how liberals have to deal with populism.

2.1 The Liberal Theory of Nation

Liberals are traditionally opponents rather than supporters of the nation and, see themselves, like Kant, as cosmopolitans. As Martha Nussbaum writes in a much-discussed article on patriotism and cosmopolitanism, nationality is a "morally irrelevant characteristic". (Nussbaum 1994: 3) Liberals are primarily concerned with the freedom of individuals. However, they face the problem of defining freedom. Liberals in the tradition of Kant and Mill consider persons to be free, insofar as they determine their will and its principles on the basis of reason. From this point of view, nationalism contributes to heteronomy and thus to the immaturity of human beings, given that it prescribes external practical principles and duties. (Kant 1974) Rawls expands the notion of autonomy in *Political Liberalism* (1993) and includes not only strictly moral conceptions, but also reasonable, comprehensive doctrines, such as religious but also patriotic doctrines. Yet, the pluralism of reasonable, comprehensive doctrines requires that none of these doctrines overrides others and that all accept liberalism as a constitutional principle.

Some liberals claim that autonomy is not subject to the internal condition of an adequate use of reason, but that it is related to external conditions. Joseph Raz uses the examples of the "Man in the Pit" and "The Hounded Woman" (1986: 373f.) to show that freedom is dependent on a range of available options. Regarding liberalism, Raz notes: "Much liberal thought has been dedicated to exploring the ways in which restrictions on individual choices, be they legal or social, can be removed, and obstacles to choice — due to poverty, lack of education, or other limitations on access to goods — overcome." (1994: 176).

However, it is not enough in order to lead a free life to have any kind of possibilities, but the options available must have value and implement the good. Raz defends the thesis that "our conception of Freedom is bounded by our notions of what might be worthwhile." (1986: 378f.) Only a good life can be a truly free life. He continues: "Autonomy is valuable only if exercised in pursuit of the good. The ideal of autonomy requires only the availability of morally acceptable options." (Raz 1986: 381).

Raz goes a step further, claiming that his concept of freedom, based on a reasonable range of choices, entails value pluralism – "valuing autonomy leads to the endorsement of moral pluralism." (Raz 1986: 399) Since freedom requires the possibility of choosing between various morally acceptable goods, "the morally acceptable options must [therefore] themselves vary in the reasons which speak in favour of each of them. There are, in other words, more valuable options than can be chosen, and they must be significantly different or else the requirements of variety which is a precondition of the adequacy of options will not be met." (Raz 1986: 398).

Raz in the following has to answer the question, what it is that determines the value of a given choice. One answer would be "that all value derives from choice which is itself not guided by value and is therefore free, i.e. arbitrary." (Raz 1986: 387 f.) This is, for example, the position of Rawls above, but also of Christine Korsgaard (1996) and Harry Frankfurt (2006). Raz, on the other hand, assumes "independently existing values which are transformed and added to by the development of one's projects and commitments." (Raz 1986: 388) According to Raz, values are given in the world.

The question remains, if the different values are really incompatible and there are "several maximal forms of life" making "complete moral perfection" (Raz 1986: 396) unachievable, how we can take a decision between the life forms available. If all values are on the same level and cannot be further ranked and if it is not us who decide on value or non-value, how can we make a decision between the different options? Would it then not be the same for us to lead a life as a Muslim or Christian, German or Turk, should we assume that all these life forms realize different, but morally equivalent goods?

The realization of a free, autonomous life is therefore, according to Raz, related to another condition. Autonomy requires not only a reasonable range of morally valuable possible choices, but also that the options available have some *meaning* for the person. "The ideal of autonomy (…) requires (…) that the agent must be aware of his options and of the *meaning* of his choices."[4] (Raz 1986: 389 f.) And how does a certain life form gain meaning for a person? Why is it that for a religious person Christianity has more meaning than Islam, always under the condition that both religions instantiate equivalent but incompatible values?

Raz's answer is that the meaning that the different values have for people is derived from their national culture. It is the particular culture of the nation to which people belong, which gives meaning to certain moral options and makes them appear more interesting, perhaps more plausible, and, above all, more *natural* than other, morally no less worthy possibilities. In this picture, to come back to the previous example, most people in Germany are Christians for the very reason that the German nation has been historically influenced by Christianity, so that only Christianity has meaning for Germans.

Raz states very clearly that "options presuppose a culture. They presuppose shared meanings and common practices." (1994: 177) He specifies that "only through being socialized in a culture can one tap the options which give life a meaning. By and large one's cultural membership determines the horizon of one's opportunities, of what one may become, or (if one is older) what one might have been. Little surprise that it is in the interest of every person to be fully integrated in a cultural group." (Raz 1994: 178).

It is the meaning that the nation attributes to various moral life forms that gives it value in the eyes of certain liberals, who, like Raz, Kymlicka, or Kwame Anthony Appiah defend a form of moral realism. These liberals see in the nation an indispensable good for individuals, in the sense that only the nation provides "the core options which give meaning to our lives — the different occupations we can pursue, the friendships and relationships we can have, the loyalties and commitments which we attract and develop, the cultural, sporting, or other interests we develop."(Raz 1994: 178) It is the nation that makes freedom of choice possible.

---

[4] Emphasis mine.

Kymlicka, a pioneer of so-called liberal multiculturalism and an important representative of liberal nationalism (2001: 203–290), gets to the heart of this point of view when he writes: "Put simply, freedom involves making choices amongst various options, and our societal culture not only provides these options, but also makes them meaningful to us. People make choices about the social practices around them, based on their beliefs about the value of these practices. And to have a belief about the value of a practice is, in the first instance, a matter of understanding the meanings attached to it by our culture." (Kymlicka 1995: 83) Appiah's defense of cosmopolitan patriotism also focuses on the freedom of the individual: "The fundamental thought of the cosmopolitanism I defend is that the freedom to create oneself – the freedom that liberalism celebrates – requires a range of socially transmitted options from which to invent what we have come to call our identities. Second, they give us a language in which to think about these identities and with which we may shape new ones." (Appiah 1997: 625).

Now one could argue that this liberalism shows at most the value of culture but not that of the nation. The concept of the nation cannot be reduced to that of culture, since the former is based on a political claim that is in general alien to culture. David Miller claims that "as far as possible, each nation should have its own set of political institutions." (Miller 1995: 81).

However, if we follow Raz's concept of culture form above, according to which culture gives meaning to moral values, then it is obvious that culture is inherently related to politics and thus it is difficult to separate the concept of culture and from that of the nation. If culture has a moral quality, then it is essential to maintain a certain political autonomy of culture that is able to preserve and defend the values. That is why Kymlicka largely defines the nation as culture and vice versa. He argues that "just as societal cultures are almost invariable national cultures, so nations are almost invariably societal cultures." (Kymlicka 1995: 80).

2.2 Critique of the Liberal Theory of Nation

Raz distinguishes between two aspects of personal autonomy. On the one hand, the ideal of autonomy does not mean much more than the freedom of non-intervention: "a life freely chosen", "opposed to a life of coerced choices." (Raz 1986: 371) On the other hand, however, Raz makes autonomy dependent upon the existence of certain capacities and conditions. Freedom requires, as we have seen, a conscious decision of the person for meaningful and morally good options, which the nation ultimately provides. Negative freedom guarantees autonomy only insofar as it is complemented by a specific form of positive freedom. Raz underlines this aspect: "Negative freedom, freedom from coercive interferences, is valuable inasmuch as it serves positive freedom and autonomy. In judging the value of negative freedom one should never forget that it derives from its contribution to autonomy." (Raz 1986: 410)

Raz even goes so far as to say that "the significance of denial of options to one's autonomy depends on the circumstances one finds oneself in. In some countries the vote does not have the symbolic significance it has in our culture. Its denial to an individual may be a trivial matter. Such factors do not diminish the importance of negative freedom, but they make it more difficult to judge." (Raz 1986: 410) On the other hand, however, he claims that "autonomy is, to be sure, inconsistent with various alternative forms of valuable lives. It cannot be obtained within societies which support social forms which do not leave enough room for individual choice." (Raz 1986: 395)

Raz's point is that the role of the nation is to ensure positive freedom without fundamentally questioning negative freedom. There are two questions here. First, does the nation really guarantee positive freedom? And second, does the nation leave negative freedom untouched? In order to realize positive freedom, the value of the nation would have to be purely *instrumental*, in the sense that its value depends solely on the fact whether it gives meaning to enough objective values and thus guarantees freedom of choice between different forms of the good life. But is the relationship not exactly the opposite, namely, that the nation constitutes values and gives itself the laws? As far as negative freedom is concerned, it needs to be clarified whether the will can freely decide between the existing national values or whether the nation constitutes not only the values, but also the will of the persons.

2.2.1 Nation and the Problem of Positive Freedom

Raz emphasizes that his theory of autonomy has nothing in common with cultural relativism. He writes, "'value' is sometimes used in a relativized sense, to indicate not what is of value but what is held to be so by some person, group, culture, etc. In this chapter 'value' is non-relativized." (Raz 1986: 397) Raz is not the only one who attributes to the nation the epistemological role to uncover the moral reality and make it accessible to us. Hubert Dreyfus and Charles Taylor (2015) have a similar theory. The problems with this theory are that it, first, has very counterintuitive consequences and, second, that it cannot avoid a certain arbitrariness and relativism.

If the value of the nation depends on its moral anchoring, it means that probably not all the nations of the world have value. Several nations come immediately to mind that are more associated with tyranny and poverty than with morality. This leads first of all to the fact that one is forced to create, similar to Hegel (1961),[5] a sort of ranking of the various nations, cultures and civilizations, in which the ones ranked first come closest to the moral ideals. And as a consequence, we cannot recognize all nations and cultures equally, and may even rightly exclude some nations violating morality as inferior. In this regard, Taylor concludes that "it can't make

---

[5] See also Singh Rathore (2017), who gathers all of Hegel's writings on India.

sense to demand as a matter of right that we come up with a final concluding judgment that [the] value [of a nation] is great, or equal to others'." (Taylor 1994: 69).

The epistemological theory not only justifies us to deny some nations their moral value, while we have to recognize this value to others. It also forces us to believe that so-called rogue or poor nations cannot have subjective value for their respective compatriots. In this regard, residents of an impoverished sub-Saharan nation, for example, could not be proud of their nation. And to give a German example, let's suppose that the German Democratic Republic (GDR) was an illegitimate state and East Germany has grown together into a nation in the decades of separation. Then, in this perspective, no citizen of the former GDR could and should feel as East German and the much-vaunted 'Ostalgie' would be inappropriate. But of course it is not like that. The overwhelming majority of East Germans are in complete agreement that the GDR was an illegitimate state and nonetheless feel a certain proud of being East German.

These are all practical problems, which, though having serious political consequences, do not undermine the epistemological theory of the nation from a logical point of view. The logical problem of this theory, however, is that it cannot prove that only objective values can establish and constitute a nation. Basically, the theory shows exactly the opposite, namely that the nation itself is the origin of values and thus cannot avoid the relativism that Raz seeks to escape from.

On what basis can we say when a nation does realize objective moral goods and when not? The moral values themselves remain inaccessible to us in two ways. First, they are *meta*physical in nature and thus cannot be known through experience.[6] That is why we need the nation, in order to put the values into practice. Second, moral truth reveals itself exclusively through the meaning that the nation is able to give to certain life forms. The only access we have to moral truth is through the meaning that the nation can convey to us. It follows that we only understand the meaning and never the truth in itself. But who can guarantee us that the nation is actually tracking the truth, that it correctly interprets the moral facts? In Raz's theory, any judgment as to whether a nation has moral character and thereby allows for positive freedom is purely arbitrary, a matter of opinion. That does not mean that within a Razian framework we cannot make moral judgments, only that those cannot be based on moral truths or facts.

Liberal nationalists do not allow us to make a clear distinction between good and evil. Ultimately, what counts as a good life form depends upon which of the various historical narratives of the nation prevails in the political struggle over their legitimate interpretation.[7] Of course, the relevant life forms of a nation can always be criticized with the help of alternative narratives. (MacIntyre 1984: 13–15) Yet, it must be clear that none of the life forms, as attractive and good as they may appear

---

[6] This touches upon the very big questions of moral realism that Sayre-McCord (2014) summarizes very well: "Non-naturalism comes with two distinctive burdens: (i) accounting for how the realm of moral properties fits in with familiar natural properties and (ii) explaining how it is that we are able to learn anything about these moral properties."
[7] For the central role of narratives see in particular MacIntyre (1981: 204–225).

to us, has an independent moral justification that is not based on national myths. That is why all kinds of nationalism are always relativistic.

2.2.2 Nation and the Problem of Negative Freedom

Liberal nationalists could accept this criticism of their concept of positive freedom and still insist that nationalism nonetheless leaves the freedom of the will untouched. Be the various options that have prevailed within the nation good or bad, the nation cannot force determinate choices upon us. Despite everything, we decide freely which of the national contemporary life forms we want to follow. The fact that we can work for alternative life forms of the nation seems to support this claim. But if the focus is more on the meaning than on the actual value of the available options, then negative freedom is no longer guaranteed, as Raz's example from above on the relative importance of voting indicates.

Liberals assume that the nation gives meaning to options without creating obligations that are incompatible with individual freedom. They insist that individuals freely choose one of the meaningful options available to them. Communitarians, on the other hand, as Kymlicka writes, "deny that we can 'stand apart' from (some of) our ends. According to Michael Sandel, (…) some of our ends are 'constitutive' ends, in the sense that they define our sense of personal identity. It makes no sense, on his view, to say that my ends might not be worthy of my allegiance, for they define who I am." And Kymlicka continues: "I believe that this communitarian conception of the self is mistaken. It is not easy or enjoyable to revise one's deepest ends, but it is possible, and sometimes a regrettable necessity. New experiences or circumstances may reveal that our earlier beliefs about the good are mistaken. No end is immune from such potential revision." (Kymlicka 1995: 91)

However, liberals face the problem to show that if the creation of meaning does not affect individuals and directly involve them, how the life forms of their *own* nation make respectively more sense than those of other nations. How do these different valuations come about, if meaning is not somehow related to individuals and shapes their worldviews?

Liberal nationalism lacks a theory of how *subjective* meaning is constituted, that means how a particular meaning manifests itself as meaning *for* an individual. The insistence on freedom of choice does not reveal how meaning affects the decisions of the individual. In liberal theory, freedom and meaning are strictly separated from each other, with the result that the foundations for the creation of meaning are lacking and meaning, consequently, cannot fulfill the role liberals ascribe to it.

Communitarianism has a theory in this regard, which however questions individual freedom, as Kymlicka correctly states above. The only way to establish a connection between meaning and individuals is by way of their identity. Identity constitutes the meaning that things take on for individuals. MacIntyre clarifies this, when he writes: "We enter human society, that is, with one or more imputed characters – roles into which we have been drafted." (1981: 216) He continues: "Hence what is good for me has to be good for one who inhabits these roles. As such, I inherit from the past of my family, my city, my tribe, my nation, a variety of debts, inheritances, rightful expectations and obligations. These constitute the given of my life, my moral starting point. This is in part what gives my life moral particularity." (1981: 220)

The nation and its values have meaning for me, just because I am already the person for whom those values have meaning. It is only through my specific, given social identity that certain values promoted by the nation have meaning for me. But this also means that the nation must first form the identity of individuals, before it can have meaning and thus value for individuals.

It remains to be seen in detail how, according to communitarianism, the nation constitutes the identity of individuals. Here it is only important to note that this does not happen on the basis of a voluntary identification with the nation, since identification already presupposes identity and meaning. If autonomy requires subjective meaning and latter presupposes an already given identity, then it also follows that identity determines the will and that free will does not exist. Each of my decisions is not derived from an unconditional free choice, but is the result of the person I am and the meaning that certain actions have for me.

Now, liberal nationalism could admit that it has a defective concept of subjective meaning and acknowledge the importance of national *identity*. And yet it could insist that freedom of the will, although restricted, is not yet completely abolished. After all, each of us has several other identities besides our national identity - gender, profession, class, religion, race, etc. Each of these individual collective identities makes demands on us and we are forced to decide freely which one we want to follow. (Sen 2007)

However, if we understand the nation as a "societal culture" that brings about meaning in all areas of human activity, including social, religious, and economic life,[8] then the national culture shapes each of these particular identities. According to the theory of liberal nationalism, when we make decisions in the various roles we take on, these are always influenced by the spirit of the nation.

2.2.3 Final Thoughts

With the rise of populism, once again the opinion gains ground that we must attribute a moral status to the nation. The nation has an undeniable value for us that politics has to take into account. Interestingly, this position is not only supported by communitarians, but increasingly by liberals. They defend the theory of so-called liberal nationalism, which ascribes to the nation a moral character on the basis of individual freedom.

I have tried to show that individual freedom, in terms of both positive and negative freedom, cannot justify the value of the nation. Only communitarianism, according to which the nation constitutes the identity of individuals, would, from a logical standpoint, be able to establish the morality of the nation. This is the main conclusion of my article. However, liberals cannot endorse traditional,

---

[8] For a definition of "societal culture" see footnote 2.

communitarian nationalism. Although communitarians do not accept the rhetoric of populism, they substantially agree with its freedom-restrictive policies, which results from obligations of national solidarity.

Some liberals argue that I am indeed right and liberal nationalism fails as a theory because of its conception of the atomized individual. However, they contend that I take communitarianism too literally. Communitarianism is rightly based on the assumption that the nation constitutes the identity of individuals. Yet, individuals necessarily have to interpret the meaning that the respective identities provide. (Taylor 1985) This is enough to guarantee the right to freedom.[9]

I also think that communitarianism is not able to show why individuals must necessarily accept their identity and cannot question the meaning that it brings about. Insofar as identity is largely based on practical reason, it is unclear to what extent communitarians can avoid Kant's conception of autonomy.

However, I believe that communitarianism is right to stress that we have no choice with regard to our national identity. We *feel* committed to the nation, even though many of us are unaware of this feeling and would deny it. When Kymlicka wonders why the nation binds us psychologically, I agree with him that "a full explanation would involve aspects of psychology, sociology, linguistics, the philosophy of mind, and even neurology." (Kymlicka 1995: 90)

The problem, in my view, is that liberals under no circumstances want to acknowledge the conditioning effects of the nation in individual behavior, but also of other collective identities. Any kind of liberalism believes that in some way we can distance ourselves from our collective identities and are free to question our identity. Therefore, liberals do not consider it necessary that our collective identities themselves must be *governed*. However, as long as nations play a moral and political role, they must be shaped accordingly and cannot be left to themselves. At first sight, this sounds very illiberal, but it only requires the implementation of a theory of justice that, like Rawls' (1971), takes human nature seriously.

In terms of populism, this would mean that the new inequalities created by globalization and immigration in Western countries (Rodrik 2018) are to be addressed and to be at the center of politics. At the same time, nations do not have to be sealed off and national equality has not to be played off against global poverty. It only entails that the participation of the most disadvantaged groups in economic, cultural and political life needs to be ensured. Populist nationalism has no other basis than a grudge against state institutions and the political and economic elite for insufficiently defending the interests of the disadvantaged of their own nation. For this reason, cosmopolitans face the task of reconciling the idea of an open world with the idea of equality over the next few years. (Kaul 2018b)

---

[9] I would like to thank Alessandro Ferrara for this valuable objection.

References

Appiah, Kwame Anthony. 1997. Cosmopolitan Patriots. *Critical Inquiry* 23 (3): 617–639.
———. 2005. *The Ethics of Identity*. Princeton: Princeton University Press.
Azmanova, Albena. 2018. The Populist Catharsis: On the Revival of the Political. *Philosophy & Social Criticism* 44 (4): 399–411. Special issue on "The Populist Upsurge and the Decline of Diversity Capital. Reset DOC Seminars 2017" (edited by Alessandro Ferrara, Volker Kaul and David Rasmussen).
Bilgrami, Akeel. 2018. Reflections on Three Populisms. *Philosophy & Social Criticism* 44 (4): 453–462. Special issue on "The Populist Upsurge and the Decline of Diversity Capital. Reset DOC Seminars 2017" (edited by Alessandro Ferrara, Volker Kaul and David Rasmussen).
Dreyfus, Herbert, and Charles Taylor. 2015. *Retrieving Realism*. Cambridge, MA: Harvard University Press.
Eichengreen, Barry. 2018. *The Populist Temptation: Economic Grievance and Political Reaction in the Modern Era*. Oxford: Oxford University Press.
Frankfurt, Harry. 2006. *The Reasons of Love*. Princeton: Princeton University Press.
Galston, William. 2018. *Anti-Pluralism: The Populist Threat to Liberal Democracy*. New Haven: Yale University Press.
Hegel, G.W.F. 1961. *Vorlesungen über die Philosophie der Geschichte*. Stuttgart: Reclam.
Kant, Immanuel. 1974. Beantwortung der Frage: Was ist Aufklärung? In *Was ist Aufklärung?* ed. Ehrhard Bahr, 8–17. Reclam: Stuttgart.
Kaul, Volker. 2018a. Populism and the Crisis of Liberalism. *Philosophy & Social Criticism* 44 (4): 346–352. Special issue on "The Populist Upsurge and the Decline of Diversity Capital. Reset DOC Seminars 2017" (edited by Alessandro Ferrara, Volker Kaul and David Rasmussen).
———. 2018b. Pluralismus, die Wiege des Populismus? Plädoyer für einen institutionellen Kosmopolitismus. In *PraeFaktisch*. https://www.praefaktisch.de/postfaktisch/pluralismus-die-wiege-des-populismus-plaedoyer-fuer-einen-institutionellen-kosmopolitismus/#more-534.
———. 2020. On How to Deal with Populism. In *Minorities and Populism: Reimagining Pluralism in the South Asian and European Context*, ed. Volker Kaul and Ananya Vajpeyi. Basel: Springer.
Korsgaard, Christine. 1996. *The Sources of Normativity*. Cambridge: Cambridge University Press.
Kymlicka, Will. 1995. *Multicultural Citizenship: A Liberal Theory of Minority Rights*. Oxford: Clarendon Press.
———. 2001. Politics in the Vernacular. In *Nationalism, Multiculturalism, and Citizenship*. Oxford: Oxford University Press.
Laclau, Ernesto. 2005. *On Populist Reason*. London: Verso Books.
Lilla, Mark. 2017. *The Once and Future Liberal: After Identity Politics*. Harper: New York City.
MacIntyre, Alasdair. 1981. *After Virtue*. London: Duckworth.
———. 1984. *Is Patriotism a Virtue?*. The Lindley Lecture, University of Kansas, March 26, 1984. https://mirror.explodie.org/Is%20Patriotism%20a%20Virtue-1984.pdf.
Miller, David. 1995. *On Nationality*. Oxford: Clarendon Press.
Mounk, Yasha. 2018. *The People vs. Democracy: Why Our Freedom Is in Danger and How to Save It*. Cambridge, MA: Harvard University Press.
Müller, Jan-Werner. 2016. *What is Populism?* Philadelphia: University of Pennsylvania Press.
Nussbaum, Martha. 1994. Patriotism and Cosmopolitanism. In *Boston Review*, Oct.-Nov. 1994.
Rawls, John. 1971. *A Theory of Justice*. Cambridge, MA: Belknap Press.
———. 1993. *Political Liberalism*. New York City: Columbia University Press.
Raz, Joseph. 1986. *The Morality of Freedom*. Oxford: Oxford University Press.
———. 1994. *Ethics in the Public Domain: Essays in the Morality of Law and Politics*. Oxford: Clarendon Press.
Rodrik, Dani. 2018. Populism and the Economics of Globalization. *Journal of International Business Policy* 1 (1–2): 12–33.

Sandel, Michael. 2010. *Justice: What's the Right Thing to Do?* New York, Farrar, Straus and Giroux.
———. 2018. Populism, Liberalism, and Democracy. *Philosophy & Social Criticism* 44 (4): 353–359. Special issue on "The Populist Upsurge and the Decline of Diversity Capital. Reset DOC Seminars 2017" (edited by Alessandro Ferrara, Volker Kaul and David Rasmussen).
Sayre-McCord, Geoff. 2014. Metaethics. In *The Stanford Encyclopedia of Philosophy* (Summer 2014 Edition), ed. Edward N. Zalta. https://plato.stanford.edu/archives/sum2014/entries/metaethics/.
Sen, Amartya. 2007. *Identity and Violence: The Illusion of Destiny.* New York, W. W. Norton & Company.
Singh Rathore, Aakash. 2017. *Hegel's India: A Reinterpretation.* Oxford: Oxford University Press.
Taylor, Charles. 1985. Self-Interpreting Animals. In *Philosophical Papers*, Human Agency and Language, ed. C. Taylor, vol. 1. Cambridge: Cambridge University Press.
———. 1994. Multiculturalism. In *Examining the Politics of Recognition*, ed. Amy Gutmann. Princeton: Princeton University Press.

Chapter 3
Freedom and Identity

Abstract As show the partly violent clashes between liberal secularists and Islamists in the aftermath of the Arab spring, the two fractions certainly defend two diametrically opposite political points of view. For liberals, politics finds its ultimate justification in the protection of individual freedom. For Islamists, only the application of the moral code and religious law codified in the Sharia can justify politics. Contrary to what is sustained by a theory of situated agency, there is no easy and definite reconciliation between the two positions. And this depends precisely upon the fact that both political models are based upon the very same idealist conception of the individual, namely the assumption, that we, as persons, have a free will and are not determined by the law of causality. Paradoxical as it might sound, it is our freedom that gives rise to the problem of identity and lends force to the Islamist argumentation. If freedom as such cannot bring about practical reason and also liberals recognize that the ultimate source of normativity is identity, there is a point in the Islamist and, more general, communitarian claim that we are not free to choose our identity. In order that identity does the normative work it is supposed to do, it must be given and not chosen. What remains, however, unclear in the communitarian picture is how the norms of our community can come to constitute our will without a process of active identification. If we cannot identify voluntarily with our community's norms, then only emotional attachment to our community can explain identification and the normative grip communitarian norms have upon us. Yet, attachment is conditioned by the effective satisfaction of our psychological and physical needs. The problem is that our need for freedom and liberty can become overshadowed by our more immediate needs based, for example, upon resentment and revenge and that today make in particular Muslims to be so hostile towards liberal ideas. I suggest that conciliatory trust-building measures can help to surmount the anger, fear, mistrust and suspicion Muslims feel vis-à-vis the West and that are at the origin of today's conflict between freedom and identity in the Muslim world.

Keywords Identity · Freedom · Practical reason · Attachment · Human needs · Islam · Communitarianism · Immanuel Kant · John Rawls

One of the predominant concerns with regard to the democratic revolutions in the Arab world is the question if they can bring forth a political order that is able to reconcile individual freedom and religious identity, a political system that is able to guarantee civil rights within a Muslim public culture. The often irreconcilable conflict and violent clashes between those who advocate for individual freedom and the promoters of one form or another of political Islam make many political observers fear, however, that the Arab spring is turning into an Arab winter.

Yet, only few political theorists actually think that there is a contradiction between the claims of freedom and the struggle for identity. And these few thinkers, sustaining Samuel Huntington's thesis of the clash of civilizations, come to the little constructive conclusion that Islam is the enemy of liberalism and Western culture and that Islam therefore needs to be fought and contained in the best manners of the cold war.[1] The large majority of contemporary political philosophers believe, on the contrary, that freedom and identity are perfectly compatible with each other and that the current opposition between liberal secularists and the religious faithful is purely artificial and invented, fostered by serious misconceptions of both freedom and identity. It is only once we consider our true self to be autonomous from its social context that identities and their claims start to give us anxiety and come to be conceived as a danger for our freedom. And vice versa, it is just in case that we think our autonomy to coincide with our identity that aspirations for freedom are judged as a threat to our integrity and the authenticity of our community and religion. But freedom and identity are always interdependent; the self is never entirely transcendent, nor fully embedded. The self rather displays both the properties of transcendence and embeddedness simultaneously, the self is constituted and free at the same time. If it is true that social norms give content to our will, we still have the freedom to interpret and dislocate the meaning of these very norms.[2]

Therefore our fears that the Arab revolutions will give rise to some version of Islamic theocracy is "motivated by entrenched cultural prejudice against Muslims and their capacity for self-governance" rooted in our Western-centric worldview. "There are multiple historical and institutional models to choose from in reconciling Islam and democracy. Rather than shying away from the contentious debate which will now break out in these countries (...), we should celebrate it as an aspect of pluralist democratization,"[3] writes Seyla Benhabib in the early days of the revolution. In reality, the current conflict must be understood as a democratic process in

---

[1] See for instance Paul Berman (2004): *Terror and Liberalism*, New York, W. W. Norton & Company.

[2] Seyla Benhabib's theory of democratic iterations and Judith Butler's theory of gender performativity render very well this process of continuous interaction between our identity and freedom. See S. Benhabib (2006): *Another Cosmopolitanism*, New York, Oxford University Press and Judith Butler (2006): *Gender Trouble: Feminism and the Subversion of Identity*, New York/London, Routledge.

[3] Seyla Benhabib (2011): "The Arab Spring: Religion, Revolution and the Public Sphere", in *Eurozine* (published on May 10, 2011) (http://www.eurozine.com/articles/2011-05-10-benhabib-en.html)

which political actors come to appropriate, redefine and transform the traditional interpretations of Islam, as a process that contributes to an "interpenetration and dialogical relation" between secularism and Islamism, "unsettling the fixity of positions and oppositional categories," as Nilüfer Göle claims with regard to the Turkish experience of the place of Islam in the public sphere.[4] Our freedom gives way to an hybridization of identity[5] that, as Roger Cohen observes in the case of Egypt, allows people to have their passion for Islam to be equaled only by their passion for free speech and free press. And Cohen sees these examples of Muslims who are religious liberals or liberal believers as "a living repudiation of all the trite religious-secular, either-or, clash-of-civilizations intellectual constructs through which the world has tried to address the Arab Spring".[6]

Yet, from the possibility of a hybridization of secular and religious identities we cannot deduce any necessity. Since we cannot only quote positions of the Muslim Brotherhood that actually stand in strong contrast with any sort of secular thought, but a theory of situated agency also cannot exclude categorically traditional religious commitments that are hostile to individual rights. A theory of situated agency cannot prescribe content and direction of the reiterations of the social norms that come to constitute us. Even if we presuppose cross-cultural contaminations and religious norms to be historically indeterminate and hybrid, nothing in our freedom inhibits us to interpret these norms in a more traditionalist and archaic manner. Our interpretations and the kind of identities we eventually come to endorse aren't bound by any independent moral criteria and have no objective measure outside the internal point of the view of the respective individuals themselves. Benhabib clearly sees this danger when she warns that "because they are dependent on contingent processes of democratic will-formation, not all jurisgenerative politics yields positive results". Therefore "*the validity of cosmopolitan norms* is not dependent on jurisgenerative and democratic iterations".[7] But then, in the last instance, freedom tends to trump identity and to precede any ethics of identity.

There is a lot at stakes, if eventually we have to choose between freedom and identity. Not only will the West continue to be in conflict with cultures and civilizations that currently deny negative rights, but also will these societies remain stuck in their struggle for recognition without actually addressing the roots causes for which they are unable to account for individual liberties. I am going to claim that the either/or choice between freedom and identity goes back to an idealist conception

---

[4] Nilüfer Göle (2002), "Islam in Public: New Visibilities and New Imaginaries", in *Public Culture* 14 (1), pp. 174 and 189.

[5] For the thesis on hybrid identity see in particular Jean-François Bayart (2005): *The Illusion of Cultural Identity*, London, Hurst and Achille Mbembe (2001): *On the Postcolony*, Berkeley and Los Angeles, University of California Press.

[6] Roger Cohen (2012): "A Place for Religion", in *International Herald Tribune Magazine* (November 30, 2012), p. 17.

[7] Benhabib, *Another Cosmopolitanism*, p. 49. Whereas jurisgenerative politics is defined as processes in which "a democratic people, which considers itself bound by certain guiding norms and principles, engages in iterative acts by reappropriating and reinterpreting these" (ibid.).

of the self and that, in fact, the liberal position itself is rather unstable and that only an identitarian theory of agency can account for the obligatory character of our will, with all the problems this entails for individual freedom. I am suggesting, however, that identity is not simply given to us by the fact of our social embeddedness, as communitarian theory claims, but that identity is the result of an attachment we have towards a community that is responsive to our fundamental needs as human beings. In this perspective, if circumstances are favorable, identity and freedom tend to stand in continuity and not in conflict with each other.

3.1 The Idealist Self

In a certain sense, this harsh opposition between liberalism and Islam comes as a surprise and the political theorists insisting on the compatibility between freedom and identity seem to be up to something very important. Islam as such does not exist and what we encounter in social reality is rather a variety of Islams, Islamic pluralism, as Clifford Geertz demonstrates exemplarily in his seminal study of the contrasting development of Islam in Morocco and Indonesia.[8] Islamists seem to be rather pretentious when they require Muslims to follow a literal interpretation of the Sharia. Don't we have the freedom to interpret Islam in the light of today's necessities, in line with modernity and globalization,[9] and develop a contemporary Islam, a European Islam, for example, as Tariq Ramadan suggests to Muslims living in Europe[10]? Yet, the reason why Islamists categorically dismiss and reject religious pluralism is precisely, and oddly enough, the same reason with which liberals justify a Muslim's autonomy in interpreting Islam: the freedom of human beings. Interestingly, both liberals and Islamists start from the very same transcendental (or idealist) conception of the self and draw exactly opposite conclusions with liberals claiming individual rights and Islamists imposing the law of God. And the even more interesting thing is that Islamists are right in insisting that our identity constitutes our freedom. Let's understand why.

Paradoxical as it might sound, it is our freedom that gives rise to the problem of identity and lends force to the Islamist argumentation. To be free means to not underlie the laws of causation. As physical and psychological beings we obviously are affected by the causal forces of nature, but insofar as we have a will, agency, these forces do not determine our actions. As we saw during the Arab Spring, people can withstand the worst forms of oppression, terror and

---

[8] Clifford Geertz (1971): *Islam Observed: Religious Development in Morocco and Indonesia*, Chicago (Il.), University of Chicago Press.

[9] See the proposals of Nasr Abu-Zayd (2010): "The 'Others' in the Qur'an: A Hermeneutical Approach", in *Philosophy & Social Criticism* 36 (3–4), pp. 281–94 and Abdelmajid Charfi (2010): "Islam: the Test of Globalization", in *Philosophy & Social Criticism* 36 (3–4), pp. 295–307.

[10] Tariq Ramadan (2004): *Western Muslims and the Future of Islam*, New York, Oxford University Press.

3.1 The Idealist Self

intimidation and rebel themselves against tyranny, even at the cost of losing their lives. It seems that people have a will that cannot be caused by any natural force, however strong and mighty it be. As Immanuel Kant maintains, our true self is at home in the transcendental world and not in the world of nature. Yet, how can we be sure that we really act freely and that the reasons of our actions, even if only unconsciously, are not determined by some empirical content? We, Westerners, often tend to interpret the Arab Spring as a revolution in the name of freedom and human rights, but who could assure us that, in reality, it wasn't the outcome of a deep-felt resentment and hate of the tyrannous regime and driven by motives of economic well-being? Acting upon principles is the only proof of our freedom, even if never ultimate given the intransparency of our mind. Only if an action is done for no other sake than that of a law, can we say that an action is really free. The fact that we can act upon obligations is the only evidence we have of our freedom.[11]

The next problem is to determine which exactly is the law of the free will. It is on this point that liberals and Islamists depart; they disagree upon the question of where the law of the will comes from. Whereas liberals tend to believe that the law is one of our own making, Islamists maintain that the law is given to us, that the law of the will has its origin in Islam itself. All the conflict between liberals and Islamists turns around the question if the law of the will has its source internal to the individual or if it is given by an external source, namely the Koran.

There is a profound reason why liberals sustain that the law of the will is within us. Kant says the following in this regard: "Supposing that a will is free, to find the law which alone is competent to determine it necessarily. Since the matter of the practical law, i.e., an object of the maxim, can never be given otherwise than empirically, and the free will is independent on empirical conditions (that is, conditions belonging to the world of sense) and yet is determinable, consequently a free will must find its principle of determination in the law, and yet independently of the matter of the law. But, besides the matter of the law, nothing is contained in it except the legislative form. It is the legislative form, then, contained in the maxim, which can alone constitute a principle of determination of the [free] will."[12] Kant maintains that we aren't really free if we act upon principles that have an empirical ground, may it be of psychological or communitarian nature. So, if our obligations can have no other source than the will itself – otherwise only the external grounds or choices upon which our obligations depend are the reasons for action, but never the obligation itself –, then the will must auto-determine its own laws. But given that freedom by definition cannot have any content, a free will can only be constituted by a law that commands our actions to have a law-like character. The reasons of our actions underlie the categorical imperative and have

---

[11] See Christine Korsgaard (1996): "Morality as freedom", in her *Creating the Kingdom of Ends*, Cambridge, Cambridge University Press, pp. 159–187.

[12] Immanuel Kant: "Critique of Practical Reason" in *Kant's Critique of Practical Reason and Other Works on the Theory of Ethics*, translated by Thomas Kingsmill Abbott, 6th edition (1909), London, Longmans, p. 117 (A 52).

to be universalizable. As Christine Korsgaard concludes, "in a sense, the Formula of the Universal Law simply describes the function or task of an autonomous will".[13]

The standard critique of Kant's moral law is that the universal law is empty, that it has no content. Hegel objects that the universalization test of our maxims is not providing the substantial moral principles Kant is hoping for; in fact, whatever action can be universalized without running into any sort of contradiction.[14] Yet, this is not the direction in which the Islamists' critique of liberalism pushes. Their problem is not so much the emptiness of the moral law than its unbinding character. They claim that an autonomous will and the individual rights which it justifies give rise to nothing less than arbitrariness and a sort of moral relativism that capitulates society into chaos. It is true that John Rawls' political constructivism has provided liberalism with a substantial foundation of the laws of practical reason that Kantian liberalism might lack.[15] But also Rawls' political liberalism runs into the problem pointed out by Islamists and of which already Kant has been very much aware: the problem of normativity. Since Rawls must suppose, once he has constructed the laws of public reason, that citizens effectively have the desire to act upon those reasonable principles "that regulate how a plurality of agents (...) are to conduct themselves in their relations with one another".[16] He must assume that "the conception-dependent desire to act in ways worthy of a reasonable and equal citizen, becomes one of the desires by which we are moved".[17] And the way these principle-dependent desires enter as elements into a person's motivational set is simply by "desiring to be this kind of person",[18] to be a worthy reasonable and equal citizen. Yet, why should we desire to be a reasonable citizen?

Kant himself is quite aware that, whatever our transcendental self might command us to do, the action has to be undertaken by the empirical self, the action must take place in our world in which no effect can be without a cause. Since the moral law has its origin in practical reason and "reason of itself", as Hume shows, "is utterly impotent in (...) produc[ing] or prevent[ing] actions",[19] the moral law itself cannot be the cause of any action. "For", and herein Kant agrees with Hume, "all inclination and every sensible impulse is founded on feeling, and the negative effect produced on feeling (by the check on the inclinations) is itself feeling."[20] In order

---

[13] Korsgaard: "Morality as freedom", in her *Creating the Kingdom of Ends*, p. 166.

[14] See Korsgaard: "Kant's Formula of Universal Law", in her *Creating the Kingdom of Ends*, pp. 77–105, for how willing to universalize maxims may give rise to contradictions and the Hegelian objections to this thesis.

[15] John Rawls (1993): *Political Liberalism*, New York, Columbia University Press, pp. 89–129.

[16] Ibid., p. 83.

[17] Ibid., p. 85.

[18] Ibid., p.84.

[19] David Hume (1978): *A Treatise of Human Nature*, L.A. Selby-Bigge & P.H. Nidditch (eds.), Oxford, Oxford University Press, p. 457.

[20] Kant: *Critique of Practical Reason*, p. 165 (A 128, 129). Note what Hume says in this regard: "Nothing can oppose or retard the impulse of passion, but a contrary impulse" (*A Treatise of Human Nature*, p. 415).

3.1 The Idealist Self

that our will becomes effective, it has therefore to produce some motivational state and affect the agent's psychology. We must somehow develop a desire to follow the laws of our will. Now Kant claims that "this feeling (which we call the moral feeling) is produced simply by reason. It does not serve for the estimation of actions nor for the foundation of the objective moral law itself, but merely as a motive to make this of itself a maxim."[21] "Consequently", continues Kant, "we can see a priori that the moral law, as a determining principle of the will, must by thwarting all our inclinations produce a feeling which may be called pain; and in this we have the first, perhaps the only, instance in which we are able from a priori considerations to determine the relation of a cognition (in this case of pure practical reason) to the feeling of pleasure or displeasure."[22] Now the question is how practical reason could ever be the cause of such a moral, or how Kant also sometimes calls it, practical feeling, if Kant, as we have seen, doesn't dispute Hume's claim that empirically there can ever be a causal relationship between reason and our passions?

Kant's solutions to this problem is, in fact, identity. It is through our moral or practical identity that the empirical self comes to coincide with the transcendental self. The moral law is the source of our self-esteem and personal worth, which, as Kant states, "in the absence of agreement with the moral law, is reduced to nothing".[23] Violating the moral law we are betraying ourselves, and it is this self-deceit that generates the feelings of humiliation, disgust and repulsion. The moral law is constitutive of our identity and identity gives rise to moral feelings. Following passage renders explicit Kant's thesis on identity as source of normativity of the moral law: "When an upright man is in the greatest distress, which he might have avoided if he could only have disregarded duty, is he not sustained by the consciousness that he has maintained humanity in its proper dignity in his own person and honoured it, that he has no reason to be ashamed of himself in his own sight, or to dread the inward glance of self-examination? He cannot endure that he should be in his own eyes unworthy of life."[24]

Yet, if identity indeed can confer the moral law a binding character, it is not clear why we should actually come to identify with the moral law. Why should we, as persons, have such a moral identity? Kant's answer is the following: "Man alone, and with him every rational creature, is an *end in himself*. By virtue of the autonomy of his freedom he is the subject of the moral law, which is holy. Man (…) must regard humanity in his own person as holy."[25] We come to identify with the moral law, because we are stunned and glorify its almightiness and purity and feel a profound sense of love for the holiness of the moral law. It is self-love, love of our holiness as authors of the moral law, that explains our identification with the moral

---

[21] Ibid., p. 169 (A 136).
[22] Ibid., p. 165 (A 129).
[23] Ibid., p. 171 (A 140).
[24] Ibid., p. 181 (A 156, 157).
[25] Ibid., pp. 180–181 (A 155, 156).

law. And this love is the outcome of admiration and illumination, of an awe-inspiring experience. Yet, this is not the way how our psychology seems to work. Love is not the result of respect, but arises only within a relationship that is based upon sympathy, empathy and compassion. Children, for example, don't love their parents because they recognize their superiority, but because parents take care of their basic needs. Discussing moral development, Rawls holds the following concerning the psychological law of love: "Given that family institutions are just and that the parents love the child and manifestly express their love by caring for his good, then the child, recognizing their evident love of him, comes to love them."[26] The transcendental self with its relentless commandments doesn't take care at all of our needs and, on the contrary, commands us to disregard, neglect and even despise them. Hence, if psychologists are right, it is impossible that we can love the moral law and have a moral identity.

3.2 The Psychological Self

Liberals face the problem that the practical principles inherent to our freedom lack normativity. Although we are ourselves the sources of our practical reasons, we still need a desire to follow our will, the desire Rawls calls principle-dependent desire. However, given the independence of our agency and will from our psychology, this desire can have its foundation only in our identity. It is our identity which provides us with a desire to follow the moral law. As we have seen, it is however quite dubious that we identify ourselves with the moral law. The will cannot constitute our identity, as long as its practical laws are given a priori and identification has to take place a posteriori. Therefore contemporary liberals give up on the idea that the laws of the will are given and sustain that we ourselves are choosing our own identity. They establish a direct link between the will and identity, making the will the source of our identification and avoiding thereby the difficulty Kant is facing in explaining how we actually come to have the identity which gives normative force to our will. And by way of a transcendental argument liberals establish that next to our particular identities we also must have a moral identity: Since it is the fact of being a human being that allows us to have a will and to be who we are, we must also value and identify ourselves with our humanity.[27] This way liberals seem finally to assure that individuals truly have inescapable ethical and moral obligations.

---

[26] John Rawls (1999): *A Theory of Justice*, Cambridge (Mass.), Harvard University Press, p. 429.

[27] I paraphrased here Korsgaard's concept of moral obligation: "Since (…) your humanity is the source of your reasons, you must value your own humanity if you are to act at all." Or: "It is because we are such animals that our practical identities are normative for us, and, once you see this, you must take this more fundamental identity, being such an animal, to be normative as well. You must value your humanity if you are to value anything at all" (Christine Korsgaard (1994): *The Sources of Normativity*, Cambridge, Cambridge University Press, p. 123).

Korsgaard puts it the following way: "The reflective structure of the mind forces us to have a conception of ourselves"[28] and "identify [ourselves] with some law or principle which will govern [our] choices".[29] "It is the conceptions of ourselves that are most important to us that give rise to unconditional obligations. For to violate them is to lose your integrity and so your identity, and to no longer be who you are."[30] But of course, if identity is chosen and not given by our will, there are two immediate objections. First, what could we actually will in complete autonomy and independence from our actual desires, if there is no law internal to the will? The problem is that an autonomous will is literally forced to make an arbitrary choice between the identities available, if it remains undetermined by any empirical content. And from this first objection follows a second problem. If all of our identifications are arbitrary, in what sense could they ever be normative for us? If I choose to be a Muslim for no reason at all, how could violating Islamic principles "be worse than death"[31]? Korsgaard is certainly well aware of these problems when she states that "you can stop being yourself for a bit and still get back home".[32] And she proposes that "a commitment to your own identity" is the solution to the problem: "We must commit ourselves to a kind of second-order integrity, a commitment to not letting these problems get out of hand."[33] But she herself admits that "the problem reiterates within the commitment to your own integrity".[34] Why could an arbitrary second-order commitment to Islam not be shed in favor of another commitment? Korsgaard eventually concludes that "obligation is always unconditional, but it is only when it concerns really important matters that it is *deep*".[35]

And the Islamists' argument precisely aims to provide this depth to our identity that liberal theory, emphasizing the freedom of choice, is unable to account for. The depth of our identity depends upon the very fact that it is given to us and not chosen, we simply are the persons we are and there is nothing we can choose to be. Yet, we are not moral persons commanded by the moral law, but individuals whose personal identity is deeply intertwined with their collective identities, with the communities, cultures and religions they are born into and in which they grew up. There is just nothing we can choose about our origins, nor can we simply shed them off: We are who we are! There is no transcendental, free self, as in liberalism, that "is detachable from its social and historical roles and statuses" and "can always, if [it] wishes to, put into question what are taken to be the merely contingent social features of [our] existence".[36] Islamists, in this regard, are undistinguishable from communitar-

---

[28] Ibid., p. 100.
[29] Ibid,. p. 103.
[30] Ibid., p. 102.
[31] Ibid., p. 18.
[32] Ibid., p. 102.
[33] Ibid., p. 103.
[34] Ibid..
[35] Ibid..
[36] Alasdair MacIntyre (2007): *After Virtue*, London, Duckworth, pp. 220–221.

ians[37] who hold that "[we] inherit from the past of [our] family, [our] city, [our] tribe, [our] nation, a variety of debts, inheritances, rightful expectations and obligations. These constitute the given of [our] life, [our] moral starting point."[38] "Shorn of these we would cease to be ourselves, (...) our existence as persons (...) would be impossible outside the horizon of these evaluations."[39] "For the story of [our] life is always embedded in the story of these communities from which [we] derive [our] identity."[40]

Islamists eventually seem to have discovered the necessarily binding laws of our freedom that both Kant and contemporary liberals were looking for in vain. Our identity constitutes our freedom, and not vice versa. Muslims are truly free persons, they fully realize their freedom only in case they follow the precepts of the Koran and not when they contest the authority of the Sharia over their lives. It is not that Islamists contest Muslims' freedom of the will, they just believe that Muslims' individual freedom is not independent of their being Muslims, but coincides with their Muslimhood. Their freedom relies in their being Muslims. Muslims are free when they follow the principles of Islam, not because they somehow willingly do so, but because they simply realize and live up to the laws of their pure will without being affected in whatsoever sense by their desires, emotions and needs, in short by their psychology. Any contestation of Islam, any attempts to reform Islam and to interpret Islam in the lights of modernity, presuppose either the idea of a pure free will or must have empirical grounds originating in the idea of individual well-being that puts into question the normative force of Islam and, hence, a Muslim's freedom and dignity. Those philosophers who think there can be a reconciliation between individual rights and identity are, in fact, liberals in disguise.

But does identity in the Islamists' conception really constitute our freedom and agency? What remains somewhat unclear in this picture is the question of how we come to be the Muslims we actually are. How do Islamic principles enter our mind and make up our agency without causing our will? Two are the standard explanations: volition and love. Islamists must, of course, exclude the possibility that Muslims come to willingly identify, endorse or commit themselves to Islamic principles. This would, presuppose the idea of a will that is independent of a Muslim's identity, making identity a matter of choice. It is neither quite plausible, as Harry

---

[37] I am considering political Islam here to be an identitarian rather than a realist argument. This means that Islamists consider the Sharia to be the law of Muslim societies, not of any society. Sharia is not about the revelation of truth but about what it means to be a good Muslim. The Egyptian president Morsi, a Muslim Brother, said recently: "My religion instructs me to believe in all the prophets and to respect all religions as well as every person's freedom of religion" ("Morsi Rejects Calls for New Unity Government in Egypt", in *International Herald Tribune*, January 31, 2013, p. 4). Fundamentalism and Islamic terrorism certainly blurs this distinction between an identitarian and realist interpretation of Islamism, as for example Al-Qaeda's rampant critique and violent rejection of Western lifestyles shows.

[38] McIntyre: *After Virtue*, p. 220.

[39] Charles Taylor (1985): *Philosophical Papers: Human Agency and Language* (Volume 1), Cambridge, Cambridge University Press, pp. 34–35.

[40] McIntyre: *After Virtue*, p. 221.

3.2 The Psychological Self

Frankfurt claims, that we just happen to have the commitments we have, that we happen to be or become Muslims independent of whatsoever – our family, education or community. Frankfurt considers our loves, that in his theory are constitutive of our identity, to be independent from agency, cognition and psychology. He argues that love "is neither affective nor cognitive. It is volitional".[41] According to Frankfurt, love is the cause of itself; it is self-generated. Love is autonomous and "the motivations that love engenders are not merely adventitious or (…) heteronomous".[42] However, given that love is as much an emotion as fear or resentment, it is quite strange that love stands outside of the chain of causation and the realm of nature and cannot be considered an emotional response triggered by external events. Hence, if Muslims neither can identify voluntarily with Islamic norms nor simply happen to be Muslims, then only emotional attachment to Islam can explain their identification and the normative grip Islamic norms undoubtedly have upon them. Only a psychological mechanism can account for our being a Muslim. But then we make a step outside of the transcendental or idealist framework of agency and communitarianism and enter the grounds of empiricism and non-cognitivism, in which freedom of the will and normativity notoriously play no role at all.

According to Akeel Bilgrami, the reason for which Muslims today are so attached to the principles of Islam is resentment. Bilgrami sees Islamism and fundamentalism to be a "defensive reaction caused not only by the scars and memories of Western colonial rule but by the failure of successive governments to break out of the models of development imposed on them by a dominating neocolonial presence of the superpowers through much of the cold war".[43] In this perspective, Muslims have become pious believers because of (post-)colonial humiliation and depravation. Muslims come to consider Islam as an appropriate answer to Western subjugation and condescension that restitutes them a sense of autonomy and dignity. Political Islam plays a precise function in a Muslim's psychological economy. In fact, John Bowlby explains our attachment to our parents with the fact that they are sensitive and responsive to our needs, taking care of our well-being.[44] I want to suggest that we can explain our being a Muslim with the very same psychological mechanism. Our identification with Islam is caused by the satisfaction of our psychological and physical needs. As, moreover, many scholars of political Islam point out, Islamic organizations such Hamas, Hezbollah or the Muslim Brotherhood gained their popularity above all with the social services they provide to the poor and deprived. They grant universal access to schools and hospitals and offer better services than those provided by secular NGOs or the feeble Arab states.[45]

---

[41] Harry Frankfurt (2006): *The Reasons of Love*, Princeton (NJ), Princeton University Press, pp. 42–43.

[42] Ibid., p. 48.

[43] Akeel Bilgrami (1992): "What is a Muslim? Fundamental Commitment and Cultural Identity", in *Critical Inquiry* 18 (4), p. 209.

[44] John Bowlby (1982): *Attachment: Attachment and Loss* (Volume One), New York, Basic Books.

[45] See for example Sara Roy (2011): *Hamas and Civil Society in Gaza: Engaging the Islamist Social Sector*, Princeton (NJ), Princeton University Press.

In a psychological theory, our identity is not somehow miraculously given to us, as it sometimes seems to be the case in communitarianism, but is the outcome of a precise psychological process that is driven by our human needs. It is not identity as such that is normative and constitutive of our will and agency; we follow the principles incorporated by our identity because of the attachment and love we feel for a religion, culture or community that takes care of our well-being. Of course in a psychological theory of identity, in which freedom is understood in negative terms to "be left to do or be what [one] is able to do or be, without interference by other persons",[46] there is no principled reason for which identity and freedom must be compatible. As shows the case of political Islam and Islamic fundamentalism, in particularly pathological political, social and economic contexts such as those in the Arab and Islamic world, where the idea of freedom and liberalism has been for centuries a vector for colonization and oppression, freedom comes to be marked somatically in extremely negative terms.[47] For many Muslims, the idea of freedom, being connoted as a Western value, provokes simply the emotions of disgust and repulsion. This explains the harsh opposition secular and liberal movements face today in Islamic countries. However, if we are thinking a psychological theory of identity through, identities that limit our freedom are anything than stable. As many examples of Muslims, such as Ayaan Hirsi Ali and Magdi Allam, who developed a profound hate and distaste for Islam as a religion and committed apostasy, demonstrate, identities that oppress our longing for freedom and liberty, a fundamental human need as universal political and social history teaches us, become quickly objects of hostility and attacks and often see themselves obliged to recur and rely on sheer force and violence, further depriving us of other basic needs. This suggests also that identity is not, as Bernard Williams claims, reducible to the emotion of shame only.[48] We embrace wholeheartedly and unconditionally only those identities that respond comprehensively to our various needs.

What conclusion can we draw? In the context of the Arab Spring, the electoral successes of the Muslim Brotherhood can be explained by the fact that they effectively respond to certain needs of the Muslim population. They are openly hostile to the West and they offer grassroots social services that benefit large parts of the impoverished societies. But as the very conflicts between the Muslim Brothers and liberal and secular movements show, Islamic organizations, due to their profound anti-Western attitude, fail to see the value of freedom and risk to become either oppressive, just think of the violence that is currently committed by Islamists, or irrelevant in the long term. For that freedom and identity can coexist in the Muslim

---

[46] Isaiah Berlin (1969): "Two Concepts of Liberty", in his *Four Essays on Liberty*, Oxford, Oxford University Press, pp. 121–122.

[47] Antonio Damasio maintains that our somatic markers guide our behavior and decision-making. A. Damasio (2005): *Descartes' Error: Emotion, Reason, and the Human Brain*, New York, Penguin.

[48] Williams holds that "shame looks to what I am"; "the structures of shame (…) give a conception of one's ethical identity" (B. Williams (1993): *Shame and Necessity*, Berkeley and Los Angeles, University of California Press, p. 93).

world, Muslims must overcome the trap of resentment[49] and conceive freedom not as a Western invention and product, but as a universal human need. Yet, if our psychological thesis is right, then Muslims won't achieve this simply by "liv[ing] up to the basic conditions of free agency" and adopting a first-person point of view, as for example Bilgrami calls for.[50] Only conciliatory trust-building measures can help to surmount the anger, fear, mistrust and suspicion Muslims feel vis-à-vis the West and that are at the origin of today's conflict between freedom and identity in the Muslim world. From this perspective, we, Westerners, must above all stop to think of ourselves and our culture as the true and only heirs of Enlightenment. Moreover, the West must engage in substantial common political projects and cooperation with the Muslim world, such as initially envisaged by the Mediterranean Union, that generate wealth and foster well-being.

References

Abu-Zayd, Nasr. 2010. The 'Others' in the Qur'an: A Hermeneutical Approach. *Philosophy & Social Criticism* 36 (3–4): 281–294.
Bayart, Jean-François. 2005. *The Illusion of Cultural Identity*. London: Hurst.
Benhabib, Seyla. 2006. *Another Cosmopolitanism*. New York: Oxford University Press.
———. 2011. The Arab Spring: Religion, Revolution and the Public Sphere. In *Eurozine* (published on May 10, 2011). http://www.eurozine.com/articles/2011-05-10-benhabib-en.html.
Berlin, Isaiah. 1969. *Four Essays on Liberty*. Oxford: Oxford University Press.
Berman, Paul. 2004. *Terror and Liberalism*. New York: W. W. Norton & Company.
Bilgrami, Akeel. 1992. What is a Muslim? Fundamental Commitment and Cultural Identity. *Critical Inquiry* 18 (4): 821–842.
Bowlby, John. 1982. *Attachment: Attachment and Loss (Volume One)*. New York: Basic Books.
Butler, Judith. 2006. *Gender Trouble: Feminism and the Subversion of Identity*. New York/London: Routledge.
Charfi, Abdelmajid. 2010. Islam: The Test of Globalization. *Philosophy & Social Criticism* 36 (3–4): 295–307.
Cohen, Roger. 2012. A Place for Religion. In *International Herald Tribune Magazine* (November 30, 2012), p. 17.
Damasio, Antonio. 2005. *Descartes' Error: Emotion, Reason, and the Human Brain*. New York: Penguin.
Frankfurt, Harry. 2006. *The Reasons of Love*. Princeton: Princeton University Press.
Geertz, Clifford. 1971. *Islam Observed: Religious Development in Morocco and Indonesia*. Chicago: University of Chicago Press.
Hume, David. 1978. In *A Treatise of Human Nature*, ed. L.A. Selby-Bigge and P.H. Nidditch. Oxford: Oxford University Press.
Kant, Immanuel. 1909. Critique of Practical Reason. In *Kant's Critique of Practical Reason and Other Works on the Theory of Ethics*. 6th ed. Trans. Thomas Kingsmill Abbott. London: Longmans.

---

[49] Istanbul Seminars '11 discussed various ways how the postcolonial world can escape the trap of resentment. See the special issue of *Philosophy & Social Criticism* 38 (4–5) 2012 on "Overcoming the Trap of Resentment" edited by Alessandro Ferrara, Volker Kaul and David Rasmussen.
[50] Bilgrami: "What is a Muslim?", in *Critical Inquiry*, p. 213.

Korsgaard, Christine. 1994. *The Sources of Normativity*. Cambridge: Cambridge University Press.
———. 1996. *Creating the Kingdom of Ends*. Cambridge: Cambridge University Press.
MacIntyre, Alasdair. 2007. *After Virtue*. London: Duckworth.
Mbembe, Achille. 2001. *On the Postcolony*. Berkeley/Los Angeles: University of California Press.
Ramadan, Tariq. 2004. *Western Muslims and the Future of Islam*. New York: Oxford University Press.
Rawls, John. 1993. *Political Liberalism*. New York: Columbia University Press.
———. 1999. *A Theory of Justice*. Cambridge, MA: Harvard University Press.
Roy, Sara. 2011. *Hamas and Civil Society in Gaza: Engaging the Islamist Social Sector*. Princeton: Princeton University Press.
Taylor, Charles. 1985. *Philosophical Papers: Human Agency and Language*. Vol. 1. Cambridge: Cambridge University Press.
Williams, Bernard. 1993. *Shame and Necessity*. Berkeley and Los Angeles: University of California Press.

Chapter 4
Psychology, Autonomy, and Liberalism

Abstract This chapter discusses an alternative approach to liberalism in the empiricist tradition that goes along with the names of Harry Frankfurt and Isaiah Berlin. Although this approach makes non-cognitive states such as desires, preferences and loves foundational of a person's reasons, it also argues that these are properly constitutive of a person's freedom, agency and autonomy. Hence, it does not ground liberalism on the premises of public reason, but on the basis of individual identities that are of psychological origin. Accordingly, the political advantage of Frankfurt's and Berlin's theories with respect to Kantian moral theories is that they ground negative freedom precisely in a psychological account of agency and do not have to recur to any arguments of transcendental reason. The chapter argues that Frankfurt's effort to make identity central to morality and Berlin's struggle to ground liberalism in identity are of great value, even though it also shows the limits of an approach that makes psychology the foundation of agency. The chapter concludes that eventually both Frankfurt and Berlin risk to collapse into a Kantian-style theory of agency.

Keywords Harry Frankfurt · Isaiah Berlin · David Hume · Liberalism · Empiricism · Causal theory of action · Behaviorism · Non-cognitivism · Agency · Autonomy · Second-order desires · Love · Volitional necessity · Positive and negative freedom

The philosophies of Kant and Rawls are the dominant approach in liberal political theory, despite the problems we pointed out in the previous chapter. Theories that start from a Humean, behaviorist perspective, such as Richard Thaler's and Cass Sunstein's 'nudge theory',[1] run into the problem that they do not take people really seriously and take them necessarily at their word. People might be ignorant about their motives and needs (see chapter 'Agency, Psychology and the Self: The Case of

---

[1] Richard Thaler & Cass Sunstein, 2009, *Nudge: Improving Decisions About Health, Wealth, and Happiness*. London: Penguin.

Religious Fundamentalism' in this volume), some sort of victims of themselves and therefore we need institutions to govern their behavior. This obviously stands in a very stark contrast with liberal political theory, that people have transparent reasons for which they can be hold accountable. Empiricism questions the very foundations of democracy, since it undermines the ideas of freedom, agency, autonomy and the first-person perspective.

There is however an alternative approach to liberalism in the empiricist tradition that goes along with the names of Harry Frankfurt and Isaiah Berlin. Although it makes non-cognitive states such as desires, preferences and loves foundational of a person's reasons, it also argues that these are properly constitutive of a person's freedom, agency and autonomy. Hence, it does not ground liberalism on the premises of public reason, but on the basis of individual identities that are of psychological origin. Accordingly, the political advantage of Frankfurt's and Berlin's theories with respect to Kantian moral theories is that they ground negative freedom precisely in a psychological account of agency and do not have to recur to any arguments of transcendental reason.

This chapter argues that Frankfurt's effort to make identity central to morality and Berlin's struggle to ground liberalism in identity are of great value, even though it also shows the limits of an approach that makes psychology the foundation of agency. The chapter concludes that eventually both Frankfurt and Berlin risk to collapse into a Kantian-style theory of agency.

The essay introduces first Frankfurt's account of autonomy and then Berlin's conception of liberalism.

4.1 Identity and Autonomy

According to Harry Frankfurt, it is the will that is distinguishing a person from other individuals. The property of having a will makes an individual a person and is constitutive of the class of persons. The will is essential or necessary for being a person.

Frankfurt contrasts his concept of a person with that of philosophers such as Peter Strawson or Alfred Ayer that reduce personhood to the fact of an individual having mental and physical properties. In fact, Frankfurt opposes all those philosophers that identify persons by the same criteria by which they identify individuals in general, namely natural properties. Frankfurt's theory of a person is fundamentally non-reductionist.

Non-reductionist theories of personhood are those that consider persons only those individuals that are endowed with a will and able to control natural intentional states, such as desires and emotions in the case of human beings. A person's will can motivate desires and thereby cause a person's action independent from what the actual desires of a person might be. Hence, if a person is a maker and agent rather than being simply made and broken by its nature, it has to be the will that characterizes a person.

4.1 Identity and Autonomy

Frankfurt's conception of the will is very interesting, since he neither wants us to be Humean victims of ourselves, nor Kantian supermen. In a sense, he has a very commonsensical understanding of the person. He is convinced that we have an irreducible will (and do we moderns really doubt that we are caused by something else than ourselves?), but that this will cannot just will anything and must be somehow anchored in ourselves (and doesn't our psychic integrity depend upon the knowledge and acceptance of who we are?). Frankfurt's very plausible intuitions face however certain philosophical problems which I would like to discuss here.

Frankfurt's first idea is that non-reductionists misconceive the problem of personal autonomy. He criticizes "Roderick Chisholm's quaint version of the doctrine that human freedom entails an absence of causal determination"[2] as inadequate. Frankfurt thinks that personal autonomy does not consist in the autonomy of the will, but in a person's endorsement of his desires. All the distinction between an autonomous and a non-autonomous person lies in the fact if a person acts upon desires that he can motivate or identify with (second-order volitions), or if he is simply caused by his first-order desires. Frankfurt's initial concept of personal autonomy combines a reductionist content of the will with a non-reductionist theory of endorsement or agency, avoiding the problems of Kant's theory of personal autonomy according to which "a free agent has (…) 'a prerogative which some would attribute only to God: (…) [being] a prime mover unmoved.'"[3]

Frankfurt comes to realize though that eventually there might be no difference between an autonomous person endorsing his will and a wanton simply being moved by his desires. After all, the endorsement of desires risks to be as arbitrary as the desires themselves. Facing this problem, Frankfurt adapts his theory of personal autonomy and sees himself constrained to give up on the idea of endorsement and agency more generally. Realizing that a person's will cannot depend upon a reductionist content and willing to save his intuition that we have no superhuman will, Frankfurt develops a theory of the will in terms of love that separates rigorously the will from our capacity to choose (which I call 'agency').

Frankfurt adopts the structure of the standard non-reductionist conception according to which personal autonomy consists in the autonomy of the will. Yet, he cannot conceive the will in terms of practical reason, that is generally considered to be the source of our agency and capacity to choose, and identifies it with a person's wholehearted loves. His strategy is to find a conception of the will that is not going to solve the Kantian problem of practical reason, but which renders it completely irrelevant, given that agency and love are two distinct faculties. The question I would like to answer here is if Frankfurt can really succeed in doing so. Can his conception of a person and his will get rid of agency altogether?

In the first part, I will briefly reconstruct the reasons for which Frankfurt's non-reductionist position is constrained to conceive the will in terms of autonomy. In the

---

[2] Harry Frankfurt, "Freedom of the Will and the Concept of a Person," in H. Frankfurt, *The Importance of What We Care About*, Cambridge: Cambridge University Press 1988, p. 23.
[3] ibid.

second part, I will argue that Frankfurt's identification of the will with the loves of a person fails, since a person's loves are dependent upon his agency.

4.1.1 Autonomy and Love

At the outset, Frankfurt considers the will to be constituted by the desires a person endorses or his second-order volitions. Yet, if second-order volitions are chosen, don't they have to be confirmed by third-order volitions, which in return have to be confirmed by fourth-order volitions and so forth? What could make a choice definitive, avoiding arbitrariness of the will and an infinite regress of higher-order volitions that eventually leads to the destruction of any volition whatsoever? Frankfurt suggests that "the decisiveness of the commitment [a person] has made means that he has decided that no further question about his second-order volition, at any higher order, remains to be asked."[4]

He maintains that each person underlies certain volitional necessities. Those are given by what a person cares about: He cannot help but to identify with what is dear to him. Frankfurt writes that "a person who is subject to volitional necessity finds that he must act as he does."[5] The volitional necessity provided by what a person cares about makes alternative courses of action unthinkable and prevent a person "from *making use of* his own capacities."[6] As Frankfurt clearly states "what [a person is] unable to muster [is] not the *power* to forebear, but the *will*."[7]

Yet, the volitional necessity becomes a *true* volitional necessity only at the moment that the individual endorses or identifies *voluntarily* with what he cares about. Frankfurt writes that "there is something which [a person] cannot do but only because he does not really want to do it."[8] Frankfurt concludes that "it may seem difficult to understand how volitional necessity can possibly be at the same time both self-imposed and imposed involuntarily."[9]

As long as Frankfurt does not conceive volitional necessities as independent from a person's agency, those remain always dependent upon agency. And we could always ask why personhood and a person's will do not simply coincide with an individual's agency to "care about caring about it".[10] Frankfurt clearly sees the danger that his theory of endorsement eventually collapses with more traditional

---

[4] ibid., p. 22.
[5] Harry Frankfurt, "The Importance of What We Care About," in H. Frankfurt, *The Importance of What We Care About*, op. cit., p. 86.
[6] ibid.
[7] ibid.
[8] ibid., p. 87.
[9] ibid., p. 88.
[10] ibid., p. 87.

non-reductionist positions. Hence, he conceives the will as independent from the agency of a person.

Frankfurt elaborates further the concept of caring and identifies the will of a person with what he loves. And he defines a person's love to be independent from both his agency and psychology. A person does not love because he perceives the intrinsic value of the object of his love. Love is neither caused naturally – it has not to be confused "with infatuation, lust, obsession, possessiveness, and dependency in their various forms."[11] Those are not congruent with the essential nature of love as a mode of *disinterested* concern for the beloved. Frankfurt concludes that love "is neither affective nor cognitive. It is volitional. Loving something has less to do with what a person believes, or with how he feels, than with a configuration of the will that consists in a practical concern for what is good for the beloved."[12]

In Frankfurt's conception of love persons love for no reason at all; love is caused by anything than itself. Love is the cause of itself; it is self-generated. Love is autonomous and "the motivations that love engenders are not merely adventitious or (…) heteronomous."[13]

4.1.2 Transcendental Love

The question is if this concept of the will in terms of love can do without agency. If the will is love, it may happen that a person has no will. This is the case if a person loves nothing or if his loves contrast each other. Love, in contrast to our faculty to choose, is not at our disposition. "It is a necessary feature of love that it is not under our direct and immediate voluntary control."[14] Whereas we cannot get rid of or loose our agency, our loves may vanish and are often rather unstable – they come and go whenever they like. Love is capricious.

Given that love is autonomous and not under our control, it is not at all uncommon in Frankfurt's conception of the will that a person comes to have no will at all. But if having a will and consequentially loving is essential to being a person, a person that does not love stops being a person. If an individual loves, it becomes a person, otherwise it remains a mere wanton.[15] It seems that this is the price Frankfurt has to pay for equating the will with love. Frankfurt is not only not ready to pay this price; it is even impossible for him to pay it. And this has major consequences for his theory of the will.

---

[11] Harry Frankfurt, *The Reasons of Love*, Princeton and Oxford: Princeton University Press 2004, p. 43.
[12] ibid., pp. 42–3.
[13] ibid., p. 48.
[14] ibid., p. 44.
[15] H. Frankfurt, "Freedom of the Will and the Concept of a Person," op. cit., p. 16.

The question is if an individual with the capacity to love could possibly not love. Frankfurt holds that without love "a major aspect of our reflective connection to ourselves, in which our distinctive character as human beings lies, would thus be severed."[16] An individual with the capacity to love that does not realize this capacity does suffer from some disorder and violates his own nature. Yet, is this all the story that if we do not love, we somehow do not live up to ourselves? Isn't the point rather that it is utterly impossible for us not to love if we have the capacity to love?

It is a feature of the very structure of the will that an individual with the capacity to will, has no choice than to will. If an individual has the faculty of will, he is constrained or obligated to will. Even a wanton that acts arbitrarily upon his most immediate desires, must *willingly* do so. This means nothing less than that a person with the faculty of love is obligated to love, if will and love are identical. If we are able to love, well, then we have to love or will to love.

I suggest that Frankfurt is perfectly aware of this problem. This has to be the sense of his insistence on the importance of loving and our interest in love.[17] However, it is also clear that a person's intrinsic interest in love would reintroduce agency through the backdoor.[18] Therefore Frankfurt tries to seal the cracks of his edifice recurring to the notion of self-love.

Self-love has the same volitional structure as love "independent of contingencies."[19] Unlike most our loves however self-love is "deeply entrenched in our nature."[20] We cannot help but loving ourselves. Moreover, "(…) self-love as such has no specific content. (…) It has no essential evaluational vector."[21] Self-love is defined as a person's "disinterested concern for whatever it is that the person loves."[22] If a person is unable to love – should it be for the reason that a person's loves are inauthentic and his true loves unconscious or that the self is ambivalent and divided between his conflicting loves –, the love of himself and his concern for his own good help the person to identify what he wholeheartedly loves.

Self-love constitutes a second-order will due to which a person comes to love to love and wills to love. The reason of love is self-love. Given that self-love is a form of love that a person has to have given his human nature and that commands to love, self-love provides the obligation to love that the faculty of love already entails; except that self-love does not originate in a person's agency. Self-love is not under our voluntary control. Frankfurt eventually grounds personhood in self-love and a person's capacity to will or love and not any longer in the will or love itself. An individual with the capacity to will is a person a priori. With the concept of self-love

---

[16] H. Frankfurt, *The Reasons of Love*, op. cit., p. 53.

[17] ibid., pp. 53–5, 57–62.

[18] Frankfurt speaks of "the intrinsically valuable goal of having something worthwhile to do," (ibid., p. 59) which means that a person intrinsically values loving.

[19] ibid., p. 82.

[20] ibid.

[21] ibid., p. 98.

[22] ibid., p. 85.

he seems to have found a plausible theory of the will, if we ignore the fact that self-love is simply an annex and not a substitution of our agency to love.

This conclusion would be too hasty. Frankfurt's concept of self-love faces two criticisms, a reductionist and a non-reductionist one. If the necessity of self-love is grounded in our human nature, self-love can be reduced to some natural state or property. It is our nature that causes us to love ourselves and to will to love. Hence, the self-loving person is not autonomous and actually has no will of its own. Frankfurt risks to fall into the reductionist trap. Moreover, self-love is tantamount to our agency to love. Self-love provides a person with the faculty to manage and control his loves and commitments. We could also say that by way of self-love a person is able to auto-determine and choose his life. Self-love enables the person to reflect upon his love and is therefore a form of transcendental love. But then self-love is nothing else than a person's transcendental self or at least a property of it, a pure will totally empty and formal that meditates and generates mental states. But why should a pure will will to love? And at that point the standard non-reductionist problem of determining a pure will arises.

We could conclude that Frankfurt's theory of the lover's autonomy fails to provide an alternative non-reductionist concept of a person and falls back to the standard problems of agency. After all, the reasons *of* love are not independent from our reasons *to* love.

4.2 Identity and Liberalism

Isaiah Berlin develops a similar approach as Frankfurt in politics and his theory of liberalism is precisely based upon an account of individual identities that does away with the concept of agency and reason. The question is if his theory can avoid the shortcomings of Frankfurt's account. I am arguing that Berlin in "Two Concepts of Liberty" is distinguishing between his two concepts of liberty through a *rational* and an *identitarian understanding of autonomy*. Yet, contrary to Berlin's own premises, the frontiers of 'negative freedom' are not constituted by subjective standards of identity, but refer instead to some objective standards of rationality. Berlin, as much as Frankfurt before, cannot demonstrate to what extent identity can be a source of autonomy.

Berlin maintains that in the history of political philosophy we can distinguish between two justifications for two divergent conceptions of freedom. We want to have *'positive' freedom* because we want to be the source of control of our actions. To act freely in this sense means being the proper master of one's choices and actions and being self-determined. Freedom means having *autonomous* reasons. Berlin opposes *'negative' freedom* to the positive concept of freedom. According to him negative freedom is not justified by considerations of autonomy but by our will to live our life according to our own ideas and preferences and to fulfil our deepest desires whatever might be the source of reasons. For "the only freedom which deserves the name is that of pursuing our own good in our own way."[23] Negative freedom can be defined as the area within which the individual "is or should be left to do or be what he is able to do or be, without interference by other persons."[24]

In my view, both justifications, for negative and positive freedom, recur to the notion of autonomy, although, as we will see later on, to different understandings of autonomy. The will to be left alone and "to do my own thing" and to live up to my own notion of what constitutes a fulfilled human life is a clear claim for autonomy even though it is negative one. Without *being left autonomous* I cannot develop my individuality. It is our longing for autonomy – in the sense of being left alone – that makes us "protest against the encroachment of public authority, or the mass hypnosis of custom or organized propaganda",[25] that makes our claims for rights and frontiers within which men should be inviolable intelligible and justifiable.[26]

If both concepts of liberty share a fundamental concern for personal autonomy, why does Berlin oppose so vigorously the notion of autonomy that constitutes the positive concept of freedom? This is due to the fact that for Berlin there exist two opposite understandings of what it does mean to be autonomous: one recurs to *rationality as the source of autonomy* and the other to *identity as the source of autonomy*. Berlin contests the rationality model of autonomy that is at the origin of the concept of positive freedom. Let us shortly see why.

Berlin maintains that the *rationality model of autonomy* opens largely the door for political tyranny. The 'real', or 'ideal', or 'autonomous' self, the self 'at its best',[27] is variously identified with reason. As this emphasis on rationality makes autonomy very much a matter of *truth*, Berlin fears that the scope of self-realization can be manipulated by those who see the real self as being part of a social 'whole' or are hold or feel entitled to discern clearer the rational interest of the individuals than the individuals themselves. As being autonomous means having the *right reasons* – the reasons which are given by my ideal, properly self-determined self – an individual is supposed to have reasons for action even if she presently cannot perceive them. Autonomy becomes an equivalent of external reason statements, of living according to rationally intelligible objective reasons. In the end, this conception of autonomy might lead "to ignore the actual wishes of men or societies, to bully, oppress, torture them in the name, and on behalf, of their 'real' selves",[28] and implies that "there can, in principle, be only one correct way of life."[29]

Berlin continues that on the contrary, the *identitarian model of autonomy* does not provide reasons for paternalism in politics. In this conception being autonomous

---

[23] J.S. Mill quoted in Isaiah Berlin, „Two Concepts of Liberty", in his *Four Essays on Liberty*, Oxford University Press, Oxford 1969, p. 127.
[24] I. Berlin, *Two Concepts of Liberty*, op. cit., pp. 121–122.
[25] Ibid., p. 128.
[26] Ibid., p. 165.
[27] Ibid., p. 132.
[28] Ibid., p. 133.
[29] Ibid., p. 155.

4.2 Identity and Liberalism

simply means living out one's identity. Reasons are not required to correspond to a standard of rationality in so far as they are conceived of being constituted by the subjective understanding of the person. Reasons are internal to a person and depend "on how we determine good and evil, that is to say, on our moral, religious, intellectual, economic, and aesthetic values."[30] Reasons are constituted by what is conceived of being a fulfilled life by the individual. If the only source for reasons is the individual's *actual* conception of the good life, there is no ground for paternalistic interference into the life of individuals. Given that in the world we encounter a multiplicity of individual values that all look incompatible, incommensurable and hypothetically in conflict Berlin denies that there are any external reasons that can be discovered commonly through rationality.[31] For Berlin it is clear that only identification can be a foundation of reason statements.

Indeed, the identitarian model of autonomy looks like the ultimate justification for negative freedom and the liberal state. If *we* are the author of values and ultimate authority, "then nothing is worse than to treat [us] as if [we] were not autonomous."[32] The relevance of identity justifies our claim to be left autonomous in living out our identity. The concept of freedom is derived from what constitutes a person, in short her identity.

Berlin recognizes that individuals' reasons might by times conflict and make individuals irrespective of each others' freedom. Therefore, an area of non-interference must be drawn for each individual in which the absolutely necessary minimum of personal freedom can be preserved. The frontiers of negative freedom which nobody should be permitted to cross must be accepted by all individuals, because otherwise they would be constituted by some unacceptable external reasons. For in Berlin it can be only autonomy – the identitarian model – that provides reasons for respecting the autonomy of others. In this sense, autonomy does not only justify negative freedom but also *constitutes* the realm of negative freedom. So, what reasons do people have to commonly agree upon some standards for negative freedom? Berlin recurs here to "what are fundamental needs of men as men, in a good (or, indeed, any) society",[33] to a "conception of what it is to be a normal human being, and, therefore, also of what it is to act inhumanly or insanely"[34] and to a notion of rules, which one could not break easily without a qualm of revulsion.[35] In other paragraphs Berlin refers to natural rights, religion, utility or the social contract as the defining principles for negative freedom.[36]

I think that Berlin fails to show to what degree identity provides autonomy in the sense of being constitutive of the standards for negative freedom. To show this

---

[30] Ibid., p. 169.
[31] Ibid., p. 168.
[32] Ibid., pp. 136–137.
[33] Ibid., p. 169.
[34] Ibid., p. 165.
[35] Ibid., p. 166.
[36] Ibid., pp. 127, 165.

Berlin would need to prove that there are subjective standards for drawing the frontiers of negative freedom, in so far as he claims that identity is the only source for us having reasons. He does not explain why living according to one's identity provides reasons for respecting or tolerating a realm of freedom of other individuals. Instead, Berlin recurs to a minimum notion of rationality and objectivity that must inform each others' reasons: fundamental needs in a good society or 'being normal' or having revulsions takes a common standard of evaluation for granted. As a consequence, being autonomous for Berlin entails objective standards of rationality and cannot be a mere matter of identity. In this sense, contrary to what Berlin says, individual freedom is not a standard for which a merely subjective status is claimed,[37] but a criterion with objective status.

The manner how Berlin conceives negative freedom presupposes rationality at the core of autonomy, and which alone can be seen as an individual's source to accept a society in which every individual enjoys equal negative freedom. To gain a right to identity and internal reasons involves the acceptance of some external reasons and standards of rationality. Berlin is unable to show that identity alone give us a right to identity.

4.3 Conclusion

In moral philosophy, Frankfurt develops the perhaps most viable alternative to Kantian moral autonomy. Whereas Humeans, such as Bernard Williams and Simon Blackburn, stress the non-cognitive elements and in particular desires in our reasons to act,[38] about which we might have consciousness and knowledge or not, Frankfurt puts at the center our identities, what we care about and what we love. Our psychological identity is supposed to provide us freedom of the will and autonomy. But what happens if we haven't managed to develop those identities? Eventually Frankfurt's theory cannot do without some form of transcendentalism

In political philosophy, Berlin's theory of liberalism constitutes the background of what goes today with the name of *modus vivendi* liberalism.[39] *Modus vivendi* liberalism seeks to do away with any form of moral foundations and defends liberalism as the most rational result under the conditions of pluralism. Yet, without a proper basic structure that shapes and moderates political identities through policies

---

[37] Ibid., p. 170.

[38] See Bernard Williams. 1981. *Moral Luck*, Cambridge: Cambridge University Press, pp. 101–113 and Simon Blackburn. 1998. *Ruling Passions*. Cambridge: Cambridge University Press.

[39] See Alessandro Ferrara (2018), "How to Accommodate Modus Vivendi Within Normative Political Theory," in *Biblioteca della libertà*, LIII, n. 222; Raymond Geuss (2008), *Philosophy and Real Politics*, Princeton (NJ): Princeton University Press; John Gray (2000), *Two Faces of Liberalism*, Cambridge: Polity Press; Bernard Williams (2005), *In the Beginning Was the Deed. Realism and Moralism in Political Argument*, Princeton (NJ): Princeton University Press.

such as Rawls envisages in *A Theory of Justice*,[40] we have no guarantee that identities do not radicalize and put the liberal consensus in question. In the current political situation, not only religious fundamentalism, but also nationalism oppose and undermine the liberal framework. (see 'Agency, Psychology and the Self: The Case of Religious Fundamentalism' and 'Liberal Nationalism', in this volume). If 'nudging' seems somewhat too much of a radical solution in a liberal democracy, a critical reformulation of Frankfurt's concept of autonomy could provide valuable insights into how to give liberal democracy a new foundation.

References

Berlin, Isaiah. 1969. Two Concepts of Liberty. In *Four Essays on Liberty*, ed. I. Berlin. Oxford: Oxford University Press.
Blackburn, Simon. 1998. *Ruling Passions*. Cambridge: Cambridge University Press.
Ferrara, Alessandro. 2018. How to Accommodate Modus Vivendi Within Normative Political Theory. In *Biblioteca della libertà* LIII, n. 222.
Frankfurt, Harry. 2004. *The Reasons of Love*, 2004. Princeton and Oxford: Princeton University Press.
———. 2008. *The Importance of What We Care About*. Cambridge: Cambridge University Press.
Geuss, Raymond. 2008. *Philosophy and Real Politics*. Princeton: Princeton University Press.
Gray, John. 2000. *Two Faces of Liberalism*. Cambridge: Polity Press.
Rawls, John. 1971. *A Theory of Justice*. Cambridge, MA: Belknap Press.
Thaler, Richard, and Cass Sunstein. 2009. *Nudge: Improving Decisions About Health, Wealth, and Happiness*. London: Penguin.
Williams, Bernard. 2005. *In the Beginning Was the Deed. Realism and Moralism in Political Argument*. Princeton: Princeton University Press.
———. 1981. *Moral Luck*. Cambridge: Cambridge University Press.

---

[40] John Rawls (1971), *A Theory of Justice*, Cambridge (Mass.): Belknap Press.

Chapter 5
Identity, Difference and Anti-essentialism

Abstract This chapter analyzes poststructural theories of difference that question the grand narratives and rationality of Enlightenment liberalism and pay close attention to subjugated knowledges and the diversity of social and cultural contexts. Foucault individuates the will of the persons, their agency, as the criterion of personal identity, since it does not "force the individual back on himself and ties him to his own identity in a constraining way" – we have a certain freedom to be what we want to be. Foucault ultimately has a Kantian and thus a liberal conception of identity. Derrida, on the contrary, in his theory of *différance*, gives up on the notion of agency and puts the very concept of identity, in the name of difference, radically into question. According to Derrida, individuals are already constituted within a structure of linguistic, cultural and historical difference that is detrimental to any form of identity statement. To be truly ourselves is to accept this structure of difference. However, also Derrida's deconstructionism and ethics of difference are grounded in a form of transcendentalism.

Keywords Michel Foucault · Jacques Derrida · Judith Butler · Frantz Fanon · Martin Heidegger · Poststructuralism · Identity · Politics of difference · Self-constitution · Technologies of the self · Subjectivation · Différance · Deconstructionism · Gender

No better way to introduce the ethics and politics of difference than with a definition of Michel Foucault: "They are struggles that question the status of the individual: on the one hand, they assert the right to be different and they underline everything which makes individuals truly individual. On the other hand, they attack everything which separates the individual, breaks his links with others, splits up community life, forces the individual back on himself and ties him to his own identity in a constraining way. These struggles are not exactly for or against the 'individual,' but rather they are struggles against the 'government of individualization.'" (Foucault 1983, 211–12).

Theories of difference are based upon a beautiful, profoundly humanistic ideal that gave rise to the anti-colonial, feminist and civil rights movements of the last century: Nobody should ever be discriminated and oppressed for reasons that are related to his or her identity – natural differences such as that of sex and race but also cultural, ethnic, religious or social differences do not justify any form of injustices or inequalities – "Look how handsome that Negro is!" "Kiss the handsome Negro's ass, madame!" (Fanon 1986, 86)

Yet, all the point and, in a sense, all the originality of theories of difference is that they do not defend their political program of anti-discrimination on a basis of equality, like liberalism does, but that they do this properly on the basis of difference, the very difference that they set off to battle in the first place. And the positive intuition theories of difference are built upon is again good: Each one of us is the particular person he or she is and moral and political reasoning should somehow account for this fact, account for "everything which makes individuals truly individual," as Foucault puts it. Now, here start all the problems of theories of difference: What exactly is it that makes us the person we are? Is there a criterion of personal identity and to what extent is it opposed to the "government of individualization"? Or does difference resist the logic of identity? It is on these points that the various theories of difference disagree profoundly and irreconcilably. The schism within the theories of difference runs basically between Foucaultian and Derridean theories.

Foucault individuates the will of the persons, their agency, as the criterion of personal identity, since it does not "force the individual back on himself and ties him to his own identity in a constraining way" – we have a certain freedom to be what we want to be. Not so Jacques Derrida: He rightly contests the idea that it is the will of a person that gives rise to difference – in fact, the will and identitarian theories à la Foucault sometimes risk to suspend individual difference in the life of the community. According to Derrida, individuals are already constituted within a structure of linguistic, cultural and historical difference that is detrimental to any form of identity statement. To be truly ourselves is to accept this structure of difference. Yet, also Derrida's ethics of difference faces the challenge of individualism.

In the first part I analyze identitarian theories of difference, and in the second section I examine difference *tout court*, difference without identity.

5.1 Difference with Identity

Let's start again with Foucault. As we saw, Foucault opposes "these abstractions, of economic and ideological state violence which ignore who we are individually" and insists on the fact that "all these present struggles revolve around the question: Who are we?" (Foucault 1983, 212) It is our identity that gives us a right to difference. Yet, if we are not what tell us the authorities, the church, the colonizers, our husbands and parents, if we refute the "scientific and administrative inquisition which determines who one is" (Foucault 1983, 240), if "the ways in which women are said to 'know' or to 'be known' are already orchestrated by power" (Butler 2004, 215),

5.1 Difference with Identity

in short if our identity cannot be defined from the outside by others from a more or less objective point of view, then only we, the single individuals, are in a position to say who we really are. No one else than myself can say who I am; it is from a subjective point of view that we determine our identity. Foucault claims that "we have to create ourselves as a work of art" (Foucault 1989, 237). We have to invent our identity.

But certainly if our identity is not given but chosen, individuals must have some form of freedom in determining their identity. We must be agents with a will in order to be other than we actually are. Only insofar as I have a will, I am not determined or caused by the biology of my sex, for example, my "'I' is [not] undone by being a gender", as Judith Butler puts it (2004, 16) – it is only in case that I exist as an agent over and above my physical and psychological constitution with a minimum degree of autonomy, that I can honestly say not to be a man; I might be a man from a theoretical point of view, but not from the practical point of view, unless I do not decide to be so. Who we are is a matter of practical identity, of what we choose to be, identity is a matter of practice and not of metaphysics.

Put like this, Foucault risks to be easily confounded with the liberal tradition he is criticizing so vehemently. He could sound like Christine Korsgaard (2009) whose theory on self-constitution assumes the existence of a choosing and constituting agent prior to its social embeddedness. Yet, as Butler maintains, "the critical task for feminism is not to establish a point of view outside of constructed identities; that conceit is the construction of an epistemological model that would disavow its own cultural location and, hence, promote itself as a global subject, a position that deploys precisely the imperialist strategies that feminism ought to criticize." (Butler 1990b, 201). And in fact Foucault denies that we choose our identity freely. Foucault maintains on the contrary that the subject "is constituted in real practices – historically analysable practices. There is a technology of the constitution of the self which cuts across symbolic system while using them." (Foucault 1983, 250). Technologies of the self, these are terms with which Foucault refers to the possibility of self-constitution, are frequently related to the so-called governmental technologies, exercises of power that are at the origin of the representations imposed upon the individuals. This means that self-constitution takes place within a determined social context, we do not have, as Korsgaard believes, the absolute freedom of Gods to create the world at will unbound by any rules and conventions; the freedom we have to create ourselves as a work of art is limited by the social material we come across. Our identity is therefore "neither fatally determined nor fully artificial and arbitrary" (Butler 2004, 211).

And it is precisely our power to dislocate the meaning of social norms, the hermeneutics of the self (Foucault 2005), that gives rise to difference between individuals. Butler's theory of gender performativity makes this point quite evident. According to Butler, gender is a "corporeal enactment that constitutes its "interior" signification on its surface;" (Butler 1990b, 189) gender is an "'act' which is both intentional and performative, where *performative* suggests a dramatic and contingent construction of meaning." (Butler 1990b, 190). Accordingly, "the possibilities of gender transformation are to be found in the arbitrary relation between such acts, in the possibility of a different sort of repeating, in the breaking or subversive repetition of that style" (Butler 1990a, 271). In the postcolony, situated agency consents individuals to "guide, deceive, and toy with power" (Mbembe 2001, 128), "to manage not just a single identity, but several – flexible enough to negotiate as and when necessary" (Mbembe 2001, 104), escaping tyranny and deceiving autocratic power.

Theories of difference clearly want to have an emancipatory character. Yet, a theory of difference based upon a conception of situated agency must not necessarily bring about the emancipation of individuals from objectifying and oppressive collective identities (Bazzicalupo 2009). There must not inevitably be a dissonance between our constructed individual identities and our given collective identities. It is not by chance that Butler closes *Gender Trouble* claiming that "the task is not whether to repeat, but how to repeat the gender norms" (Butler 1990b, 202–203); she understandingly comes to have anxiety about which difference and what gender identities have value and increase the possibility of a livable life (2004, 218–19). Since it is obvious that not all repetitions dislocate the norms that characterize our collective identities in the same way. Some repetitions and interpretations stand in a greater contrast to social norms than others. We certainly have the possibility to reinterpret the social norms that come to constitute us, but a theory of situated agency cannot prescribe the content and direction of the reiterations. A Foucaultian theory of agency does not allow us to make any moral claims about the identities individuals eventually come to choose. We have no objective measure outside the internal point of the view of the respective individuals themselves to say which reproduction, contestation or alteration is better or more subversive and valuable than another. It is only a matter of ideology to see the drag rather than common housewives as a more subversive and emancipatory interpretation of gender norms.

Listen to Frantz Fanon's account of what the *black* man wants: "What! When it was I who had every reason to hate, to despise, I was rejected? When I should have been begged, implored, I was denied the slightest recognition? I resolved, since it was impossible for me to get away from an *inborn complex*, to assert myself as a BLACK MAN" (Fanon 1986, 87). "I wanted to be typically Negro" (1986, 101). It is not at all the case that the performance of resistance entails the displacement or subversion of hegemonic norms. On the contrary, a huge part of the resistance in the postcolony but also of certain feminist movements[1] follows the pattern of an explicit endorsement of the norms which provided the justification for the discrimination, subjugation and colonization of cultures, races and sexes. It does not matter that, as Edward Said (1979) illustrates effectively in *Orientalism*, it has been we, the European colonizers, who have constructed the very idea of the Orient, of what it means to be Oriental, Muslim, Arab or Black – that the properties that go along with these collective identities are purely invented. As Butler rightly maintains, in a theory of situated agency "there is no possibility of agency or reality outside of the

---

[1] "Feminists assert the validity of feminine sensitivity and the positive value of nurturing behavior." (Young 1990, 166).

discursive practices that give those terms the intelligibility that they have." (Butler 1990b, 202). But then it should not come as a surprise that a profound sense of dignity virtually requires the colonized individuals to show that there is just nothing wrong with the properties that are supposed to constitute Blackness or Muslimhood – subversion of these norms could actually be considered as an act of cowardice, escaping rather than confronting the oppressors. A truly proud black person asks for recognition. Hence, "this politics asserts that oppressed groups have distinct cultures, experiences, and perspectives on social life with humanly positive meaning" (Young 1990, 166), the politics of difference turns into the claim of group rights. But then, of course, the difference holds between social groups and not any longer between individuals. And how could these politics of difference be distinguished from more standard versions of communitarianism? Not really, as Iris Marion Young herself admits: "To be sure, it is difficult to articulate positive elements of group affinity without essentializing them" (Young 1990, 172). Certainly, Young is anything but a communitarian and rather considers antiracist racism in the wake of Jean-Paul Sartre as the negative moment that prepares the sublation, the realization of humanity in a society without races. Other than Aimé Césaire (1972), she does not believe Negritude to have whatsoever ontological foundation. But, as Fanon astutely remarks, in order that this strategy works, "I needed to lose myself completely in negritude." (Fanon 1986, 103) and expose myself, the individual, to all the risks that are inherent to communitarianism. And that these risks are quite real is exemplified by the authoritarian turn the Iranian revolution took in the last decades, the Islamic Shiite revolution against the pro-western Shah of 1979, so wholeheartedly endorsed by Foucault.

All the point is that Foucault's theory of situated agency is susceptible to this communitarian drift of the politics of difference. In order to foreclose this possibility, while maintaining that "the masses *know* perfectly well" (Foucault quoted in Spivak 1994, 69), Foucault must somehow assure that "the person who speaks and acts (…) is always a multiplicity" (Spivak 1994, 70). And he does this eventually presupposing the intransitivity of freedom (Foucault 1983, 222), the free subject that stands out of the realm of causality (Foucault 1983, 221). In order that Foucault's emancipatory political project works he must take for granted the existence of an autonomous, self-knowing (self-proximate, if not self-identical) and transparent subject, in fact, the Kantian moral person. But then, as Gayatri Spivak maintains, a "politics of the oppressed 'speaking for themselves', restore[s] the category of the sovereign subject within the theory that seems most to question it" (Spivak 1994, 73) and "leads to an essentialist, utopian politics" (Spivak 1994, 71).

5.2 Difference Without Identity

We have seen that a theory of difference conceived in terms of situated agency collapses eventually into some form of egalitarianism based upon the notion of the autonomous and free agent, when it tries to stay clear of the dangers of communitarianism. It is intentionality, or our capacity to choose, our agency, and the identities that come along that risk to undermine the project of difference. Hence, the solution must be to give up on the idea of intentionality – and this is the starting point of Derrida's theory of difference. Derrida contests profoundly the idea of a transcendental self, the idea that there is something that is *you* and that *chooses* among alternative courses of action. Derrida criticizes Heidegger precisely for distinguishing ontological difference from sexual difference – Heidegger quite in accordance with Foucault's conception of the will understands being (Dasein) to be irreducible to metaphysics, ethics, anthropology or biology and to be nothing else than a relation to itself: "The interpretation of this being – which *we* are – must be carried out *prior to* and *outside* of a concretion of [our sexuality]" (Derrida 2008, 12), before "dispersion and distraction (*Zerstreuung* in both senses) characterize the inauthentic ipseity of *Dasein*" (2008, 25). And Derrida questions Heidegger's "metaphysical isolation of man" as follows: "What if 'sexuality' already marked the most originary *Selbstheit?* What if it were an ontological structure of ipseity? What if the *Da* of *Dasein* were already 'sexual'? And what if sexual difference were already marked in the opening to the question of the meaning of Being and to ontological difference? And what if neutralization, which does not happen all by itself, were a violent operation?" (Derrida 2008, 17) It is not me who chooses to be man or woman, my self is already constituted by sexual difference.

Now, when Derrida maintains that being is already sexual, that ipseity is characterized by sexuality, he does not want to say that there is anything essential in our sexuality that determines our being; he does not want to introduce any causal relationship between our biological constitution and our being as such. In fact, his criticism of Heidegger wants to "open thinking to a sexual difference that would not yet be sexual duality, difference as dual" (Derrida 2008, 26). Derrida does not believe that sexual difference has anything to do with being a man or a woman, that sexual difference can be reduced to any biological difference, or that the order of difference that constitutes being in general has anything to with and refers to the empirical differences we find in the world. Not that empiricism would not allow for a theory of difference – David Hume, after all, is a theorist of difference par excellence. The fact that there is a causal connection between our sexuality and our desires must not give rise to any idea of personal identity, given that we, as human beings, underlie a large variety of causes that cannot be reduced to sexuality alone – and hence, since "there is no impression constant and invariable" (Hume 1978, 251–52), no idea of the self can be derived. And yet, empiricism cannot exclude categorically the possibility of essentialism. Spivak, when she discusses the Hindu practice of self-immolation of widows on their husband's funeral pyre, claims that the causal constitution "between patriarchy and imperialism" makes "the figure of the woman disappear (…) [leaving] no space from which the sexed subaltern subject can speak" (Spivak 1994, 102–3). This is the reason why Derrida does not want to reduce ontological and sexual difference to some form of empirical difference (Derrida 2001, 351–70).

What does Derrida refer to when he talks about sexual difference, if it is neither us, persons, who invent the difference (existentialism), nor difference has anything

5.2 Difference Without Identity

to do with being biologically a man or a woman (empiricism)? Derrida claims that whenever we try to define ourselves as either a man or a woman, when we try to fix our identity as a man or a woman, the identity claim disappears in the structure of differences that characterizes language. We are always already both, man and woman. His argument is that identity statements of any sort are *a priori* impossible and this for two reasons: First, meaning is not determined by the psychological state or 'intention' of the speaker. Secondly, language is the result of "effects which do not find their cause in a subject or a substance, in a thing in general, a being that is somewhere present" (Derrida 1982, 11), signs and symbols are not simply substitutions for the thing itself. On the contrary, as in Ferdinand de Saussure's semiology, "the elements of signification function due not to the compact force of their nuclei but rather to the network of oppositions that distinguishes them, and then relates them one to another" (Derrida 1982, 10). But, of course, if the meaning of a word is given solely by the way it differs from other words, then meaning must be a function of differences *"without positive terms"* (Derrida 1982, 11), which means that the meaning of a word actually defers to the meaning of the words it differs from, which in their turn defer to the meaning of the words they differ from, and so on. Derrida labels this relation of both difference and deferral between signifiers as 'différance'. Thus, it is impossible for me to identify as man or woman – whenever I want to fix the meaning of what it means to be a man or a woman, I have to refer to other identities, which in their turn have to refer to other identities, etc., with the result that we end up in an infinite regress, whenever we want to specify the meaning of an identity: "The signified concept is never present in and of itself, in a sufficient presence that would refer only to itself." (Derrida 1982, 11). Hence, when Derrida maintains that the self cannot be conceived independently from a structure of (sexual) difference, he in fact claims that the self itself is constituted by différance and which in turn does not allow the formation of binary gender identities.

But how could différance then ever give rise to a politics and ethics of difference, when whenever we try to mark a difference and claim an identity, the very difference disappears in différance and language games? Homi Bhabha's answer in this regard is that since "it is this *structure of difference* that produces the hybridity of race and sexuality in the postcolonial discourse" (Bhabha 1994, 53), it is the structure of difference that characterizes culture that destabilizes and eventually suspends colonial power (and any form of stereotypization and identitarian discrimination), insofar as it gives rise to identity games of the oppressed in form of mimicry and sly civility. Hence, the ethical implications of différance are not the recognition of difference as in Foucaultian theories, but, on the contrary, the impossibility of individuating cultures, the impossibility of any sort of identity politics. Différance does not imply respect for individual difference, but for the differential structure of being as such. Accordingly, Derrida deduces from différance an ethics of undecidability – "I believe there is no responsibility, no ethico-political decision, that must not pass through the proofs of the incalculable or the undecidable" (Derrida 1995, 273). But are we sure that it is différance itself that impedes us to make identity claims?

The ethics of undecidability is based upon the idea that the structure of difference defers my decision endlessly and for this reason I must act as if a finite decision can never be taken, act in the shadow of the undecidable, place my actions "under the heel of ontology" (Derrida 2001, 169). Yet, what happens if I violate "the universalist, law of difference or doubling" (Bhabha 1994, 57), what happens if I take a decision where in principle no decision can be taken? In fact, nothing at all, since it is impossible to criticize an action as morally wrong without violating in turn the very principle of difference. Différance cannot provide an independent criteria to distinguish between right and wrong that does not underlie the logic of différance; it cannot even establish the criteria of undecidability, given that nothing can stop the infinite regress of substituting one concept for the other and make us come to the conclusion that there is something undecidable. Différance keeps us like a hamster spinning in the wheel, not helping us to stop it. The practical law of difference and of the undecidable must therefore have its origin outside of the structure of difference, and in Derrida's account this source can only be *Kantian* practical reason.

As Jürgen Habermas (2008, 271–311) concludes, différance gives rise to moral relativism rather than to moral individualism or Bhabha's vernacular cosmopolitanism: It does not protect the individual from identitarian politics. Individualism and rights, after all, suspend the logic of différance.

Two words of conclusion: As we have seen, theories of difference try to provide an alternative to the oppressiveness of egalitarianism and the essentialism of communitarianism. My suggestion in this article has been that there is no space left in-between liberalism and communitarianism: Either we are liberals, or we are communitarians, there are just no identitarian liberals or liberal communitarians. I think that Derrida, obscure and convoluted as he may seem, is on the right track – agency as it is conceived in Kantian and Hegelian theories is problematic. But maybe we should not dismiss too quickly empiricism and the possibility of a psychological account of identity.

References

Bazzicalupo, Laura. 2009. *Postcolonial Studies*: tra decostruzione e antagonismo. *Politica & Società* 2: 29–49.
Bhabha, Homi. 1994. *The Location of Culture*. London/New York: Routledge.
Butler, Judith. 1990a. Performative Acts and Gender Constitution: An Essay in Phenomenology and Feminist Theory. In *Performing Feminisms: Feminist Critical Theory and Theatre*, ed. Sue-Ellen Case. Baltimore: Johns Hopkins University Press.
———. 1990b. *Gender Trouble. Feminism and the Subversion of Identity*. London/New York: Routledge.
———. 2004. *Undoing Gender*. London/New York: Routledge.
Césaire, Aimé. 1972. *Discourse on Colonialism*. New York: Monthly Review Press.
Derrida, Jacques. 2001. *Writing and Difference*, ed. Alan Bass. London/New York: Routledge Classics.
———. 1995. *Points: Interviews, 1974–1994*, ed. Elisabeth Weber. Stanford: Stanford University Press.

———. 1982. *Margins of Philosophy*. Brighton: The Harvester Press.
———. 2008. *Geschlecht* I: Sexual Difference, Ontological Difference. In *Psyché. Inventions of the Other*, ed. J. Derrida, vol. 2, 7–26. Stanford: Stanford University Press.
Fanon, Frantz. 1986. *Black Skin, White Masks*. London: Pluto Press.
Foucault, Michel. 1983. "The Subject and Power" and "On the Genealogy of Ethics: An Overview of Work in Progress". In *Michel Foucault: Beyond Structuralism and Hermeneutics*, ed. Hubert Dreyfus and Paul Rabinow, 208–252. Chicago: The University of Chicago Press.
———. 2005. *The Hermeneutics of the Subject. Lectures at the Collège de France (1981–1982)*. New York: Picador.
Habermas, Jürgen. 2008. *Between Naturalism and Religion*. Cambridge: Polity Press.
Hume, David. 1978. *A Treatise of Human Nature*, ed L.A. Selby-Bigge and P.H. Nidditch. Oxford: Oxford University Press.
Korsgaard, Christine. 2009. *Self-Constitution. Agency, Identity, and Integrity*. Oxford: Oxford University Press.
Mbembe, Achille. 2001. *On the Postcolony*. Berkeley/Los Angeles: University of California Press.
Said, Edward. 1979. *Orientalism*. New York: Vintage Books.
Spivak, Gayatri Chakravorty. 1994. Can the Subaltern Speak. In *Colonial Discourse and Post-Colonial Theory*, ed. Patrick Williams and Laura Chrisman, 66–111. New York: Columbia University Press.
Young, Iris Marion. 1990. *The Politics of Difference*. Princeton: Princeton University Press.

Chapter 6
Agency, Psychology and the Self: The Case of Religious Fundamentalism

Abstract The chapter analyzes the motivations of religious fundamentalists. Typically, fundamentalism is considered to have its origin in determinate cultural or religious systems of beliefs and norms. In this regard, it can be distinguished between metaphysical and moral accounts of fundamentalism. First state that fundamentalism makes claims concerning the reality of cultures and religions. Latter hold fundamentalism to be of practical, not of theoretical nature. This essay argues, on the contrary, that fundamentalism does not have its source in religion or culture. Fundamentalists are not motivated by cultural or religious beliefs and reasons. Their intolerance is, in contrast, caused and driven by purely emotional reactions. What makes a fundamentalist is the emotional non-distinction between the intentions and actions of others and the proper behavior in matters of culture and religion. A fundamentalist has equally strong and intense emotional reactions when it comes to others' integrity as with regard to his or her own piety.

Keywords Fundamentalism · Islam · Essentialism · Pluralism · Autonomy · Non-cognitivism · Emotions · Moral psychology · Ideology · Self-knowledge

How can we explain religious fundamentalism? We can distinguish between two very distinctive, but opposite approaches. A first explanation believes fundamentalism to be related to the reasons individuals have for action. A second explanation holds fundamentalism to be caused by states over which individuals do not have any sort of power. This chapter analyzes in depth arguments in favor and against both positions. It comes to the conclusion that although *prima facie* fundamentalism seems to be related to the agency of an individual, there are strong grounds to believe that fundamentalism has its origin in the psychology of an individual. Accordingly, this chapter introduces a new model of fundamentalism.

I am going to present first the arguments that rely upon the first-person perspective of fundamentalists and proceeds then to introduce and defend a causal conception of fundamentalism.

6.1 Agency and Fundamentalism

There is a long lasting debate in political philosophy as to what extent pluralism and, more specifically, religious pluralism is a matter of justice. It is a discussion that goes back at least to Hobbes' *Leviathan*. According to the social contract tradition, religious pluralism and tolerance is neither natural nor spontaneous, but occurs only in political circumstances that guarantee some form of justice, last but not least, social and economic justice. This thesis stands in clear contrast to the position that holds pluralism to depend upon the respective religious doctrines themselves and the degree to which they allow for differences. According to this theory, religions can be more or less tolerant – and this entirely independent from the social and political context. The most extreme formulation of this theory we can find in Samuel Huntington's *The Clash of Civilizations*.

My goal in this first part is to review the lightest and most moderate versions of the latter, anti-reductionist thesis. Although those theories are not defending any form of religious essentialism, they do sketch out the argument that we cannot ignore the constitutive role that religious beliefs and norms play in the motivation of extremism and intolerance. Accordingly, religious pluralism is not solely the result of institutions. Reductive theories that emphasize the ideological character of religion or stress religious extremists' lack of self-knowledge run into a variety of problems that concern, in particular, agency, subjectivity and first-person authority.

A methodological point: I use the terms religious extremism and intolerance as more or less synonymous and the terms religious pluralism and moderatism as antonyms. Extremists believe that in one way or another religion may actually legitimate acts of discrimination and the use of violence. Moderates, on the other hand, do not commit acts of intolerance on religious grounds.

6.1.1 Religious Extremism and Agency

It is a recurrent debate, in particular with regard to the emergence of Islamism, that religious extremism has its cause in poverty, frustration, repression, hatred, etc., rather than in God's law. There are good grounds to believe that radicalization has other origins than religion itself. Sociologists and economists show that correlations exist between certain social factors and extremism and violence.[1] Psychologists demonstrate that personality disorders rather than particular belief systems explain violence. In fact, certain studies can be interpreted, although with great caution and inconclusively, as indicating that extremists tend to have some common

---

[1] See in particular Paul Collier and Anke Hoeffler, "On Economic Causes of Civil War". *Oxford Economic Papers* (50)4: 563–573, 1998.

psychological and social features.² It is very plausible to think that psychological and social factors explain extremism rather than a religious doctrine that is moreover often shared by moderates too.³ (see also the Chap. 11 on 'Populism', in this volume)

It is not the place here to flesh out a causal theory of religious extremism in detail. As an empirical theory, it requires not only data but also rather complex theories of causation and the human mind. Whereas Seyla Benhabib emphasizes the role of negative emotions such as anger and hatred in the emergence of fundamentalism,⁴ other analysts, such as Scott Atran, stress rather the attractive features of terrorist networks and the positive feelings they bring about.⁵ The point I want, however, to analyze here is whether causal theories can really deny the foundational function that beliefs have in the motivation of an action. Despite the evidence that speaks in favor of causal theories, one crucial aspect is left out: namely that religious beliefs, though perhaps insufficient, are nevertheless necessary in the psychology of the extremist. For an Islamist to attack a bareheaded woman because she does not wear a head covering, for example, requires the belief that women should cover their heads.

I would like to discuss here one particularly hard objection to those causal theses that reject the relevance of religion in the explanation of extremism. The hard objection holds that causal theories depict extremists as a sort of victim of their psychology, family background as well as social and economic circumstances, thereby denying their agency as actors. Seen from their own perspective, however, extremists are absolutely not victims, they are just the contrary. They consider themselves to be moral heroes that, unlike their moderate peers, have the courage to speak out and act in accordance with religious values and God's commandments. They are the epitome of integrity, refusing, contrary to moderates, any kind of compromise and utilitarian calculus. If anyone is a victim, the godless moderates are. Such strong convictions become manifest in their self-righteous and cruel action. Extremists present themselves as highly-stylized and display very elaborated aesthetics of their own in the way they dress, move and talk – a phenomenon that we can observe also

---

²See Bundesamt für Verfassungsschutz, Bundeskriminalamt (KI11, ST33), Hessisches Informations- und Kompetenzzentrum gegen Extremismus (HKE), *Analyse der den deutschen Sicherheitsbehörden vorliegenden Informationen über die Radikalisierungshintergründe und -verläufe der Personen, die aus islamistischer Motivation aus Deutschland in Richtung Syrien ausgereist sind*, 01.12.2014, downloaded at http://www.pti kassel.de/institut/download/ praeventionsnetzwerk_salafismus_analyse.pdf

³This is the claim of Akeel Bilgrami in "What is a Muslim? Fundamental Commitment and Cultural Identity". *Critical Inquiry* 18(4):198–219, 1992.

⁴Seyla Benhabib, "Piety or Rage? On the Charlie Hebdo Massacres". In; *Reset DOC*, 11.01.2015, downloaded at http://www.resetdoc.org/story/00000022481

⁵Scott Atran with Lydia Wilson, Richard Davis, Hammad Sheikh, *The Devoted Actor, Sacred Values, and Willingness to Fight: Preliminary Studies with ISIL Volunteers and Kurdish Frontline Fighters*, Recent and ongoing research in conjunction with the U.S. Department of Defense MINERVA Initiative, November 2014, downloaded at http://artisresearch.com/wp-content/uploads/2014/11/Atran_Soccnet_MINERVA_ISIS.pdf

in respect of other violent subaltern actors, such as mafia gangsters, guerilla fighters, child soldiers etc.[6] In fact, following the Charlie Hebdo massacre, the portrayal of the attackers as victims was muted in favor of condemnations that asserted their moral agency.[7] From the extremist point of view, their actions are clearly guided by convictions, values and commitments. In this regard, causal explanations that do not take into account religious beliefs are certainly incomplete. By rejecting the agency of extremists, we risk ignoring the subjective point of view and its importance in the motivation of action.

6.1.2 Religious Extremism and Ideology

We can find two arguments that defend the causal theory against hard objection: the arguments concerning *ideology* and *self-knowledge*. Both these arguments try, in one way or another, to explain away the problem of beliefs. The first counter-thesis basically leaves intact the hard objection and its claim that beliefs motivate action. Yet, it argues that in the end, all that what we consider to be doctrines, values and subjective reasons are rather a form of ideology. People believe indeed that they are the authors of their proper beliefs, yet in reality their beliefs, at least in the Marxist tradition, are simply the results of the relations of production and, more generally, material conditions. Marx reduces and explains "the production of ideas, of conceptions, of consciousness […] with the material activity and the material intercourse of men".[8] Therefore, he can say that "religion is the sigh of the oppressed creature, the heart of a heartless world, and the soul of soulless conditions. It is the opium of

---

[6] Jean-François Bayart and Jean-Pierre Warnier (eds.), *Matière à politique. Le pouvoir, les corps et les choses*, (Paris: Karthala, 2004). See also Janet MacGaffey and Rémy Bazenguissa-Ganga, *Congo-Paris: Transnational Traders on the Margins of the Law* (Bloomington, Indiana: Indiana University Press, 2000).

[7] Michaela Wiegel, "Eine Zäsur". *Frankfurter Allgemeine Zeitung*, 8.01.15, p. 1: "All those who provided a social explanation of the worst acts of violence disappeared astonishingly quickly from the public debate. The former managing editor of *Charlie Hebdo*, Philippe Val, exhorted that society is not to be blamed for young French people with a background of living out their Islamistic fantasies of violence. He demanded, in particular from the left, a new sincerity in the overly-cautious debate on Islam and immigration in society" (translation by the author).

[8] Marx continues: "Conceiving, thinking, the mental intercourse of men, appear at this stage as the direct efflux of their material behaviour. The same applies to mental production as expressed in the language of politics, laws, morality, religion, metaphysics, etc., of a people. Men are the producers of their conceptions, ideas, etc. – real, active men, as they are conditioned by a definite development of their productive forces and of the intercourse corresponding to these, up to its furthest forms". (Karl Marx and Friedrich Engels, "Feuerbach. Gegensatz von materialistischer und idealistischer Anschauung". Karl Marx and Friedrich Engels, *Über Ludwig Feuerbach*, (Leipzig: Reclam, 1970), p. 15. Translation from the online edition of *The German Ideology*, downloaded at https://www.marxists.org/archive/marx/works/1845/german-ideology/

the people".⁹ Religion is an illusion, a false consciousness. In this regard, beliefs, although existent and powerful, are no particular big problem. At the moment that the material conditions change, extremist beliefs will, over time, disappear.

Leaving aside the complex difficulties in proving this theory, advocates of the hard objection could claim that all efforts to eliminate the first-person miss the point. The first-person perspective is irreducible. In short, the hard objection could point to the subjective nature of practical beliefs, in the sense that values and commitments are the result of our freedom and autonomy.

6.1.3 Religious Extremism and Self-Knowledge

The second counter-argument tends to dismiss the role played by beliefs and maintains that it need not necessarily be beliefs that give rise to religious intolerance, even though we tend to think they do. This theory is based upon the assumption that our mind lacks transparence: we do not always, and perhaps only rarely, have accurate access to our mind. For example, extremists who believe that non-Muslims are infidels must not automatically have this belief, despite believing that they do. Or, Islamists, claiming to act upon the obligations written in the Qur'an, might have quite different motivations for their actions, such as feelings of guilt, resentment etc. The motives or beliefs guiding their actions can in fact be hidden from them, without the need to deceive themselves. According to this theory, self-knowledge is not special with respect to other knowledge. Therefore, we do not have immediate, first-person access to our mental state nor special authority with regard to our beliefs and desires. Knowing oneself is not unlike knowing other minds. We must observe ourselves in order to know what we are really up to.

Many experiments in the cognitive sciences confirm the opacity of the mind.[10] And extremists may effectively be driven by motives other than they are aware of. It is a standard thesis in the psychology of religion that fundamentalism fulfills particular psychological needs and is an answer to the quest for meaning in an inhospitable environment.[11]

---

[9] Karl Marx, *Critique of Hegel's 'Philosophy Of Right'*, Joseph O'Malley (ed., trans.), Annette Jolin (trans.), (Cambridge: Cambridge University Press, 1977), p. 1.

[10] For the original epistemological account of self-knowledge, see Gilbert Ryle, *The Concept of Mind* (Chicago: The University of Chicago Press, 1949). For a recent study that denies privileged access to our own minds and is based upon studies and results from the cognitive sciences, see Peter Carruthers, *The Opacity of Mind: An Integrative Theory of Self-Knowledge* (Oxford: Oxford University Press, 2011).

[11] Ralph W. Hood Jr., Peter C. Hill and W. Paul Williamson, *The Psychology of Religious Fundamentalism* (New York: Guilford Press, 2005).

Nevertheless, questioning first-person authority might again fail to refute the hard objection. Lack of self-knowledge does not necessarily compromise agency.[12] Perhaps extremists are not always particularly clear on their commitments and are confused about their motivations, but their integrity and credibility in the eyes of others – and also in their own eyes – stands and falls with the extent to which they actually live up to the self-proclaimed commitments. If commitments do not reflect themselves in action – if extremists are not perceived to be authentic as well as to believe in their cause and reveal, on the contrary, only self-interest, insecurity and frustration – religious extremism may well disappear. The problem is, as the hard objection continues to insist, that beliefs and convictions are present and cannot be brushed aside.

From this perspective, religious extremists are therefore agents rather than passive victims. Treating their beliefs as only residues of various injustices suffered, without taking such beliefs seriously, risks increasing incomprehension between groups, offensive behavior and social division. Still, the question remains as to how to engage with extremist beliefs. Since refuting their claims on a cognitive or theological level, as hermeneutical readings of the sacred texts propose,[13] might nonetheless miss the point, if we do not consider extremism to be about religious truth. However, in order to address extremism effectively, it seems impossible to avoid the arduous task of understanding the nature of religious commitments from the first-person perspective.

6.2 Psychology and Fundamentalism

I turn now to arguments that question the agential perspective of fundamentalists and introduce a new theoretical framework of how to understand fundamentalism. If fundamentalists can be generally characterized by their forthright intention – in actions, words and gestures – to impose a particular cultural, ethnic, racial or religious doctrine upon others,[14] it is far less clear what precisely makes them to have such an intention. If we leave aside the rather crude analysis proposed by the school of political realism, according to which fundamentalism needs to be explained in terms of pure self-interest and rational choice, contemporary political theory commonly sees fundamentalism to arise from and be motivated by *norms*. Accordingly, fundamentalism is confronted and sought to be defeated on either the level of truth

---

[12] This is the thesis of Akeel Bilgrami in *Resentment and Self-Knowledge* (Cambridge, Mass.: Harvard University Press, 2006).

[13] See in particular Nasr Abu Zayd, *Rethinking the Qu'ran: Towards a Humanistic Hermeneutics* (Amsterdam, SWP Publishing, 2004).

[14] I am not discussing here moral and political fundamentalism, a fundamentalism that emerges from moral and political doctrines and that is the target of Isaiah Berlin's analysis in "Two Concepts of Liberty," in I. Berlin (1969), *Four Essays on Liberty*, Oxford, Oxford University Press. My interest is limited to what we might call ethical or thick fundamentalism.

or normativity. A first strategy is to demonstrate that fundamentalists misunderstand the very nature of the norms they propagate and to defend pluralism in *metaphysical* terms. Another approach is to show that whatever norms fundamentalists might come to hold, they are not justified to impose these norms upon others. Pluralism is defended here as a matter of *morality*. As a result, these political theories come to imply that moderates either have more correct and sophisticated ontological insights or are morally more competent agents than fundamentalists.

The intuition is, however, that the fault line between fundamentalists and moderates is neither metaphysics nor morality. On the contrary, moderates attribute most probably the same ontological status to norms as fundamentalists and are just as little moral agents as are fundamentalists. I am going to suggest, as a working hypothesis, that fundamentalists and moderates have different *psychologies*. I propose that moderates and fundamentalists have different emotional reactions with regard to what others do and say in matters of culture and religion, the latter's being much more intense and violent. This is due to the fact that fundamentalists are emotionally unable to distinguish between themselves violating a norm and others not respecting a norm, a distinction moderates are emotionally perfectly able to do. Whereas moderates become emotionally highly troubled when they themselves entertain ideas or desires that break cultural or religious norms, their emotions drastically cool down when others disregard these norms. This difference in the emotional engagement with oneself and with others contributes, so my thesis, to moderatism and tolerance. Whereas the emotional non-discrimination between oneself and others results in fundamentalism and intolerance. I conclude this section with some policy implications of this psychological theory of fundamentalism.

6.2.1 Metaphysics

The paradigm case today is, of course, Islamic fundamentalism. There have been made enormous efforts to deconstruct the Islamists' narrative and to reveal the wrongness of their discourse showing that nothing in Islam makes it incompatible with democracy, secularism, liberalism and modernity at large. The main objection is that Islamists go wrong about the nature of Islam, that they do not really understand what Islam is all about. The metaphysical assault on fundamentalism, aiming at reestablishing an authentic Islam or at least at grounding some truths concerning Islam, can be divided into two strands: the *foundational* and the *anti-foundational critique*.

The foundational critique, that is probably best represented by the work of Abdullahi An'-Naim,[15] argues that the norms Islamists endorse are simply un-Islamic and therefore illegitimate. Fundamentalists' norms do not correspond to the

---

[15] Abdullahi An-Na'im (2010), *Islam and the Secular State: Negotiating the Future of Shari'a*, Cambridge, Mass., Harvard University Press.

core or essence of Islam, so as it has been revealed in the Koran and the millennial history of Islam. An'-Naim et al. suppose that Islam exists as much as other types or kinds exist, such as 'chair', 'horse', etc.. Insofar as we can individuate an object as a chair qua its chair-ness or its property of being a chair, we can identify intentions, utterances and actions as Islamic qua their Islam-ness. Note that fundamentalists plainly agree with approaching Islam in foundational terms. The only disagreement is about what exactly are the foundations of Islam.

Many political philosophers, who share the metaphysical stance on fundamentalism, do not necessarily agree with the foundationalist strategy. In fact, they very much doubt that there exists Islam as such and that we can discern the true and authentic Islam with the help of universals. Their claim is precisely that foundationalism is the very sin that leads to fundamentalist thought. Anti-foundationslists are either outright skeptical with regard to norms, conceiving norms to be a matter of language and practice rather than of reality (e.g. postcolonial criticism in the wake of Derridean deconstructionism).[16] Or, they maintain that human agency is a constitutive element of norms. Norms are instantiated by way of an interpretative process, that is always and already contextual and historical in nature (this hermeneutical approach to Islam is most famously defended by Nasr Abu Zayd and Tariq Ramadan).[17] Islam exists as a human construction, constantly in flux, and not as an independent universal. 'Being Islamic' is not an inherent property of Islamic norms, but a property that we at least partly come to attribute to those norms without necessarily having any further grounds or ontological justification. From this theoretical insight into the nature of norms, anti-foundationalists draw a moral conclusion. Since there exists not one Islam but a plurality of Islams, fundamentalists are not justified to impose their interpretation of Islam.

6.2.2 Morality

Still, according to a great deal of political theorists the metaphysical confrontation with fundamentalism misses entirely the point. It is at the same moment too illiberal and too accommodating with fundamentalism. Is not freedom of thought one of the cornerstones of liberalism? Thoughts, ideas and desires, no matter what might be

---

[16] For the origins of skeptical anti-foundationalism see in particular Ludwig Wittgenstein (1953), *Philosophical Investigations*, G.E.M. Anscombe and R. Rhees (eds.), G.E.M. Anscombe (trans.), Oxford, Blackwell.

[17] Nasr Abu Zayd (2004), *Rethinking the Qu'ran: Towards a Humanistic Hermeneutics*, Amsterdam, SWP Publishing. See also Nasr Abu Zayd (2010) "The 'Others' in the Qur'an: A Hermeneutical Approach," in Alessandro Ferrara, Volker Kaul, David Rasmussen (eds.), "Postsecularism and Multicultural Jurisdictions," special issue of *Philosophy & Social Criticism* 36 (4), pp. 281–294. And Tariq Ramadan (2005), *Western Muslims and the Future of Islam*, Oxford/New York, Oxford University Press.

their nature, are part of the material that constitutes the most intimate kernel of our private sphere. Why do fundamentalists not have a right to privacy? On the other hand, the metaphysical critique grants far too much to fundamentalism. How can we seriously try to discuss metaphysics with people who stone women for committing adultery or crash airplanes into the twin towers? Fundamentalists are mad! No metaphysical argument can overcome this simple truth. What allows people to be fundamentalist, are not their views about the world, but their incapacity to be moral agents, agents who make autonomous use of their proper reason, respecting others as free and equal despite their differences. The problem with fundamentalism is of moral nature and needs to be confronted on the practical and not on the theoretical level.[18]

Whereas moralists and liberals are certainly right on both points of their critique of metaphysics, their solution is not entirely without problems. At the very end of the day, moralists can only come to the conclusion that it must be indeed religion, Islam, that impedes moral agency. Accordingly, they find themselves to have either no other solution than to declare Islam the enemy of liberal democracy and to begin to wage a war against Islam.[19] Or, to take Islam to be a basically liberal religion, thereby risking to fall into the essentialist trap of metaphysical foundationalism.[20]

6.2.3 Psychology

As I see the problem, both metaphysicians and moralists do not get the difference between fundamentalists and moderates right. Fundamentalism is not a problem of norms. I think that both fundamentalists and moderates hold more or less the same views concerning culture and religion. Insofar as I understand moderate Muslims and religious people in general, they do not believe their faith to be a matter of interpretation, but to be more or less grounded in God's word. Moreover, as Akeel Bilgrami illustrates in *What is a Muslim?*,[21] moderates have, even though perhaps only unwillingly, due to the oppressions of colonialism, pretty much the same value system as fundamentalists sharing most of their extremist views: The West and liberal culture in general are suspicious, the Koran constitutes the foundation of the state, of public and civil law as well as of the economy, it regulates marriage, divorce, the condition of women in the private and public sphere, heritage, etc..

---

[18] This is of course the Kantian strategy of John Rawls (1993), *Political Liberalism*, New York, Columbia University Press and Jürgen Habermas (1990), *Moral Consciousness and Communicative Action*, Cambridge (Mass.), MIT Press.

[19] As an example of liberal hawkishness see in particular Paul Berman (2004), *Terror and Liberalism*, New York, W. W. Norton.

[20] Andrew March (2009), *Islam and Liberal Citizenship: The Search for an Overlapping Consensus*, Oxford/New York, Oxford University Press.

[21] Akeel Bilgrami (1992), "What is a Muslim? Fundamental Commitment and Cultural Identity," in *Critical Inquiry* 18(4), pp. 198–219.

Fundamentalists and moderates are not divided on metaphysical grounds. They do not disagree about what Islam really is.

As much as I do not believe that we can distinguish fundamentalists from moderates in terms of morality. Moderate Muslims are morally not more competent persons. Moderates do not go for global *jihad*, because they believe it to be morally somewhat unjustified. On the contrary, as we just said above, they consider Western culture to be the enemy of Islam and feel certainly to some extent even obliged to resist and fight Western civilization. If they are not going to join Al-Qaeda right away, then for the simple fact that they are emotionally far less involved with matters concerning the West than fundamentalists. The idea of infidels triggers diversely intense emotional reactions in moderates and fundamentalists. Whereas moderates might feel at unease thinking about the West and remain with a slight sensation of disgust and anger or perhaps only feel pity for Westerners, fundamentalists become fully outraged by the very idea of the West. This different emotivity with regard to others explains, in my view, the different behavior of moderates and fundamentalists.

Moderates are emotionally able to distinguish between what they themselves think, desire, say and do and the intentions of others. While their emotional alarm bells ring in case they themselves are going to transgress in thoughts, words or actions Islamic norms or rules, while their emotional reaction makes it unthinkable for them to live a life outside Islam (just think of the violent feelings a believing Muslim woman might experience imagining herself leaving the house bareheaded), they react emotionally very differently in case that others intend or decide to deviate from the good life as it is outlined in the Koran. What enables them to tolerate nonbelievers is the relative emotional calm they have in confront of them. Fundamentalists, on the other hand, are psychologically incapacitated to make a distinction between themselves thinking and doing something and others thinking and doing something. They are as furious with others breaking the norms as they are with themselves when they come to have infidel tendencies. It is this undistinguished psychological reaction between themselves and others that makes them fundamentalists. Not that moderates never get offended and outraged by others' behavior. They clearly do so with regard to moral questions and matters of justice. Yet, their psychologies enable them to distinguish between ethics and morality, religion and politics, private and public.

6.3 Conclusion

The most interesting question is of course why fundamentalists are emotionally impaired to make those distinctions, a question I hope to deal with on another occasion. Still, the psychological approach to fundamentalism already brings along some policy implications. It seems that as much as we are not able to easily change the emotional reactions we have with regard to ourselves, in the same sense fundamentalists are unable to change their reactions concerning others. If our actions are

6.3 Conclusion

most of the time necessitated by our psychology, fundamentalists similarly appear to have no choice than to give in to their hostile reactions towards others. If we understand this structural similarity between a moderate psychology and a fundamentalist psychology, if we understand that they are as much caused by the psychological category of the 'unthinkable' as we are, we probably condemn fundamentalism a little bit less and begin to slightly empathize with fundamentalists with regard to the difficult psychological condition they find themselves in. This does not mean that relativism slips in through the back door. But it enables us to get engaged with fundamentalism on the only level that really makes the difference: psychology.

Part II
Identity and the Quest for Multiculturalism

Chapter 7
Multiculturalism, Islam and Suicide Bombers

Abstract Is a Muslim still a Muslim when he crashes airplanes into the twin towers? Any serious theory of multiculturalism has to deny that Islam could ever come to justify suicide bombing and terrorism. My thesis is that none of the contemporary multicultural theories manages to do so, or at least not without collapsing into a Kantian conception of personal autonomy and, consequently, into some standard version of liberalism. Communitarianism, trying to demonstrate that fundamentalism has nothing to do with the true and authentic Islam and that it does not take into account the pluralism prevailing in Islam, has to moralize Islam. A Humean position, which takes Islamic fundamentalism to be merely a pathology, the product of resentment and Western neocolonialism, eventually could come to the conclusion that good an upright Muslims today cannot help but to become suicide bombers. Liberal multiculturalism, considering identity to be a matter of choice, must suppose that an active agent with self-knowledge is by definition a responsible person with a moral identity. In conclusion, multiculturalism, in its effort to make the good identities prevail the bad and the ugly identities, risks to adopt some of the same righteous attitudes towards Islam as traditional liberalism.

Keywords Multiculturalism · Personal autonomy · Identity · Islam · Terrorism · Communitarianism · Moral psychology · David Hume

In a sense, 9/11 and the terrorist attacks in Paris, Brussels, Berlin, London and Madrid have come to constitute a major challenge to the paradigm of multiculturalism and constrain multicultural theories to reason and argue about the question if Muslims can be suicide bombers. Any multicultural theory has to avoid at whatever cost the impression that Islam could give rise to anything such as suicide bombing and terrorism. My thesis is that theories of multiculturalism cannot deny the claim that Islamic fundamentalists crashing airplanes into the twin towers realize their true and inner selves, at least not without adopting the classical liberal conception of autonomy, according to which cultural identity and religious commitments are obstacles to the realization of the person's true will. Multicultural theories cannot avoid the conclusion that under certain circumstances devout Muslims cannot help but become suicide bombers. They collapse into the paradoxical claim that Muslims gain only full autonomy in their proper death. The problem is certainly not Islam in itself or cultures and religions in general; the problem is a philosophy that makes Islam the foundation of personal autonomy.

There exist three theories of multiculturalism: a communitarian version, a psychological account and a liberal approach to multiculturalism. All three theories of multiculturalism have in common that they conceive identity to somehow constitute personal autonomy and practical reason and that they are critical of the liberal, Kantian conception of agency and the self. But just because they conceive identity to be the source of normativity, all the three theories run fundamentally into the same problem, once culture and religion come to justify oppression, discrimination and belligerence, in the way Islam is currently be used to justify terrorism and fundamentalism. Hence, it comes as no surprise that multiculturalists are extremely sensitive to the criticism of liberal hawks, such as Paul Berman and Christopher Hitchens, that accuse them to be the intellectual allies of Bin Laden and co. But at the same time, none of the multiculturalists does want to fall into the trap of the liberals that consider Islam to be the political problem underlying suicide bombing, justifying surveillance and assimilation of Muslim minorities at home and forced interventions in Muslim countries abroad. That's why they are multiculturalists in the first place.

The classical paradigm of multiculturalism is certainly communitarianism and has its foundation in Hegel's theory of freedom. Only communitarianism attributes intrinsic value to communities, cultures and religions, whereas the psychological and liberal theory of multiculturalism consider them to be rather of extrinsic and contingent value. And since communitarianism makes our agency entirely dependent upon the values of our community, it seems as if it were the communitarians who have the real trouble with cultural and religious fundamentalism such as radical Islam. After all, the psychological account, whose origins can be traced back to David Hume, criticizes the communitarian thesis that individuals have an irreducible interest in culture and considers fundamentalism to be merely the product of resentment and to play only a functional role in a person's psychological economy depending upon the particular historical context. And the liberal model of multiculturalism is precisely conceived to give the voice back to the individual reintroducing the agential first-person point of view and to avoid any form of cultural and historical determinism.

Yet, even if the Hegelian and Humean theories have very different, actually opposing starting points, considering themselves to be the worst foes, communitarian and certain neo-Humean positions that endorse a conception of personal autonomy[1] tend to converge on the question of suicide bombing: Both come to agree that the reason why Muslims blow themselves up is because of their commitments to the community, that if they would not do this, they couldn't any longer consider

---

[1] Some neo-Humeans, such as Harry Frankfurt and Bernard Williams, make, contrary to Hume, psychology the foundation of personal autonomy and normativity (see also Sect. 7.2).

themselves to be the persons they actually are, good and upright Muslims. Hegelians and Humeans would certainly tell us very different stories about how it comes that Muslims have the fundamentalist commitments they have, but at the end of these stories they both could arrive at the conclusion that Muslims cannot help but to become suicide bombers. For sure, both Hegelians and Humeans try desperately to avoid such an outcome, according to which it seems that Muslims can realize their freedom and autonomy only through terrorist attacks. But as I would like to maintain here, both strategies are not particularly promising and convincing: Hegelians and in particular certain neo-Humeans must eventually concede that in their respective theories suicide bombers realize themselves *as* Muslims.

According to liberal multiculturalism, self-constitution is not merely reactive and defensive, but the product of our agency and freedom of the will. However, in order to criticize the excesses of identity politics, liberal multiculturalism has to presuppose that an active agent with self-knowledge is by definition a responsible person with a moral identity. Still, if a Muslim's moral identity trumps his Islamic identity, Islam stops to be the source of normativity and multiculturalism is heavily watered down becoming undistinguishable from liberalism.

The structure of the essay is the following: In a first part, I discuss the communitarian's difficulties with Islamic fundamentalism. In a second moment, I illustrate the Humean helplessness in front of suicide bombers. The concluding remarks shed some doubts on the strategy of liberal multiculturalism to distance itself from radical Islam.

7.1 Communitarianism in the Face of Islamic Suicide Bombing

No communitarian would ever want to maintain that Islam is motivating terrorist attacks – communitarians criticize their liberal counterparts precisely for making Islam responsible for such actions. But it is certainly a core claim of communitarianism that our cultures and religions provide us with the values and ethical frameworks within which we are organizing our lives. Communitarians disagree fundamentally with Humean theories of action that consider values to be merely the product of our projections, expressions of our desires, feelings and tastes, a matter of what gives us pleasure and what causes us pain: "The complete Utilitarian would be an impossibly shallow character" (Taylor 1985: 26).[2] Yet, they also deeply contest the existentialist claim that we have a choice about our values, that we invent values rather than discover them, that values are creations of our free will: "A choice utterly unrelated to the desirability of the alternatives (…) falls ultimately into a criteria-less leap which can not properly be described as choice at all" (Taylor 1985: 32–3).

---

[2] See also Alasdair MacIntyre's polemic against emotivism (McIntyre 2007: 6–35).

Hence, in order to choose anything and to act as a person at all our will needs to be bound by values that are given and have their source outside of the individual. According to communitarians, our individual volitions are constituted by the ethical life of our community and are deeply embedded in culture (Taylor 1985: 111). Thus, our cultural identity is constitutive of our agency, our personal autonomy; stepping outside the limits of the strongly qualified horizons of our cultural identity "would be tantamount to stepping outside what we would recognize as integral, that is, undamaged human personhood" (Taylor 1992: 27), "shorn of these we would cease to be ourselves, (…) our existence as persons (…) would be impossible outside the horizon of these evaluations" (Taylor 1985: 34–5).

Given this premise, communitarians cannot just ask suicide bombers not to act upon their Muslim identity and condemn them for having violated some universal moral principles – as persons, they have no other choice than to act as Muslims; they are free and autonomous only insofar as they act as Muslims. Since communitarians cannot question identity as the source of normativity, the only instrument at their disposal to stop suicide bombers is to question if a pious and upright Muslim really has to engage in terrorist attacks against infidels – they have to put into question the specific *content* of a person's Muslim identity that makes him or her to become a terrorist. Communitarians must maintain that he or she, as a Muslim, gets it wrong to kill innocent people. If it is true that we "become incapable of understanding any moral argument at all", if we abstract from what we are "morally moved by", then the only way we have to convince fundamentalists of the irrationality and wrongness of their acts is to change "[their] reading of [their] moral experience" (Taylor 1992: 73). And we do this by way of "comparative propositions" showing "that the move from [fundamentalism] to [moderate Islam, for example] constitutes a gain epistemically", demonstrating "for instance, that we get from [fundamentalism] to [moderate Islam] by identifying and resolving a contradiction in [fundamentalism] or a confusion [fundamentalism] relied on, or by acknowledging the importance of some factor which [fundamentalism] screened out, or something of the sort" (Taylor 1992: 72). We try to convince fundamentalists that a moderate interpretation of Islam is a superior perspective to fundamentalism and contributes to moral growth (Taylor 1992: 71–2).

If practical reason is rooted in the specific cultural and religious identity of a person, communitarianism has to *moralize* this very identity if it wants to avoid relativism and nihilism. In a communitarian theory the moral law must be part of and literally inscribed in a culture and religion. There are two ways communitarians can get the moral law inside Islam, either through a perspective from within Islam or trough an external perspective on Islam: Either communitarians enter into a theological debate about what it is to be a Muslim or they emphasize the pluralism that must prevail in Islam. For what concerns the internal approach, reformists have to demonstrate that Islamic fundamentalism is an inadequate and wrong interpretation of the Koran. Abdullahi An-Na'im (2010) argues, for example, that the Koran's insistence on voluntary acceptance of Islam makes Islamic principles more consistent with the ideas of human rights and liberal citizenship than with the coercive enforcement of Sharia. Or, Andrew March (2009) maintains that Islamic theology and history provide very strong arguments for accepting the principles of liberal democracy.

The obvious problem with the internal strategy is that it has to presuppose an authentic and true Islam and has to essentialize Islam distinguishing between a good and a bad Muslim, a strategy actually not dissimilar to the one used by fundamentalists. And, I, personally, would not dare to challenge suicide bombers on any account of coherence and consistency, conjecturing a conflict within their value system; it seems impossible to have a more integrated value system than a person who is ready to die for his or her ideas.

Most communitarians are notoriously known for avoiding and actually dismissing any claims that go into the direction of an objectification and reification of cultures. Their strategy for rejecting fundamentalism is, on the contrary, to show that there does not exist just one, true interpretation of Islam, but that Islam is pluralist in nature – and they do this precisely by emphasizing the many possible interpretations that have been given and could be given of Islam. Nasr Abu-Zayd, for example, insists on a hermeneutical and historical reading of the Koran and invites us to understand the justification of the use of force against non-Muslim communities in the Koran against the background of the political dangers Muslims had to confront. Therefore, "it is absurd to think that [the practical and legal norms of the Koran] could or should be transferred into today's world in their exact form" (Abu-Zayd 2010: 293) and that "the spirit and culture of Islam can be found in those early years and in the foundational scripture" (Abu-Zayd 2010: 283), as it is maintained by Islamic fundamentalists. Also Seyla Benhabib (2010) stresses the fact that the meaning of Islamic norms underlies a process of 'democratic iterations', renegotiations and appropriations, and is determined by the subjective choices and attitudes of Muslims.

Yet, this approach risks to impose the moral law upon Islam from outside and not gain a moral perspective from within Muslim identity. If communitarianism does not want to fall into the essentialist trap, it has to allow fundamentalism to be one possible interpretation of Islam. But why should the fundamentalist then accept moderate versions of Islam? Fundamentalists certainly cannot tolerate dissidents from within their own Muslim identity – it just tells them to kill the infidel. It must therefore be a voice independent of and contrary to their own Muslim values telling them to have a more complete and broader picture of what it actually means to be a Muslim and to accept pluralism within Islam – and this is the voice of the Kantian moral agent.

Eventually, the communitarian line of argumentation against suicide bombers and Islamic fundamentalism collapses into the very position that liberalism sustains: Suicide bombers are victims of their religious identity; Islam is the culprit. If liberals claim that Islam makes Muslims blind to the principles of morality, communitarians maintain that some forms of Islam are backward, incoherent, confused, ignorant and morally inferior. Certainly, liberals tend to accuse Islam as such and communitarians limit their critique to certain tendencies in Islam only, but in the final outcome, the problem is and remains a person's particular Muslim identity.

7.2 The Moral Psychology of Suicide Bombers

Humeans are not known for being diehard multiculturalists. Indeed, they criticize communitarians for "reversing the critical sense of the contingency of [social and cultural] arrangements to an elite, perhaps, or at the limit, to the theorist himself" (Williams 2005: 33). Not only do they question the normativity of identity – after all Hume has a causal and not normative concept of action; but, traditionally, Humeans are also very critical of the very idea of personal identity (Hume 1978: 251–63). The most they could say about suicide bombers is that they "*must be crazy*", that suicide bombing is "*lunatic*", "unthinkable", that "it does not fall within the range of what we understand to be normal; rather, it strikes us as unnatural or even monstrous. That is why the notions of irrationality and insanity seem germane" (Frankfurt 1988: 185–6).

Yet, Hume famously maintains that "tis not contrary to reason to prefer the destruction of the whole world to the scratching of my finger" (Hume 1978: 416). And this for the following simple reason: "Where a passion is neither founded on false suppositions, nor chooses means insufficient for the end, the understanding can neither justify nor condemn it" (Hume 1978: 416). If reason alone or beliefs can never motivate action and are only the slaves of our passions, then just the means and never the end itself of an action can be unreasonable or irrational, as long as the end is not based upon false information. But if actions have their origin in our passions, "what is unthinkable for a person may [not only] vary from one time to another" but it is also "subject (…) to changes in the contingent circumstances from which [our passions] derive" and "susceptible to being affected by causal forces" (Frankfurt 1988: 187–8). Harry Frankfurt concludes that "the ability and the inability [to perform a certain action] depend [perhaps] on beliefs, commitments, or personal idiosyncrasies – having to do with matters of taste, politics, religion, love, or the like – with respect to which it is natural and in no way pathological for people to be diverse. We know that preferences or types of conduct that are irrational in one cultural locale may often be entirely rational in another" (Frankfurt 1988: 186). Humeans would like to make their theory of action immune to any philosophy of history and culture, to any form of Hegelianism – and this for the obvious reasons that we have seen above. But eventually they cannot!

Human nature is supposed to limit the ends a person can possibly adopt. "There are certain things that no thoroughly rational individual [or basically sane person] would ever consider doing "(Frankfurt 1988: 189). First, it lies in our human nature "that when we have the prospect of pain or pleasure from any object, we feel a consequent emotion of aversion or propensity, and are carry'd to avoid or embrace what will give us this uneasiness or satisfaction" (Hume 1978: 414). Secondly, "the minds of all men are similar in their feelings and operations, nor can any one be actuated by any affection, of which all others are not, in some degree, susceptible. Thus it appears, *that* sympathy is a very powerful principle in human nature, (…) and *that* it produces our sentiments of morals" (Hume 1978: 575–7).

But obviously suicide bombers are neither concerned with their proper well-being, nor do they seem to have any compassionate feelings for their victims. And Humeans have an explanation of why Muslims could come to ignore their most profound interests and moral feelings: Because Muslims *find* themselves to have a value commitment to Islamic fundamentalism. In the last centuries, humiliation and resentment have been central elements in the self-constitution of the Muslim world. Akeel Bilgrami claims that we have to understand Islamic revivalism as a "defensive reaction caused not only by the scars and memories of Western colonial rule but by the failure of successive governments to break out of the models of development imposed on them by a dominating neocolonial presence of the superpowers through much of the cold war" (Bilgrami 1992: 209). In order to compensate the subsequent loss of the sense of autonomy and dignity and protect themselves against Western subjugation and condescension, Muslims have come to endorse not only their religion and culture in general, but particular aspects of Islam that stand in strong opposition to their enemies. In accordance with the proverb "the enemy of my enemy is my friend" resentment has made Muslims identify with those parts of the Koran that call for a holy war and depict the infidel as the enemy. And this defensive function of commitments to Islam "leaves [also moderate Muslims] open to be exploited by the political efforts of absolutist movements," who accuse more accommodating positions to "surrender to the forces of the West" (Bilgrami 1992: 212) and to betray the cause of Islam. A proper Muslim today has to be fundamentalist.

The fact that "cultural identities arise (…) as the consequence, not the cause, of conflicts" and enmity between cultures (Appiah 2005: 64, see also 114–141) explains Islamic fundamentalism, but not necessarily suicide bombing. Humeans could in a certain sense accept fundamentalism as one possible result of their projectivist theory of value, but they could still claim that a Muslim's other fundamental projects and loves balance and actually outweigh the most extreme demands of Islamism. Muslims have to kill and, if necessary, sacrifice their life for the sake of Islam, for sure, but isn't their love for their family, children and other ideals impeding them to live up in all respects to their commitments to Islam? Muslims are not only Muslims, but they are most probably also parents, lovers, women, laborers, human beings belonging to a specific class, ethnic group and nation. Muslims, as any other person, have a plurality of identities and loyalties and their value system is not exhausted by religious commitments alone.

Yet again, the psychological approach has an explanation of why Muslims today may not only sacrifice all of their values and interests for the sake of Islam, but also their life, if the fundamentalist ideology requires this. Our identity tends to create practical and volitional necessities precisely because of its psychological foundation. Bernard Williams shows the intrinsic connection between our identity and the emotion of shame. "Shame looks to what I am"; "the structures of shame (…) give a conception of one's ethical identity" (Williams 1993: 93). Our identity is given and revealed by what Williams calls the internalized other, who "is indeed abstracted and generalized and idealized, but he is potentially somebody rather than nobody, and somebody other than me" (Williams 1993: 84). We discover our identity in our conscience, in the super-ego, to use Freud's term, that represents the values of our community and gives voice to other people's expectations about us. Their imagined gaze, their imagined contempt or derision or avoidance, in case that we do not live up to the expectations the world has about the kind of person we are, arouses our shame and lowers our self-respect to such a degree that we do not see any other possibility than to conform to our role, if we want to go on having the life with others as we know it. Given the present value structure of Muslim communities, Muslims could gain recognition only as suicide bombers.

Hany Abu-Assad's film *Paradise Now* (2005) illustrates brilliantly the role shame plays in motivating suicide bombing. At first, Said, one of the two protagonists from Nablus, only reluctantly accepts to engage in a suicide bombing mission in Tel Aviv having all the 'Humean' scruples described above: He is in love, has to take care of his mother, enjoys his social life and is appalled by the idea of murder. Yet, the profound shame he feels for his father, who was executed when he was 10 years old because he was a 'collaborator' with the Israelis, helps him to overcome all his qualms and gives him the deep and strong conviction that, as a Palestinian and Muslim, he has to engage in the mission in order to restore honor upon his family's name.

Traditional Humeans could accept that in their theory social pathologies could indeed give rise to such extreme hostilities. Yet, they would insist on the point that suicide bombing is after all the result of a psychological aberration, of a pathology, that suicide bombing has nothing to do with auto-realization, autonomy and freedom. Certain neo-Humeans, however, such as Frankfurt and Williams, who make psychology and identity the foundation of a conception of personal autonomy (Frankfurt 1988, 2006; Williams 1981, 1993), find themselves in the same dilemma as communitarianism: They lack arguments against the claim that truly autonomous Muslims today have to be suicide bombers.

7.3 In Lieu of Conclusion: Multiculturalism in Search of the Emergency Exit

Both Anthony Appiah and Bilgrami are sympathetic with identity politics that aims to redress past injustices. In certain contexts, such as that of (post-)colonialism, being treated with equal dignity might not be enough, "and so one will end up asking to be respected [*as a Muslim*]" (Appiah 1998: 98). Yet, "the acute consciousness of and obsession with the historical cause of their commitment has made [Muslims] incapable of critical reflection about the commitment itself" and, therefore, they fail "to live up to the basic conditions of free agency" (Bilgrami 1992: 213). Making the first-person point of view central to our self-conception, Appiah and Bilgrami hope to liberate Muslims from an identity that is "too tightly scripted" and "too constrained by the demands and expectations of others" (Appiah 1998: 99) and to introduce the possibility of self-constitution: Muslims are free to distance themselves from certain doctrinal commitments and can choose what sort of Muslims they want to be – it is up to them to determine what it is to be a Muslim. For Bilgrami, Muslims with a critical self-conception have to become some kind of reformers who oppose fundamentalism and endorse the Koranic verses "with the more purely universalist and spiritual claims and commitments" (Bilgrami 1992: 216) – they are certainly not fond of suicide bombing.

Yet, it is not clear why self-reflective Muslims have to be *moral* persons. If Muslims are free to choose their values and identity, why should their freedom prevent them from becoming fundamentalists? Bilgrami recognizes the possibility that someone with Islamic commitments might have a second-order commitment that "entrenches them and guards them against a time when there might well be a weakening or a loss of the commitments" (Bilgrami 2006: 9). Muslims in fact are not simply passive and reactive treating themselves as objects, when they endorse an anti-reformist, fundamentalist stance, even in times in which this attitude could seem to be rather obsolete. Reflective endorsement does not limit the range of our possible identifications – at least, unless we do not consider our freedom to have transcendental implications. Christine Korsgaard argues that we have a free will only qua human being and that "if we do not treat our humanity as a normative identity, none of our other identities can be normative. Moral identity is therefore inescapable (...) and exerts a kind of governing role over the other kinds" (Korsgaard 1994: 129–30). Muslims are given a human identity that they cannot violate if they want to be Muslims at all.

Liberal multiculturalism, making identity a matter of choice rather than pure discovery, tries to distinguish the good from the bad and the ugly of identity politics (Gutmann 2003). Yet, for that the good identities prevail the bad and the ugly identities, liberal multiculturalism must come dangerously close to a Kantian conception of moral autonomy and risks, in fact, to adopt the same righteous attitude towards Islam as traditional liberalism. The emergency exit for multiculturalism remains, after all, liberalism, criticizing but also victimizing Muslims as alienated from their true moral nature by Islam. Isaiah Berlin (1966) perfectly sees these problems underlying the theory of positive liberty based upon a conception of personal autonomy. Yet, should we give up on the notion of autonomy, it is not at all clear how we can save Berlin's beautiful intuition that we nevertheless have a right to negative liberty or to freedom from interference, *despite* the fact that we might not be autonomous. (see also Chap. 4 "Psychology, Autonomy, and Liberalism", in this volume)

References

Abu-Zayd, Nasr. 2010. The 'Others' in the Qur'an: A Hermeneutical Approach. *Philosophy & Social Criticism* 36 (3–4): 281–294.

Appiah, Anthony. 1998. Race, Culture, Identity: Misunderstood Connections. In *Color Conscious. The Political Morality of Race*, ed. A. Appiah and Amy Gutmann, 30–105. Princeton: Princeton University Press.

———. 2005. *The Ethics of Identity*. Princeton: Princeton University Press.

An-Na'im, Abdullahi. 2010. *Islam and the Secular State: Negotiating the Future of Shari`a*. Cambridge, MA: Harvard University Press.

Benhabib, Seyla. 2010. The Return of Political Theology: The Scarf Affair in Comparative Constitutional Perspective in France, Germany and Turkey. *Philosophy & Social Criticism* 36 (3-4): 451–471.
Berlin, Isaiah. 1966. *Two Concepts of Liberty*. Oxford: Clarendon Press.
Bilgrami, Akeel. 1992. What is a Muslim? Fundamental Commitment and Cultural Identity. *Critical Inquiry* 18 (4): 198–219.
———. 2006. Notes Toward the Definition of 'Identity'. *Daedalus* 135 (4): 5–14.
Frankfurt, Harry. 1988. *The Importance of What We Care About*. Cambridge: Cambridge University Press.
———. 2006. *The Reasons of Love*. Princeton: Princeton University Press.
Gutmann, Amy. 2003. *Identity in Democracy*. Princeton: Princeton University Press.
Hume, David. 1978. In *A Treatise of Human Nature*, ed. L.A. Selby-Bigge and P.H. Nidditch. Oxford: Oxford University Press.
Korsgaard, Christine. 1994. *The Sources of Normativity*. Cambridge: Cambridge University Press.
MacIntyre, Alasdair. 2007. *After Virtue*. London: Duckworth.
March, Andrew. 2009. *Islam and Liberal Citizenship: The Search for an Overlapping Consensus*. Oxford: Oxford University Press.
Taylor, Charles. 1985. *Philosophical Papers: Human Agency and Language*. Vol. 1. Cambridge: Cambridge University Press.
———. 1992. *Sources of the Self: The Making of the Modern Identity*. Cambridge, MA: Harvard University Press.
Williams, Bernard. 1981. *Moral Luck*. Cambridge: Cambridge University Press.
———. 1993. *Shame and Necessity*. Berkeley/Los Angeles: University of California Press.
———. 2005. *In the Beginning Was the Deed: Realism and Moralism in Political Argument*. Princeton: Princeton University Press.

Chapter 8
Foundations of Multiculturalism (1): Self-Knowledge

Abstract Today we can identify two challenges of pluralism: the ever-growing conflicts between religious, national and ethnic groups on the one hand and the oppression of dissenting individuals by their respective communities on the other hand. Both intercommunitarian and intracommunitarian conflicts find their origin in a communitarian conception of our political, cultural or religious identities. After presenting some of the problems of the communitarian solution in particular with regard to the challenge of internal pluralism, I introduce alternative conceptions of multiculturalism that consider our commitments to be part of our *personal* or *individual* identity. Distinguishing a conception of identity based upon self-knowledge from liberal, postmodern (Richard Rorty) and alternative non-cognitive theories (Bernard Williams) that consider identity to be individual in nature, I propose that the awareness of the individual nature of commitments makes it possible for us to not impose our values upon other individuals, who do not share them, while at the same time justifying the multicultural project.

Keywords Multiculturalism · Pluralism · Commitments · Personal identity · Personal autonomy · Self-knowledge · Bernard Williams · Richard Rorty

Multiculturalism is today the focus of the widely discussed challenge of pluralism. Samuel Huntington (1998) summarizes this challenge famously as the "clash of civilizations" according to which certain religions, nations, ethnic groups or more generally communities with different civilizational backgrounds stand in an irreducible conflict with each other. For many political analysts the actual cultural clash in today's world takes place between the Islamic and Western world and could be described in terms of "Jihad vs. McWorld" (Barber 1996). Hence, the possibility of intercivilizational and –religious dialogue and toleration and generally the question of how different communities can live together peacefully lie at the heart of the current debate on pluralism.

Yet, multiculturalism does not only *pose* the challenge of pluralism, it also *faces* the challenge of pluralism. If the great political challenge of multiculturalism concerns the possibility of pluralism among communities or external pluralism, multiculturalism on its own is confronted with the question of pluralism within a community or internal pluralism. Communities do not just stand externally in conflict, they are internally striven by conflict as well. In particular liberal and feminist thinkers criticize and attack multiculturalism for tolerating, and in a certain sense legitimating in the name of communitarian values and ideals, the oppression of political oppositions and non-conformist individuals as well as the patriarchal submission of women. Paul Berman (2004) reproaches multiculturalist positions with justifying totalitarian and terrorist movements in Islam and Ayaan Hirsi Ali (2008) condemns Western nations for deliberately overlooking oppressive aspects of Muslim culture – such as the "culture of virginity" that threatens the liberty and lives of Muslim women – for the sake of cultural diversity.

As a matter of fact, multicultural theory does by no means want to stand in opposition to basic human rights and individual freedoms, defending tyrannical cultural practices. From its very beginnings in German Romanticism multiculturalism is conceived as the true project of individual emancipation that, contrary to the Enlightenment philosophies and contemporary theories of liberalism, recognizes individuals as they truly are – empirical not purely rational beings with a particular psychological and social constitution. Multiculturalism wants to be in touch with the vast variety of human experiences and take seriously "affections, commitments, and projects that make people what they are or at least make their lives what they are" (Williams 2008, p. 32). A theory, that has at its core each single individual's authenticity and what makes it the specific individual it is, cannot turn against the individual it so wholeheartedly wants to flourish (Ferrara 1998).

Still, there exits in multicultural theories the serious risk that communitarian values could justifiably trump dissenting individual ideas and projects, giving rise certain political results in the Muslim world, but certainly also elsewhere, that seem to confirm the multicultural nightmares of Berman and Hirsi Ali. Given the importance of the empirical constitution of the self and the centrality of cultural, social or religious attachments and commitments for an individual's identity, it is hold to be impossible for individuals "to detach [themselves] from any particular standpoint or point of view, to step backwards, as it were, and view and judge that standpoint or point of view from the outside" (McIntyre 2007, p. 126), "to view their own culture and society as if from the outside" (McIntyre 2007, p. 125). "But just for that reason they have no doubt that reality is as they represent it to themselves." They have "a view of the world for which they claim truth" (McIntyre 2007, p. 129). In multicultural theories each community, culture or religion can legitimately claim objectivity for its own standpoint and each one has its own truth. This is not only the reason for which multiculturalism is at the root of a possible clash of civilizations and cultures, but also the reason for which multiculturalism might have serious problems with the justification of some significant form of internal pluralism. In short, multiculturalism needs to face the criticism à la Berman and Hirsi Ali.

The first scope of this essay is to suggest that there is a connection between the external and internal challenge. Both challenges have their origin in a communitarian conception of identity according to which our cultural, social or religious commitments are our source of normativity. As a consequence, not only communities might stand in conflict with each other, but also the community and the single individual. Multicultural theory, fully aware of this double impasse, has however, due to its communitarian roots, to distinguish an account of pluralism within a community clearly from pluralism among communities – with the result, that a solution to the challenge of external pluralism seems more feasible than the accommodation of internal pluralism.

My second goal is to introduce alternative conceptions of multiculturalism that consider our commitments to be part of our *personal* or *individual* identity. Those might allow us not only to treat the internal and external challenge indistinctively, but provide also more appropriate solutions to the challenge of pluralism. On the one hand, liberal multiculturalists emphasize the role of autonomous choice in an individual's self-constitution as well as the importance of recognition for individual well-being and dignity. Postmodern thinkers (Richard Rorty) and more generally non-cognitivist theories of identity[1] (Bernard Williams), on the other hand, maintain that self-consciousness makes us aware of the historically and socially contingent, relative character of commitments. However, both the liberal as well as the postmodern theory of multiculturalism, having at its center rather the individual than the community, might have difficulties to justify multiculturalism as such, dismissing too rapidly a core insight of communitarianism, namely that commitments are discovered and not chosen by the individual and that commitments make normative claims upon the individual. It seems as if there is a trade-off between multiculturalism and pluralism: The more pluralist a theory is, the less it can be multiculturalist, and vice versa.

Therefore, I am looking in this essay for a normative account of multiculturalism that can resist the challenge of pluralism. I would like to present a possible conception of identity that takes the morality of communitarian commitments fully seriously, without depriving us of any meaningful possibility to reflect on ourselves and our commitments critically. I propose that contrary to what communitarianism claims our capacity of self-reflection is fundamental for our self-understanding, and yet it does not have to presuppose the autonomous or Cartesian self central to liberal theories. It neither implies an existentialist idea, according to which we lack any ultimate criteria, principle or value. Being able to take a critical stance upon our commitments and to put them into perspective does not liberate the self from its commitments – it does not deprive the self and strip away its qualities. Our commitments do not disappear, even once we understood their true, purely contingent and relative or even irrational nature – they remain ours, fully constitutive of our self. But having knowledge of our commitments, they do not longer move us in an

---

[1] Non-cognitivist theories hold contrary to cognitivism, to which we can count communitarianism, that our commitments are expressing non-cognitive attitudes more similar to emotions rather than beliefs and have therefore no truth conditions.

unreflective, spontaneous way, they stop being our source of normativity; they can only move insofar as we *will* them to be the reason of our actions, we have to accept and endorse our inner commitments. The fact that individuals have to endorse their commitments deprives the community of its categorical and unlimited normative force and hold on the individual and gives rise to the possibility of internal pluralism. At the same time, a theory of identity that conceives commitments in individual terms – our social, cultural or religious commitments are only true about us and not the others – provides also a solution to the problem of external pluralism and the challenge of a possible clash of cultures.

In the first part, I introduce the external and internal challenge of multiculturalism and present the efforts of communitarianism to deal with them. In the second part, I review liberal, non-cognitive and postmodern approaches to multiculturalism and indicate the contours of a conception of identity based upon self-knowledge that is able to address the challenge of pluralism.

8.1 Multiculturalism and the Challenge of External and Internal Pluralism

Multiculturalism is the theory that our moral outlooks, ways of life, habits, tastes and preferences are shaped by the communities we belong to. "Our categories, relationships, commitments, aspirations are all shaped by, expressed in term of, the existing morality" (Walzer 1985, p. 20). Occupying a social role and being embedded in a community, we discover to have social, cultural or religious commitments that are of foremost importance in our moral life; they structure our actions and life and provide us with a sense of who we are. "That morality is authoritative for us because it is only by virtue of its existence that we exist as the moral beings we are" (Walzer 1985, p. 20). As members of the same community we share ethical concerns and are bound by common values; hence, communities are characterized by their respective ethical frameworks. From this point of view, multiculturalism can be defined as the theory of intra-communitarian monism and inter-communitarian pluralism. It is precisely the concurrence of internal monism and external pluralism that gives rise to the political challenge of multiculturalism: Different communities have to coexist, finding political agreements in international relations as well as in multicultural societies without recurring to religious and cultural wars and national aggressions. Monism tends to put into question the possibility of inter-communitarian toleration: Values that like communitarian values are justified and absolute (McIntyre 2007, pp. x–xii) could give rise to validity claims that are not limited only to those individuals who endorse them, but hold universally. Monism and pluralism might stand in strong contradiction with each other.

In *Political Liberalism* and *The Law of Peoples* John Rawls tries to reconcile the fact that our values and political ideas might justly stand in opposition with each other with the possibility of mutual tolerance. Rawls does not directly address the multicultural challenge, since he does not conceive our comprehensive doctrines as commitments we have by way of belonging to a community, but as the result of individual reasoning: "a reasonable doctrine is an exercise of theoretical reason" as well as "practical reason" (Rawls 1994, p. 59). Still, it is maintained that the conflict between comprehensive doctrines and the clash of civilizations can be treated analogously. In this regard, Rawls would propose that irreconcilable but reasonable communitarian doctrines with no imperial or missionary zeal – to which we can count many of the prevailing cultural and religious frameworks – can find a common ground and endorse a freestanding political conception of tolerance through an overlapping consensus (Maffettone 2010). In contrast, Jürgen Habermas (1996) does not believe that there is an unbridgeable conflict between communities. Unlike Rawls, he refuses monism, though he certainly recognizes the existence and centrality of communitarian commitments. Communities do not adhere to an independently justified ideal of toleration, but find shared values engaging themselves and confronting each other in dialogue and democratic deliberation. Deliberation transforms and democratizes communitarian identities to a point in which different communities come to share a common political identity from within each tradition, despite their respective differences.

In Habermas' position communitarian values are not given and eternally fixed, but are open for renegotiation. Similarly, multiculturalism does not advocate crude communitarian monism and does allow for some form of internal pluralism within the communities themselves. Multiculturalism is not a conservative theory justifying oppressive cultural and anti-emancipatory practices (Taylor 1992). For Michael Walzer, cultural traditions indeed require social criticism; he quotes Marxism and the French revolution as examples of legitimate criticism of Western bourgeois culture and society (Walzer 1985, pp. 34–42). A thorough monist position does imply an objectified and reified concept of culture, that difficultly fits the sociological observation that members of a community disagree about which values authentically represent their community (Geertz 1977). As McIntyre writes, "traditions, when vital, embody continuities of conflict" (McIntyre 2007, p. 222). Or as Walzer maintains, "morality […] is something we have to argue about." "Common possession does not imply agreement" (Walzer 1985, p. 29). But once we admit the possibility of moral disagreement within a community, multiculturalism faces *itself* the challenge of pluralism.

Communitarianism, in fact, tries to provide an account of anti-monism. Taking a critical distance from our community does not mean that we are required to divide or double our self, stepping mentally back from the "involved, committed, parochial" self in order to take the position of the "detached, dispassionate, impartial" self that takes up the morally objective standpoint; "we don't look at ourselves from nowhere in particular" (Walzer 1985, p. 43). "[Commitments] constitute the given of my life, my moral starting point" (McIntyre 2007, p. 220). Nevertheless, we certainly are in a position and also have to interpret the meaning of social norms (Bayart 1996; Benhabib 2002; Bhabha 1994). Taylor maintains that "practice is, as it were, a continual interpretation and reinterpretation of what the rule really means" (quoted in Appiah 2005, p. 54). "Interpretation does not commit us to a positivist reading of the actually existing morality"; norms "have to be 'read,' rendered, construed, glossed, elucidated, and not merely described" (Walzer 1985, p. 27). Moral interpretation is therefore an intrinsically critical enterprise fully internal to the tradition of a specific culture and might potentially challenge received opinion. The range of the possible interpretations of social norms is necessarily limited – a norm cannot be interpreted in whatsoever sense: "While the contours of my identity will in some ways be open and subject to revision, they are not wholly without shape" (Sandel 1982, p. 180). But within certain constraints we are free to develop our understanding of our place in the community. Thus our social identities can take multiple though not infinitively many forms within a community.

Communitarianism tries to vigorously defend an anti-monist position, emphasizing the dynamic and plural character of our commitments that "requires a thickly differentiated society". "But if I am Don Quixote, lance in hand, tilting at windmills, I will be mismatched and overmatched" (Walzer 1994, p. 102), since any given society can only respond to a limited number of social roles. Yet, communitarians do not want to avoid Don Quixote's experience, and for this reason they propose that "points of access should always exist for deviant members" and that "we must protect their rights […] as best as we can" (Walzer 1994, p. 103). However, as pointed out by different authors, it might result incoherent to combine a *thick* theory of morality with *thin* concepts such as abstract individual rights (Barry 2001; Sen 2006). Given these difficulties, many attempts have been recently undertaken to show on an anthropological, sociological and historical level that cultures not only are plural but also incorporate individual rights. But also this solution to the challenge of internal pluralism is not unproblematic: after all, it has to make the assumption that a culture is constituted by immutable and fixed norms, a conception of culture communitarians, as we have seen, would generally like to avoid.

Although both the internal and external challenge of pluralism have their roots in a communitarian conception of our values and identity, communitarianism, given the centrality of the community, must distinguish the challenge of external pluralism from the challenge of internal pluralism (Walzer 1985, 1994) and address them with two different set of theories. Whereas Rawls and Habermas might provide, each in his own manner, reasonable solutions to the external challenge, communitarianism faces some more problems with regard to internal pluralism precisely because it cannot be as radical as external pluralism. Communitarianism has to somehow make a distinction between internal pluralism and pure individualism, without sacrificing neither the first nor the latter and this creates some trouble for it. These problems might not be insolvable; nevertheless, if we take into consideration alternative conceptions of practical identity that make us individuals the source of our communitarian commitments reducing the external and internal challenge of pluralism to *one* challenge only, we might hope to find a theory of multiculturalism that fares better in the light of the challenge of pluralism.

8.2 Multiculturalism and the Accommodation of Pluralism

Liberal authors critical of communitarianism maintain that multiculturalism is justified not because communities have an independent moral standing or because communities determine exhaustively the patterns of reasoning and ethics available to us, but only insofar as we individuals care about our communities and value our communitarian identities. In fact, they take an explicit individualist stance upon multiculturalism and defend it both upon the basis of personal autonomy and individual well-being and dignity. Christine Korsgaard (1994), who has developed a Kantian theory of identity, imagines our autonomous selves to be the author of our commitments choosing them freely. Yet, the emphasis on the possibility of choice and self-constitution within communitarian constraints does not take effectively into account the deep intuition of communitarianism that our commitments are not a matter of agency, but about the discovery of the self and its authenticity – we have commitments because we cannot help to have them. Individual choice introduces an element of arbitrariness into our commitments that, as Korsgaard admits herself, "establishes an authentic limit to the *depth* of obligation" (Korsgaard 1994, p. 103).

Other theorists emphasize the role culture and recognition plays for individual well-being and dignity. Individuals have cultural rights, insofar as communities are important sources of self-respect and provide the material for leading a meaningful life (Appiah 2005; Kymlicka 1991). Multiculturalism promotes equal respect of individuals (Galeotti 2005). Identity politics becomes a powerful instrument to counter social and political discrimination of individuals of certain minority communities (Appiah and Gutmann 1998). As a result, in a liberal multiculturalist position our communitarian identities have instrumental and not inherent value; communities are treated like primary goods, in nature not very different from other public welfare allocations. Identity can be recognized only insofar as it constitutes the source of individual well-being (Okin 1999). But irreducible commitments in the communitarian sense, that we have to take seriously at all costs, have no place in a liberal theory of multiculturalism. Liberal approaches with their emphasis on individual autonomy and dignity have less problems to face the challenge of pluralism than to justify multiculturalism properly. Once we give up on the constitutive aspects of community, multiculturalism might be the contingent product of social change and a remedy to political and social injustices, but it lacks any further normative foundation and necessity.

It is Bernard Williams who sets out to defend an individualist version of multiculturalism from within an identitarian perspective, precisely based upon the notion of commitment as such. According to him, commitments cannot be reduced to their utility for the person; on the contrary, commitments often have detrimental effects upon individual well-being (Williams 1973). Like communitarians and contrary to Kantians, Williams maintains that the source of our ethical convictions and commitments is not a decision of our free will, but that in some sense they come to us through our social context. Our values find their origin in the structure of the social world which we inhabit and are part of our way of living; they are a cultural artifact

(Williams 1985, pp. 147, 169). Yet unlike communitarians, he believes that we can take a reflective and critical stance upon our commitments. We can "stand back from the practices of the society and its use of [...] concepts" (Williams 1985, p. 147) and reason not only within, but also reflect upon the ethical categories of our commitments. For Williams, our stepping outside of the commitments and taking up the stance of an external observer requires us to analyze critically the values implicit in our commitments: We "ask whether this is the right way to go on, whether these are good ways in which to assess actions, whether the kinds of character that are admired are rightly admired" (Williams 1985, p. 147). We evaluate our morality upon the knowledge we have about our values. "We can gain knowledge about, or around, the ethical. Inside the ethical by the same process, we may gain understanding" (Williams 1985, p. 168). The more knowledge we have about human nature, history and what the world actually is, the clearer we come to see our values: they are the contingent product of our culture and history, they are non-objective and relative to our way of living. But if values have no metaphysical or religious foundation, certain ethical concepts, that stand in plain contradiction to the scientific knowledge we have about human nature and the world, become unacceptable. As a consequence, reflection might destroy ethical concepts and modifies inherently the ethical practice, although it does not make emerge an objective, universal morality. Reflection allows us to condemn and reject certain communitarian norms: "Once we regard the ethical life we now have as a genuinely historical and local structure, one that is peculiarly self-conscious about its own origins and potentialities, we shall have less temptation to assume that it is a satisfactorily functioning whole; and we shall be more likely to recognize that some widely accepted parts of it may stand condemned in the light of perfectly plausible extrapolations of other parts" (Williams 2008, pp. 36–7). Moreover, reflection "requires one to live some kind of ethical life while conscious not only that alternatives to it have existed in different social circumstances at different time and places, but also that alternatives to it may exist at our own door" (Williams 2008, p. 36). Free institutions are necessary "for free inquiry but also for diversity of life and some ethical variety" (Williams 1985, p. 172). In this way, Williams seems to have solved both the problem of internal and external pluralism, insofar as they are in an individualist conception of identity just two sides of the same coin.

Unfortunately, he does not! The Hegelian background of Williams' theory of reflectiveness that conceives history in terms of a march toward clearer self-consciousness (Williams 1985, p. 163) makes it at the same time both too relativist and too absolutist for coming to terms with the question pluralism. Let me examine Williams' relativism first. Given that toleration and liberalism are a matter of knowledge, they have become possible only in the wake of modernity with its disenchantment of the world and naturalistic conception of society. Williams is constrained to admit a "relativism of distance" (Williams 1985, p. 162), insofar as "not every society can think about its ethical life in historical and social categories (Williams 2008, p. 36). He tends to justify – although only very much reluctantly (Williams 1985, p. 166) – hierarchies in earlier societies, since "they may not have been wrong in thinking that their social order was necessary for them" (Williams 1985, p. 165).

8.2 Multiculturalism and the Accommodation of Pluralism

Hence, the justification of liberalism is contingent upon the knowledge we have about the world and depends very much upon "moral luck" – we have to find ourselves in circumstances that allow us to gain the relevant knowledge. On the other hand, the implications that Williams draws from reflection are too foundationalist. He must maintain that "relativism over merely spatial distance is of no interest or application in the modern world" (Williams 1985, p. 163). Today, ethical practices have to take into account the achievements of modernity. "The current attempts by Islamic forces in particular to reverse this process […] do not show that the process is local or reversible, only that it can generate despair" (Williams 1985, p. 165). On Williams' view, people having anti-modern commitments and attitudes should change them. Although Williams would like to avoid the conclusion that the consciousness of the nonobjectivity of our ethical outlook does require us to "switch off [our] ethical reactions when [we] are confronted with another group" – since "there is no reason why [we] should" (Williams 1985, p. 159) –, in his theory there is only one group of people who do not have to draw these consequences necessarily, namely the liberals. Only persons with a liberal attitude have some justification to not put into question their commitments and to defend them – given that only liberal positions converge upon more or less true knowledge about human nature and the world. Paradoxically, Williams does not only not give enough space, as we initially hoped, to substantial forms of pluralism, but he is also against his very best intentions critical of multiculturalism and identity politics.

As a direct consequence of his foundationalism, Williams cannot really take seriously the communitarians' claim that commitments are independent sources of value for a person – that we have commitments independent of the fact if we like them or not, consider them right or wrong, true or false. Williams' theory of self-consciousness relying upon a realist theory of knowledge combined with a philosophy of history makes it impossible for him to have a non-reductionist account of commitments. The normative claims of commitments underlie strong epistemological constraints. Science has the last word about who you can and who you cannot be and hence about the justification of multiculturalism. In some sense, anti-foundationalist non-cognitive theories, to which we can count postmodernism and most of postcolonialism, are more sensitive to our fundamental commitments than Williams' theory. Richard Rorty, for example, grounds, as Williams, self-consciousness in the knowledge we have about the nature of the values constituting our commitments. However, given that knowledge only shows us that we cannot be other than what history already made us, that there exists no truth about the world but only situated ethical standpoints, self-consciousness cannot require us to change our commitments. It only tells us to not take ourselves seriously and to adopt an ironic, quasi blasé attitude towards ourselves: "always aware that the terms in which [we] describe [ourselves] are subject to change, always aware of the contingency and fragility of [our] final vocabularies, and thus of [our] selves" (Rorty 1989, pp. 73–4). Traditionalists as well as liberals must combine "commitment with a sense of the contingency of their own commitment" (Rorty 1989, p. 61) and endorse a morality of universal toleration joining irony and liberal hope. For sure, such a position excludes identity politics,[2] but might allow for some form of weary, soft multiculturalism in the absence of any real alternative.

Both Williams and Rorty consider self-consciousness to have epistemological implications. They treat self-consciousness in terms of knowledge and not self-knowledge. They ask us to analyze the content of our commitments in the self-conscious stance and evaluate to what extent they stand in correspondence to the reality of the world. Depending on their respective theory of knowledge they can then either dismiss some of our commitments or ridicule commitments as such. But they cannot conceive commitments as being simply ours, being simply there, integral part of who we have become to be and with which we have to come to terms somehow – Williams and Rorty are judging and criticizing our commitments. Yet, dissociation or self-rejection won't make commitments disappear. The externalization of commitments might lead to the creation of an alienated self, which as a consequences contributes to an incoherent self-representation and a radical, pathological split of the self in a good and a bad self.

Approaching our commitments in terms of self-knowledge rather than knowledge, being self-conscious does not mean to take a stance upon the content of a commitment, but to simply know to *have* a commitment. Making a step out of the normative perspective of the commitment taking a perspective upon the commitment, we aren't any longer helplessly determined by it and its content. Not that detachment makes us free in the transcendental, Kantian sense or inexistent in the Buddhist sense – we have nothing else than ourselves at disposition to live our life. But in the self-conscious stance knowing about our commitments, we are autonomous, insofar as we have the possibility to *endorse* a commitment before it moves us into action.[3] Once we are in a position to endorse our commitments, they become properly *ours* and stop being part of our community. Being aware not of the relative character of the norms constituting our commitment, but of the individual nature of commitments as such once that they come to be endorsed, we do not have to change or ridicule ourselves, whatever might be the content of a commitment. This awareness makes it possible for us to not impose our values upon other individuals who do not share them. Self-knowledge is a necessary condition of personal identity, insofar as it gives us a sense of the self and its values, enabling us thereby to constitute the very self as an agent with a proper, clearly identifiable will. If we would be incapable to gain self-knowledge, David Hume (1978) after all might have been right in conceiving us as a mere succession of mental states without a stable identity.

---

[2] In particular in the postcolonial context the deconstruction of racial, ethnic and national categories manipulated by political and social power (Foucault 2004) aims to question their moral and political relevance (Bhabha 1994; Mbembe 2001; Spivak 1998).

[3] My account of the role of self-knowledge as the foundation of personal autonomy is based upon Harry Frankfurt's conception of the person in his essay "Freedom of the Will and the Concept of a Person" (Frankfurt 1988, pp. 11–26). According to Frankfurt, an individual is only insofar an autonomous person, as she endorses her desire forming a second-order desire to desire the first-order desire.

Once we give up on the idea of necessity and essence with regard to our social, cultural or religious identity, we might not be left with an unencumbered self free and superior to its commitments; self-consciousness must not have self-rejection as a consequence and self-knowledge could constitute properly our identity and freedom, a point already underlined by Spinoza. The hypothesis is that a specific theory of identity based upon self-knowledge helps us to solve the conundrum of how we can justify multiculturalism in the face of pluralism while taking ourselves seriously. Given the individual and not communitarian basis of identity and the fact that endorsement is the source of normativity of our commitments, internal pluralism is guaranteed, *pace* Berman and Hirsi Ali, without hollowing out the very idea of multiculturalism – the communitarian source and constitution of our commitments justifies the multicultural project. But once we solve the problem of internal pluralism, the issue of external pluralism might be resolved as well without having to recur to the help of Rawls and Habermas. As we have seen, only communitarianism has to distinguish between internal and external pluralism.

References

Ali, Ayaan Hirsi. 2008. *The Caged Virgin: An Emancipation Proclamation for Women and Islam.* New York: Free Press.
Appiah, Anthony. 2005. *The Ethics of Identity.* Princeton: Princeton University Press.
Appiah, Anthony, and Amy Gutmann. 1998. *Color Conscious: The Political Morality of Race.* Princeton: Princeton University Press.
Barber, Benjamin. 1996. *Jihad vs. McWorld: Terrorism's Challenge to Democracy.* New York: Ballantine Books.
Barry, Brian. 2001. *Equality and Culture: An Egalitarian Critique of Multiculturalism.* Cambridge: Polity Press.
Bayart, Jean-François. 1996. *L'illusion identitaire.* Paris: Fayard.
Benhabib, Seyla. 2002. *The Claims of Culture. Equality and Diversity in the Global Age.* Princeton: Princeton University Press.
Berman, Paul. 2004. *Terror and Liberalism.* New York: W. W. Norton & Company.
Bhabha, Homi. 1994. *The Location of Culture.* London/New York: Routledge.
Ferrara, Alessandro. 1998. *Reflective Authenticity: Rethinking the Project of Modernity.* London/New York: Routledge.
Foucault, Michel. 2004. *Society Must Be Defended. Lectures at the Collège de France 1975–76,* ed. Arnold Davidson. London: Penguin.
Frankfurt, Harry. 1988. *The Importance of What We Care About.* Cambridge: Cambridge University Press.
Galeotti, Elisabetta. 2005. *Toleration as Recognition.* Cambridge: Cambridge University Press.
Geertz, Clifford. 1977. *The Interpretation of Cultures.* New York: Basic Books.
Habermas, Jürgen. 1996. *Die Einbeziehung des Anderen.* Frankfurt a.M: Suhrkamp.
Huntington, Samuel. 1998. *The Clash of Civilizations and the Remaking of World Order.* New York: Simon & Schuster.
Hume, David. 1978. *A Treatise of Human Nature*, ed. L.A. Selby-Bigge and P.H. Nidditch. Oxford: Oxford University Press.
Korsgaard, Christine. 1994. *The Sources of Normativity.* Cambridge: Cambridge University Press.
Kymlicka, Will. 1991. *Liberalism, Community and Culture.* Oxford: Clarendon Press.
Maffettone, Sebastiano. 2010. *Rawls: An Introduction.* Cambridge: Polity Press.

Mbembe, Achille. 2001. *On the Postcolony*. Berkeley: University of California Press.
McIntyre, Alasdair. 2007. *After Virtue: A Study in Moral Theory*. London: Duckworth.
Okin, Susan Moller. 1999. *Is Multiculturalism Bad for Women?* Princeton: Princeton University Press.
Rawls, John. 1994. *Political Liberalism*. New York: Columbia University Press.
———. 2001. *The Law of Peoples*. Cambridge, MA: Harvard University Press.
Rorty, Richard. 1989. *Contingency, Irony and Solidarity*. Cambridge: Cambridge University.
Sandel, Michael. 1982. *Liberalism and the Limits of Justice*. Cambridge: Cambridge University.
Sen, Amartya. 2006. *Identity and Violence*. New York: W. W. Norton.
Spivak, Gayatri. 1998. Can the Subaltern Speak? In *Marxism and the Interpretation of Culture*, ed. Cary Nelson and Lawrence Grossberg, 271–316. Champaign: Illinois University Press.
Taylor, Charles. 1992. *Sources of the Self: The Making of Modern Identity*. Cambridge: Cambridge University Press.
Walzer, Michael (1985): Interpretation and Social Criticism, The Tanner Lectures on Human Values., http://www.tannerlectures.utah.edu/lectures/documents/walzer88.pdf.
———. 1994. *Thick and Thin. Moral Argument at Home and Abroad*. Notre Dame: Notre Dame University Press.
Williams, Bernard. 1973. A Critique of Utilitarianism. In *Utilitarianism: For and Against*, ed. J.J.C. Smart and Bernard Williams. Cambridge: Cambridge University Press.
———. 1985. *Ethics and the Limits of Philosophy*. Cambridge, MA: Harvard University Press.
———. 2008. *In the Beginning Was the Deed: Realism and Moralism in Political Argument*. Princeton: Princeton University Press.

Chapter 9
Foundations of Multiculturalism (2): Recognition

Abstract This chapter discusses the principal paradigm of multiculturalism, the struggle for recognition. The first part shows to what extent our need for recognition has epistemological grounds. The second part argues that truth cannot be the ground for cultural recognition. If truth is relative to cultures, then the grounds for recognition cease to apply. If truth is a metaphysical concept, then cultures do not provide the basis for judgment and criticism. A relativist concept lacks the grounds for understanding other cultures – what are the foundations on which to base recognition? In a realist model cultures play no foundational (epistemological) role at all and it is no clear why we owe recognition to cultures. The essay concludes that we must have an a propri reason for recognition and suggests that in an empirical concept of culture recognition would occur independent of the question of truth.

Keywords Charles Taylor · Recognition · Truth · Relativism · Metaphysical realism · Fusion of horizons · Hermeneutics · Peter Winch · Hans-Georg Gadamer

Identity conflicts are generally explained in two opposing ways: Either they are considered to have their origin in culture or religion. Or they are taken to be ideological conflicts that have their causes somewhere else, outside culture and religion. The most extreme version of the first theory is of course Samuel Huntington's thesis of the clash of civilizations that explains conflicts on the basis of incompatibilities between cultures. But some version of what we might call the 'culturalist' theory is embraced also by much more liberal approaches, who contest the incompatibility thesis and claim that identity conflicts are the result of serious misinterpretations of cultures, given that all cultures contain sources of tolerance, freedom and democracy. Still, both approaches share the assumption that identity conflicts are somehow a cultural problem.

The second theory, on the contrary, holds that identity conflicts are somewhat due to an illusion. People believe that their cultures put them in conflict with each other, but what is really motivating those conflicts is something very different, e.g. class struggles, utility maximization, structures of power, depending upon the assumptions of the respective theory. From this point of view, it makes no sense at all to address cultural issues in order to resolve identity conflicts. What has to be dealt with is the underlying reality – inequalities, poverty, Orientalism, etc. – of which cultural conflicts are merely an ideological expression.

Both paradigms are facing a series of problems, last but not least those of essentialism and self-knowledge. The 'culturalist thesis' is constrained to rely upon properties that constitute cultures and provide definitions of cultures. The 'ideologist thesis' has to discredit most central beliefs people hold about themselves and their identity.

There is a third explanation of identity conflicts: the lack of recognition or misrecognition, a thesis put forth notably by Charles Taylor. He writes, "the thesis is that a person or group of people can suffer real damage, real distortion, if the people or society around them mirror back to them a confining or demeaning or contemptible picture of themselves." (Taylor 1994, 25) "The struggle for freedom and equality must therefore pass through a revision of these images," (ibid., 66) "which takes place both within the subjugated and against the dominator." (ibid., 65)

According to Taylor, there is no inherent conflict between cultures, even if cultures may indeed promote incompatible goods and values. Conflicts arise when cultures do not recognize each other. Neither cultural reforms from within, nor other social, economic and political reforms are going to make identity conflicts disappear as long as the problem of recognition persists. In this sense, the paradigm of recognition can be understood as a third way mediating between the 'culturalist' and 'ideologist' theses: Identity conflicts are indeed cultural in nature, but their origin lies outside the cultures themselves. The recognition-thesis is from a political point of view rather attractive, since it avoids interference with thorny and sensitive issues of culture, while it takes people rather seriously as agents. Or at least, this seems to be the promise. For sure, it asks more from us than traditional liberalism does, but if recognition is the key for overcoming intricate cultural conflicts, the efforts seem worth it.

Taylor holds that "truly recognizing difference (…) means recognizing the equal value of different ways of being. It is this acknowledgement of equal value that a politics of identity-recognition requires." (Taylor 1992b, 51) One should suppose then that overcoming identity conflicts entails the attribution of equal value to different ways of life, cultures and religions. It seems as if we are simply asked to accept people as they are – not more and not less. Yet this is not Taylor's conception of recognition. He argues that "just the fact that people *choose* different ways of being doesn't make them equal; nor does the fact that they happen to *find themselves* in these different sexes, races, cultures. Mere difference can't itself be the ground of equal value." Taylor is clearly aware of the problems he is running into not attributing a priori equal value to all cultures. "If withholding the presumption [that we owe equal respect to all cultures] is tantamount to a denial of equality, and if important consequences flow for people's identity from the absence of recognition, then a case can be made for insisting on the universalization of the presumption as a logical extension of the politics of dignity. Just as all must have equal civil rights, and equal voting rights, regardless of race or culture, so all should enjoy the presumption that their traditional culture has value." (Taylor 1994, 68) Nevertheless, Taylor eventually concludes that "it can't make sense to demand as a matter of right that we come up with a final concluding judgment that their value is great, or equal to others'." (ibid., 69) "To come together on a mutual recognition of difference – that is, of the equal value of different identities – requires that we share more than a belief in this principle; we have to share also some standards of value on which the identities concerned check out as equal. There must be some substantive agreement on value, or else the formal principle of equality will be empty and a sham." (Taylor 1992b, 51–52)

Since I share Taylor's concern about recognition and agree that misrecognition is fuelling identity conflicts, I consider Taylor's refusal to recognize cultures independently from their contents as quite problematic, precisely for the reasons Taylor points out himself. Taylor sees himself constrained to hold back universal recognition, or at least so I am going to argue, because in his theory culture is closely related to truth. But this way the need for recognition turns out to be a matter of epistemology rather than of psychology. In the first section I reconstruct Taylor's argument for recognition and in the second part I claim that truth cannot be the basis for recognition. In the conclusion I briefly lay the grounds for a psychological notion of recognition.

9.1 The Structure of Recognition

The first question that needs to be clarified is why people actually need to be recognized – in particular since traditional liberalism is based upon the very refusal of any sort of moral recognition. In a nutshell, Taylor's position is the following: (1) As human agents we have necessarily and inescapably to confront questions of truth – our judgments are not reducible to simple emotional reactions. (2) Cultures provide the answers to questions about truth. (3) For that reason we cannot but start reasoning from within the evaluative frameworks cultures provide – they constitute our identity. (4) Since the sources of our judgments and values have their origin in the broader cultures we are embedded in and are not autonomously brought forth by individuals, our beliefs must be recognized by others in order that we know that we are on the right path towards the truth. (5) Hence recognition is constitutive of our identity.

(1) Taylor claims that "that it belongs to human agency to exist in a space of questions about strongly valued goods, prior to all choice or adventitious cultural change." (Taylor 1992a, 31) We cannot escape questions about truth. Yet we cannot just invent the answers to those questions or answer them "just on the basis of desires and aversions, likes and dislikes." (ibid., 30) "Answers to questions [of truth] (…) inescapably pre-exist for us, independent of our answer or inability to answer." (ibid., 30) Put differently, "one orients oneself in a space which exists independently of one's success or failure in finding one's bear-

ings." (ibid, 30) But if it is neither our reason nor emotions that enable us to discover truth, what exactly is this independent space that provides answers to question of truth?

(2) Taylor holds the Aristotelian view that all human beings have the same potentiality. "Our value terms purport to give us insight into what it is to live in the universe as a human being." (ibid. 59) But he also maintains, in line with Hegel, that it is only history that lays bare this potentiality. "What is *an sich* unfolds *für sich* in history." (Taylor 1997, 160) This means that we do not have direct access to our potentiality, but that this access has to be mediated. And what mediates our access to our own reality, but also to that of the universe, is culture. Culture constitutes the space of reasons that provide answers to questions of truth.

(3) The culture we grow into introduces us to issues of truth that as selves we inescapably have to confront. Since it is the culture in which we happen to find ourselves that provides us with the language of interpretation that puts us in touch with the truth, we cannot but *accept* this language "as a valid interpretation of these issues." (Taylor 1992a, 34) Our culture defines the issues that matter for us and gives us a sense and the idea of the good that "represent standards by which (…) desires and choices are judged." (ibid., 20). Thereby our culture becomes "constitutive of human agency" (ibid., 27) as much as of our identity. It defines 'imports' or 'desirability characterizations', "incorporating a sense of what is important for us," (Taylor 1985a, 60) "that give the grounds or basis for [our] feeling[s]," (ibid., 49) desires, and emotions.

(4) If our identity makes truth claims that are grounded in our culture and not in our reason or emotions, we can never be one hundred percent sure that we got things right and understood the full meaning of the cultural norms. In theory, your fellows and co-nationals could always contest your interpretation of cultural prescriptions, insinuating that you misunderstood what they really are about. The only way to verify the validity of our judgments and beliefs – if it is really true, as Taylor holds, that "language or culture, in forming our worlds, mediates our contact with the universe and with our human nature" (Taylor 1994, 128–129) – is their recognition by others. Only through dialogue and exchange with others we can come to understand if our good is truly worthwhile. Taylor concludes that "we define our identity always in dialogue with, sometimes in struggle against, the things our significant others want to see in us." (ibid., 32–33)

(5) Yet, as a consequence, an "identity needs and is vulnerable to the recognition given or withheld by significant others." (ibid., 36) Non-recognition "can inflict damage on those who are denied it. (…) The projection of an inferior or demeaning image on another can actually distort and oppress, to the extent that the image is internalized." (ibid., 36) If your fellows refuse to consider your interpretation of culture as legitimate and valid, you have inevitably to put into question your idea of the good and live with the nagging doubt that your commitments are insignificant and worthless. For that reason, according to Taylor, "the understanding that identities are formed in open dialogue (…) has made the politics of equal recognition more central and stressful." (ibid., 36)

9.2 Can We Recognize Other Cultures?

It becomes evident from this reconstruction of Taylor's concept that our need for recognition has purely epistemological grounds. Recognition is *not* a *psychological* need we have, in the sense that we feel the need to be recognized for what we are and have become. It is not an existential need we experience independent from the fact if our identity corresponds to some truth or not. In Taylor's theory, we want to be recognized because this is the only way we can be sure to strive towards the truth which as human selves we have to face.

9.2 Can We Recognize Other Cultures?

However, there is one problem with Taylor's model of recognition. If it shows *grosso modo* that we have a qualified obligation of recognition of members of our home culture within certain limits, it seems to not establish that we have the same obligation of recognition with respect to people from other cultures. How could we judge, and hence recognize, other cultures, if we do not understand them? Other cultures, with their own access to truth, have different languages and frameworks of significance and we do not understand the peculiar meaning things have for them. All we can say, it seems, is that "this is just their form of life" and that "there may be nothing quite corresponding to it in our society." (Taylor 1985b, 127) If culture provides the access to truth and each culture has its own truth, this "rules out an account which shows them up as wrong, confused or deluded. Each culture on this view is incorrigible." (ibid., 123) And as a matter of fact, cultural relativism, as Taylor continues, seems to be "the only real safe-guard against [ethnocentricity]. We understand each culture in its own terms, and we can never fall into the error of misunderstanding one according to the categories of another." (ibid., 125)

But this is not what other cultures want. They do not seek for mere difference, where there is nothing to engage with one another. And Taylor clearly agrees that what is at stake between cultures is recognition, not difference. In fact, according to him, recognition is the very foundation of multiculturalism. Yet why does recognition exactly matter to other cultures in Taylor's structure of recognition? If each culture has its own access to truth, what seems to matter to our self-understanding is recognition within our own culture. Other cultures cannot access the meaning and import things have for us and so, similar to the conclusion cultural relativism draws, we even should disregard their opinions about us. Taylor, on the contrary, holds that cultures are not monads, independent systems that are immune to each other. Our narratives about other cultures influence their self-interpretation and determine the perception they have of themselves with regard to their position with respect to truth. Cultures interpenetrate. And they do so because cultures can *understand* each other, they can communicate with each other, they can speak a common language. Therefore the obligation of recognition does not stop at our borders. We owe recognition also to other cultures.

The next question then is how exactly we can understand other cultures? And what seems even more important, on what basis do we judge them? Given the constitutive role cultures play in setting "the forms and limits of intelligibility" (Taylor 1997, 148) in Taylor's theory, the recognition of other cultures has to result from the standards fixed by our home culture. We cannot leave aside our cultural framework when understanding other cultures. Understanding, as Taylor argues, "is not just a matter of feeling empathy," it "is discursive understanding" (Taylor 1985b, 118) of others' identities. Yet how do we avoid then not to fall into the ethnocentric trap, namely understanding their practices in the light of our own cultural standards and judge them as deviant, backward, immoral etc.? How do we circumvent the dangers of which cultural relativism is warning? Taylor's solution is a "fusion of horizons," a method he is adopting directly from Gadamer.

Obviously, as Taylor writes, "there is a challenge because others don't really makes sense against our home understanding. The challenge can just remain at the level of the strange and bewilderment. But this is almost impossible to sustain. In fact, we almost always proceed to another stage: we find a way of placing the strange practice as corresponding to one (some) of ours." (Taylor 1997, 152) We put other cultures' practices in relation to ours and draw "comparisons or contrasts" (ibid., 152) between them. This "allows for the fact (…) that they may have activities which have no correspondent in ours." (ibid., 129) But it also presupposes that we share a common core and that the meaning of our practices at least partially overlaps. Although our practices often are very different, perhaps even incompatible, they are motivated by common intentions. Discussing the cultural relativists' interpretation of magic and rites as being incompatible with and having no correspondent in Western practices, Taylor argues that we cannot say "that they are doing *this as against* trying to control certain (…) contingencies. (…) The rites have a relation to consumption; they are undertaken to make the crops grow free of the hazards that threaten them. (…) We can all too easily find analogies between primitive magical practices and some of our own, because they *do* overlap." (Taylor 1985b, 140)

The question then is what precisely allows us to fuse cultural horizons. Do we really understand other cultures on the basis of our cultural standards? Or do comparisons and contrasts not presuppose a criteria that is entirely independent from culture? If we try to consider magic from a purely scientific point of view, it is impossible to say if they try to mimic, without the adequate knowledge, what technology does (using the causalities of the natural world) or if they do something on a completely different order. And this for the simple reason that they do not use standards that are intelligible from the point of view of science. If they do not have the criteria we have, how can we know what they are up to? In fact, there is nothing we could understand about other cultures if they use standards different from ours. And so there will be never a fusion of horizons and we are stuck in cultural relativism, with the consequence that there can be anything as recognition of cultures.

Taylor, in reality, does not ground the understanding of other cultures in a simple fusion of horizons. Taylor's thesis is that cultures have "very different way[s] of understanding, human life, the cosmos, the holy, etc" (Dreyfus and Taylor 2015, 113), whereas latter provide "standards we consider binding on us" (Taylor 1997, 160). Cultures "formulate (…) alternative possibilities in relation to some human constants (…) of birth, death, marriage, drought, plenty, etc." (Taylor 1985b,

125–127) Taylor thinks that we can understand each other because cultures, in all their diversity, have a common feature: namely, they strive to unfold truth – a truth, that even though Taylor conceives it to be plural, must be determinate in order to still count as truth. Cultures can understand each other on the basis of this common purpose and against the background of a more or less shared truth.

Since we know that at least partially cultures develop the same aspects of truth and share common goals – e.g. managing natural contingencies given our shared vulnerability –, we can say that cultural practices "are not simply different, but rather that they are incommensurable." (Taylor 1985b, 145) On this basis, we can judge what cultural practice is right (science) and which wrong (ritual), which is superior and which is inferior. "One culture can surely lay claim to a higher, or fuller, or more effective rationality, if it is in a position to achieve a more perspicuous order than another." (ibid., 150) Referring to the development of rationality and human rights in the Western civilization, Taylor states that we "tend irresistibly to define them as development or evolution, or advance, or realization of the properly human." (Taylor 1997, 161) The West provides a better account of certain aspects of the human good related to reason and freedom than other cultures.

To sum up, we understand other cultures because they have to answer the same questions of truth as we have to. We understand their practices in the light of this truth. At the same time, this puts us in a position to judge the progress different cultural practices have made towards the truth and make "valid transcultural judgments of superiority." (Taylor 1985b, 149) Because there exists an independent truth to which cultures have to live up, it cannot be "a principle of ethics" and "can't make sense to demand as a matter of right that we come up with a final concluding judgment that [a culture's] value is great, or equal to others'." (Taylor 1994, 69) Because of truth, we cannot recognize other cultures if we have progressed further to it than they – despite Taylor's claim "that the withholding of recognition can be a form of oppression" (ibid, 36).

Admittedly, unlike Hegel, Taylor does not think that there is just *one* reality that history has to unfold. "To speak of potentialities doesn't mean to suppose a unitary set. We can and increasingly do recognize diverse lines of possible development, some of which seem incompatible with each other, at least at first blush." (Taylor 1997, 162) In this sense, "all cultures allow for human flourishing." (ibid, 162) and provide access to *plural* and often incompatible aspects of reality. And this way Taylor hopes to avoid the politically rather problematic ranking of cultures. But as Taylor writes elsewhere, recognition requires judgments of value that are objective, "independent of our own wills and desires" (Taylor 1994, 69). "The validity of the claim [of the equal equality of cultures] has to be demonstrated concretely in the actual study of the culture." (ibid., 67)

But can it be really the case that cultures realize independent truth(s)? Is it really the Western civilization that has invented liberalism and democracy, if we consider those as given universal standards? If it would be indeed cultures that bring to light an independent truth, then we would not any longer know that the standards to which cultures have come to live up are indeed universal and real. If it were indeed culture that brings about certain standards, it would be impossible for us to say that those standards are universal and objective. We would be constrained to see them as *relative* to the particular culture that produced them. There would be no way to escape the cultural framework in which they raised and see their independent truth. But what Taylor says is that we know those truths and we judge cultures according to these truths – therefore we can impossibly know the truth through our culture. We know the truth independently from our culture.

But if culture can neither foster nor impede us to understand the truth, how could we judge cultures on the grounds of this very truth? If we do not live up to truth, we cannot blame our culture. In Taylor's theory there is no way to have culture and truth together and Taylor oscillates between the two. (1) Either truth is relative to culture and then the concept of truth disappears as it happens in the model of the fusion of horizons. (2) Or there is an independent and given truth that sets universal standards, as the Aristotelian human potentialities, and then culture must be something entirely different from truth. Yet in both cases the conditions for recognition are no longer fulfilled. A relativist concept lacks the grounds for understanding other cultures – what are the foundations on which to base recognition? (Please note that this problem arises not only between cultures but also within the same culture – what could decide which interpretation of culture is the right or the wrong one, if there is no foundation?). In a realist model cultures play no foundational (epistemological) role at all and it is no clear why we owe recognition to cultures.

We have seen that Taylor's model of recognition that makes cultures functions of an independent truth collapses into either relativism or realism. The consequence, however, is that in both relativism and realism we lose a clear conception of what culture actually is and why recognition is "a vital human need." (Taylor 1994, 26) If culture has nothing to do with truth, what is it then? Why do people want to be recognized for their culture, if cultures do not provide the grounds for judgment and criticism?

Given that I believe misrecognition to be central to identity conflicts, it is important to maintain a meaningful concept of culture. The big question is what will be the relationship between culture and truth in a revised concept of culture. For sure, truth cannot be relative to culture nor metaphysical in nature. But still must we presuppose some idea of truth to make sense of culture and accordingly of recognition? Is Taylor right that the need for recognition is of epistemological origin? Or can we reduce recognition to a psychological need that is independent from the fact if our culture gets things right or wrong?

Let me try to give a tentative answer. If Taylor is right and "due recognition is not just a courtesy we owe people," (Taylor 1994, 26) then we must have an a priori reason to recognize other cultures. This has two consequences: (1) The a priori reason cannot be transcendental, in the sense that it abstracts from the concrete cultural identity people happen to have. (2) What we come to recognize is not the value of other cultures. A concept of culture based upon experience seems to be the best candidate to fulfill these conditions. Following premise would frame the background: Given the experiences you have had, I can fully recognize you without necessarily agreeing with you. This would separate the need for recognition from truth, ground it in our psychology and make recognition a matter of empathy. But what exactly is culture in this conception and what does this mean for agency and first-person authority?

References

Dreyfus, Hubert, and Charles Taylor. 2015. *Retrieving Realism*. Cambridge, MA: Harvard University Press.
Taylor, Charles. 1985a. *Philosophical Papers (Vol. 1), Human Agency and Language*. Cambridge: Cambridge University Press.
———. 1985b. *Philosophical Papers (Vol. 2), Philosophy and the Human Sciences*. Cambridge: Cambridge University Press.
———. 1992a. *The Sources of the Self. The Making of Modern Identity*. Cambridge, MA: Harvard University Press.
———. 1992b. *The Ethics of Authenticity*. Cambridge, MA: Harvard University Press.
———. 1994. *Multiculturalism. Examining the Politics of Recognition*. Princeton: Princeton University Press.
———. 1997. *Philosophical Arguments*. Cambridge, MA: Harvard University Press.

Chapter 10
Islam and Democracy

Abstract This chapter provides an overview and analyzes the different contemporary theories that seek to establish the compatibility of Islam and democracy. It distinguishes between epistemological theories that, on the one hand, argue that we cannot but access Islam from the point of view of political modernity (Abu Zayd) and those that, on the other hand, maintain that Islam has to correspond to moral reality (El Fadl). Last but not least, it introduces ethical theories that evoke the freedom and agency of Muslims in the face of their understandable resentment of the West (Bilgrami).

Keywords Islam · Democracy · Epistemology · Hermeneutics · Moral realism · Ethics · Agency · Nasr Abu Zayd · Khaled Abou El Fadl · Akeel Bilgrami

This chapter addresses following fundamental question: Is Islam compatible with democracy or not? I am reviewing critically major positions taken by Islamic theorists and theologians as well as Western philosophers that were presented at the Istanbul Seminars and published in the volume *Toward New Democratic Imaginaries* (2016) edited by Seyla Benhabib and me. The positions that I am going to analyze give a rather straightforward answer: Yes, Islam and democracy are indeed compatible, even though some qualify this statement. In a sense, the theories under examination here attempt to respond to the challenge that we dealt with in Chap. 6 of this book, namely why Muslims should accept democratic pluralism and should not endorse extremism and fundamentalism (see 'Agency, Psychology and the Self: The Case of Religious Fundamentalism', in this volume). The positions discussed here address the question of democracy and fundamentalism from within Islam itself.

Michael Walzer argues that there cannot be a democratic revolution and a religious revival at the same time, in the same place.[1] Walzer claims, discussing the rise

---
[1] Walzer, *The Paradox of Liberation*.

of Islamism, that factors such as "colonialism, imperialism, and global capitalism (…) don't give us a distinguishing reason for religious zealotry" and that "surely there have to be cultural and inner-religious reasons for this appeal."[2] The theories discussed in this chapter resist this conclusion and set out to demonstrate that Islam, as a religion, does not provide any grounds for or justification of fundamentalism and extremism.

The authors under review basically provide two reasons why Islam can accommodate democracy. The first argument is based on theological considerations that concern the very nature of truth. It contests the Islamists' voluntarist conception of truth, according to which God's word, as it is revealed in the Qur'an, represents the moral and political order of things and the immutable, timeless reality of the world. It does so from either a hermeneutical perspective[3] or on the grounds of moral realism.[4] The second argument in favor of the compatibility of Islam and democracy is not based upon Islamic theology, and even admits the difficulties of reconciling Islam with secularism and democracy on account of its political history,[5] but invokes the freedom and agency of Muslims to change the course of that history.[6]

10.1 The Epistemological Argument

The contributions of Nasr Abu-Zayd, Abdelmajid Charfi, Khaled Abou El Fadl and Fred Dallmayr share and largely confirm Walzer's analysis that Islam actually makes truth claims. What distinguishes these four thinkers from Walzer is their rejection of the claim that the religious pursuit of truth stands in any sense in opposition to democracy. They do not deny the fact that there effectively exist interpretations of Islam, "Puritanical-Salafism," as Abou El Fadl calls them, that make "absolute, exclusivist and authoritarian claims to the truth"[7] that are by all means incompatible with democracy. Yet, these versions of Islam get the truth, such as it is revealed within Islam, quite wrong. Islamic fundamentalism is simply a distortion of Islam.

Yet matters are not that simple. The trouble these reformist philosophers face is the claim of Islamic extremists that they, in turn, are applying the Qur'an quite literally, interpreting their act of submission precisely, as Abou El Fadl states, "as if it [were] an act of obedience by lowly soldiers to the orders of a superior officer."[8] Therefore the reformists' claim that Islamists miss the point and go totally wrong about the nature of Islam is, to say the least, contested. What then, asks Abu-Zayd,

---

[2] Walzer, *Islamism and the Left*.
[3] See Abu Zayd, "The 'Others' in the Qur'an"; Charfi, "Islam: The Test of Globalization".
[4] See El Fadl, "The Epistemology of Truth in Modern Islam"; Dallmayr, "Whither Democracy?".
[5] See Hashemi, "Rethinking Religion and Political Legitimacy Across the Islam-West Divide".
[6] See Bilgrami, "Islam and the West"; Ahmad, "Democracy and Islam".
[7] El Fadl, "The Epistemology of Truth in Modern Islam", p. 115.
[8] El Fadl, "The Epistemology of Truth in Modern Islam", p. 116.

10.1 The Epistemological Argument

are the "incalculable misinterpretations and misunderstandings" that Islamists are guilty of when attempting to transfer relevant Qur'anic passages "literally into our era?"[9]

We can distinguish among two answers given here. Abu-Zayd and Charfi reproach Islamists, in line with the larger tradition of hermeneutics, that they fail to *contextualize* the truth as it is revealed in the Qur'an and believe truth to exist in a blank, unmediated form. Abou El Fadl and Dallmayr argue, by contrast, that truth in the Qur'an precedes and binds God's will and that the Qur'an therefore needs to be read against the background of independent moral principles. Abu-Zayd insists that "we must recognize that, even though [the Qur'an] is the speech of God, it is an historical text" and that "the Qur'an, though a given fact from the perspective of faith, exhibits a response to the factual reality of its time."[10] Abu-Zayd argues that "Islam is humanity's creation like every religion,"[11] displaying the extent to which the Qur'an, and in particular its moral, legal and political prescriptions, provide an answer to the challenges the Muslim community faced in the Arabic peninsula in the early seventh century.

Today, however, the context that Islam is confronting has radically changed, and as Charfi points out, traditions "which claims to reflect faithfully the will of the Prophet,"[12] become increasingly illusory. With globalization, democracy "has become a universal value and an integral part of the rights of man"[13] and gender equality is recognized as "a general aspiration of the younger generation."[14] Therefore, the institutionalization of the Qur'an, that would take as morally binding the actions of the Prophet and the early representatives of Islam, and which would thus legitimize religious as well as sexual inequalities, needs to be reformed in line with the necessities of globalization.

There are two possible interpretations of Abu-Zayd's and Charfi's account of the historicity of Islam and their criticism of the literalist readings of the Qur'an. According to the first, the truth in the Qur'an is laid down on the basis of conceptual schemes, values and norms that were prevalent in Arabia in the seventh century. Given that our mindset and attitudes are very much different today, Muslims are required to give a new, updated interpretation of the Qur'an and its message. In a second reading, Abu-Zayd and Charfi could be said to claim that historicity refers only to the circumstances that circumscribe the setting of the Qur'an and not to the truth itself. That is, the principles informing the actions of the Prophet and the ethics laid out in the Qur'an are still valid in our day today and claim some form of universality, even if the conditions of Muslim communities in the seventh century was

---

[9] Abu Zayd, "The 'Others' in the Qur'an", p. 98.
[10] Abu Zayd, "The 'Others' in the Qur'an", p. 98.
[11] Abu Zayd, "The 'Others' in the Qur'an", p. 99.
[12] Charfi, "Islam: The Test of Globalization", p. 146.
[13] Charfi, "Islam: The Test of Globalization", p. 142.
[14] Charfi, "Islam: The Test of Globalization", p. 143.

such as to necessitate measures that would be largely inacceptable from the point of view of today's societies.

Abu-Zayd and Charfi endorse the first interpretation, that is, the hermeneutical approach to truth. Abu-Zayd claims that it is "an unsophisticated understanding of religion [to] suggest that one need only uncover the 'correct' interpretation of the Qur'an and one will know what 'Islam' means."[15] Charfi affirms that "the first Muslims whose task it was to apply what they understood of Islam could do so only in the framework of the cognitive and social systems at their disposition."[16]

However, as Dallmayr argues, Islamists make a rather harsh objection, reproaching that the hermeneutical approach threatens their faith and endorses a form of relativism. Abu-Zayd clearly tries to resist this accusation, by claiming to "have developed (...) a historical method that enables one to recognize the core of Islam, something that is inherent in Islam, in certain convictions and principles." Yet, at the same time Abu-Zayd argues that "[the] normative sense [of religion] is historically determined, and is, thus, changeable. It is normative according to the specific milieu paradigm; any paradigm-change leads to norms-change."[17] And, as Charfi shows, today's paradigm and norms are determined by modernity, democracy and pluralism, which Islamists consider precisely to be *the* problem.

According to them, these norms, which for both Abu-Zayd and Charfi constitute the basis of any plausible version of contemporary Islam, undermine the very foundations of Islam. Describing the point of view of traditional Islamists, Dallmayr writes that "modernity or modernization means a lapse from faith into non-faith (...) and from the holistic unity of 'truth' into a radical relativism denying 'truth'. Islamists assert that modernity has replaced the reign of God (*hakimyya*) with the reign of 'man' or humanity – a replacement equaling a lapse into paganism and the state of pre-Islamic 'ignorance' (*jahiliyya*)."[18]

In fact, Abou El Fadl criticizes Muslim reformers who "in response to the challenges of modernity, and the oppressiveness of doctrinal absolutism, (...) have gravitated towards theories"[19] that emphasize the role of agency and interpretation in determining Islamic faith. He holds that "from an Islamic philosophical perspective, these approaches are not entirely satisfying,"[20] since in one way or another they give up on the idea of truth and epistemology. As we have seen, however, hermeneutics does not exactly abandon the concept of truth. Yet, according to Abou El Fadl, without assuming the existence of something like an absolute or universal truth, "our rational faculties can be used only hermeneutically in interpreting Revelation"[21] without ever putting us into a position to see and understand the truth to which

---

[15] Abu Zayd, "The 'Others' in the Qur'an", p. 98.
[16] Charfi, "Islam: The Test of Globalization", p. 145.
[17] Abu Zayd, "The 'Others' in the Qur'an", p. 100.
[18] Dallmayr, "Whither Democracy?", p. 152.
[19] El Fadl, "The Epistemology of Truth in Modern Islam", p. 118.
[20] El Fadl, "The Epistemology of Truth in Modern Islam", p. 119.
[21] El Fadl, "The Epistemology of Truth in Modern Islam", p. 121.

10.1 The Epistemological Argument

Revelation actually refers. Hermeneutics struggles to distinguish between the interpretable and the uninterpretable.

Therefore, Abou El Fadl recovers the categories of *haqq* and *hikma* from the tradition of Islamic epistemology and semiotics. He defines *haqq* as "the true nature of things or the inherent truthful nature and essence of things, (…) constant and non-shifting." Whereas *hikma* "is truth, not simply from the perspective of what the essence is, but truth [in what concerns its] relational dynamics,"[22] truth that is non-constant and shifting. The principles of justice and fairness, to take an example, are always the same, however, the means to achieve the justice and fairness change with time "as our consciousness, which is a function of our human psychology, becomes more complex, and human needs have dramatically altered."[23]

Whereas Abu-Zayd and Charfi risk to reduce *haqq* to *hikma*, Abou El Fadl seeks to distinguish the two categories and holds them to be irreducible to one another. He maintains that God's Revelation is based upon "laws of humanity that (…) are embedded in our cognition and consciousness, and are as stable and unwavering as the laws of mathematics or the logic." He concludes that "when the Qur'an invokes ethical and moral terminology, it necessarily assumes a pre-existing epistemological context in which it operates and a moral trajectory that it seeks to engage and negotiate. When the Qur'an sets out specific instructions about a particular situation or issue, these instructions must be analyzed in terms of the moral purpose and trajectory that elicited the instructions in the first place."[24]

This version of moral realism takes the Islamists' objection seriously and engages with them on the field of absolute truth. Yet, moral realists and Islamists come to quite different conclusions. For Islamists, as Abou El Fadl puts it, from the fact that "one believes in an immutable, omnipotent and all-powerful God who is the Lawgiver," it follows, "that Revelation defines what is right or wrong."[25] Realists, on the contrary, tend to point always to moral laws and principles that bind God's will. When Dallmayr discusses the proposal of certain Islamist thinkers to return to God's sovereignty as an antidote to democracy, he objects that it is impossible that God be construed "as a willful and arbitrary despot" or tyrant "untrammeled by any rational constraints or intelligible standards of justice."[26]

Yet, Islamists could make a non-negligible objection even against realists. Without even entering into a metaphysical debate with realists, Islamists could simply point out that in case that God does not constitute truth, and that man, as realists further argue, can discover the independent truth without the help of God, God becomes in many respects superfluous and even delegitimized, somewhat unworthy of the faith and trust believers put into Him. In the hands of moral realists what disappears is not only Islamism, but also Islam as a religion. Given the difficulties

---

[22] El Fadl, "The Epistemology of Truth in Modern Islam", p. 119.
[23] El Fadl, "The Epistemology of Truth in Modern Islam", p. 120.
[24] El Fadl, "The Epistemology of Truth in Modern Islam", p. 122.
[25] El Fadl, "The Epistemology of Truth in Modern Islam", p. 121.
[26] Dallmayr, "Whither Democracy?", p. 153.

for demonstrating the compatibility of Islam and democracy on epistemological grounds, some theorists hold that the Islamists' problem, despite claims to the contrary, is after all not theological truth. It lies somewhere else.

10.2 The Practical Argument

Akeel Bilgrami, Nader Hashemi as well as Irfan Ahmad agree upon the fact that the current opposition of many Muslims to democracy has little to do with the Qur'an and Islam as such. For them, the question is not if Islamic norms are compatible with democracy or not. Ahmad argues that "both the Incompatibility and the Compatibility Paradigms are premised on the notion that it is the unitary, reified normative impulse of religion that is the ultimate variable."[27] Bilgrami accuses theorists of the clash of civilizations to ignore that the religious conflict between Islam and the West is superseded by a much more serious and deeper psychological conflict that goes back to colonial conquest and subjugation. Therefore, Ahmad proposes to "shift the debate from the [textual-normative approach] to the domain of practice."[28]

Putting aside the Qur'an and shifting the focus from debates about what it is to be a proper Muslim and Islamic ethics to the social, economic and political realities with which many Muslims today are confronted, we can actually find explanations of Islam's hostility towards the West and everything thought to be western, including democracy. Bilgrami and Ahmad agree that factors external to Islam are responsible for the current impasse. Hashemi, on the other hand, believes that factors internal to Islam, that are largely related to its historical and political trajectory, complicate the relationship between religion and politics. Which precisely are these external and internal factors?

Bilgrami and Ahmad blame the West, and more in particular European colonialism and US geopolitics, for contributing either directly through the support of Islamic militants and autocratic rulers to non-democratic political systems or indirectly through (post-)colonial attitudes of condescension and superiority to anti-democratic feelings. Ahmad concludes, analyzing western foreign policy, that "it is the culture of de-democratization by the western power that renders the Middle East undemocratic."[29]

Bilgrami locates the trouble Muslims have with democracy on a purely psychological level that has its origin in (post-)colonialism. Observing that fundamentalist parties generally gain few votes whenever there are fair and open elections, Bilgrami concludes that "most Muslims are not absolutists at all, in fact they share very little with the absolutist," in the sense that in principle they are not anti-democratic and anti-modern. Yet, he notices that "members of the far larger population of ordinary

---

[27] Ahmad, "Democracy and Islam", p. 127.
[28] Ahmad, "Democracy and Islam", p. 127.
[29] Ahmad, "Democracy and Islam", p. 133.

10.2 The Practical Argument

Muslims (…) are often unwilling to come out and be openly critical of the absolutists in their midst, with whom they share so little by way of ideology and ideal."[30] Bilgrami attributes this reluctance of non-absolutist Muslims to criticize radicals to colonialism and its continuing effects. Colonialism has generated a sense of "alienation, dehumanization and resentment,"[31] turning a religious conflict, that shaped for centuries the relations between Christianity and Islam, into a material-economic and moral conflict. Therefore, "non-absolutist Muslims feel that to criticize their own people in any way is letting the side down, somehow capitulating to this long-standing history of being colonized and condescended to."[32]

Hashemi, on the contrary, tends to stress rather causes internal to Islam's political history in order to explain the Muslim malaise. After noting that "political secularism emerged in the Anglo-American tradition out of the need to negotiate and resolve an existential threat,"[33] namely the European wars of religion, Hashemi argues that in comparison, due to the relative tolerance characterizing per-modern period Muslim societies, "no political dynamic emerged within Muslim societies necessitating the development of intellectual or moral arguments favoring religion-state separation." Islam not only was not a source of political conflicts, but also "played a constructive role as an agent of socio-political stability and predictability," as "a source of social cohesion (…) and a potential ally in promoting social justice."[34] These two internal factors together with the fact that secularism in Muslim societies has been a top-down process that has gone hand in hand with "despotism, dictatorship and human rights abuses"[35] explains, according to Hashemi, that many Muslims across Europe, Asia, Africa, and the Middle East "express a desire for sharia to be recognized as the official law of their country."[36]

Still, one question remains open. Is the explanation of many Muslims' difficulties with democracy the end of the story? Do we therefore have to accept, at least for the moment and the near future, that Islam is incompatible with democracy? Do resentment and history justify not only Islam's opposition to democracy, but also the affirmation of a radical and absolutist Islam? Hashemi sees no policies or political development on the horizon that could actually reverse the contested relationship between Islam and democracy. According to him, "the decline of secular politics and the rise of a religious consciousness in Muslim societies at the end of the 20th century have deeply transformed the political culture of Muslim societies" and "will

---

[30] Bilgrami, "Islam and the West", p. 174.
[31] Bilgrami, "Islam and the West", p. 173.
[32] Bilgrami, "Islam and the West", p. 174.
[33] Hashemi, "Rethinking Religion and Political Legitimacy Across the Islam-West Divide", p. 165.
[34] Hashemi, "Rethinking Religion and Political Legitimacy Across the Islam-West Divide", p. 166.
[35] Hashemi, "Rethinking Religion and Political Legitimacy Across the Islam-West Divide", p. 167.
[36] Hashemi, "Rethinking Religion and Political Legitimacy Across the Islam-West Divide", pp. 162–63.

shape how Muslims (…) perceive and understand the relations between religion and politics in the years to come."[37]

Bilgrami and Ahmad are much less skeptical and actually make a distinction between the explanation and the justification of Muslims' hostility towards democracy. Ahmad analyzes the transformation of Jamaat-e-Islami from a staunch anti-democratic Indian political party aiming at the establishment of an Islamic state under the leadership of the Islamist thinker Abul Ala Maududi into a party participating in and strongly defending and endorsing democracy. He comes to the conclusion that this revolution has not been the outcome of a rational choice and "side effect of democracy in a Hindu-majority milieu," but the result of agency in the proper sense of the term. Muslims have been the makers and agents of this change, coming to recognize and accept, through the political discussions taking place in a democracy, the "plurality of views."[38]

Bilgrami goes one step further and makes it a matter of principle that Muslims, whether living under democratic institutions or not, cannot consider themselves to be merely victims, caused by their circumstances. "Understanding oneself is done by stepping outside of the self and looking at oneself from the outside, as a third person would. But to take that perspective on ourselves, though often necessary, cannot *exhaust* our perspective on ourselves. If it did it would destroy our freedom, which consists in the first-person point of view, the point of view of agency, the point of view of the subject rather than the point of view by which we view ourselves as objects, the objects of history and its causes."[39] Bilgrami's claim is that Muslims, as free agents, are *morally* required to accept democracy.

10.3 Conclusion

This last point connects the debate on Islam and democracy to a larger issue, namely the problem of pluralism. If we can expect that people for a variety of reasons hold different, if not opposite political points of view, how can they still live together under common political institutions? Political philosophers have given different answers to this challenge, notably the idea of an overlapping consensus and discourse ethics. And what is interesting about these answers is that they justify democracy in moral and political terms rather than on religious grounds.[40]

---

[37] Hashemi, "Rethinking Religion and Political Legitimacy Across the Islam-West Divide", p. 168.
[38] Ahmad, "Democracy and Islam", p. 131.
[39] Bilgrami, "Islam and the West", p. 177.
[40] For a further development of this point see Kaul & Salvatore, *What is Pluralism?*

References

Nasr, Abu Zayd. 2016. The 'Others' in the Qur'an: A Hermeneutical Approach. In *Toward New Democratic Imaginaries – Istanbul Seminars on Islam, Culture and Politics*, ed. Seyla Benhabib and Volker Kaul, 97–119. Basel: Springer.

Ahmad, Irfan. 2016. Democracy and Islam. In *Toward New Democratic Imaginaries – Istanbul Seminars on Islam, Culture and Politics*, ed. Seyla Benhabib and Volker Kaul, 125–136. Basel: Springer.

Benhabib, Seyla, and Volker Kaul. *Toward New Democratic Imaginaries – Istanbul Seminars on Islam, Culture and Politics*. Basel: Springer.

Bilgrami, Akeel. 2016. Islam and the West: Conflict, Democracy, Identity. In *Toward New Democratic Imaginaries – Istanbul Seminars on Islam, Culture and Politics*, ed. Seyla Benhabib and Volker Kaul, 171–177. Basel: Springer.

Charfi, Abdelmajid. 2016. Islam: The Test of Globalization. In *Toward New Democratic Imaginaries – Istanbul Seminars on Islam, Culture and Politics*, ed. Seyla Benhabib and Volker Kaul, 137–147. Basel: Springer.

Dallmayr, Fred. 2016. Whither Democracy? Religion, Politics and Islam. In *Toward New Democratic Imaginaries – Istanbul Seminars on Islam, Culture and Politics*, ed. Seyla Benhabib and Volker Kaul, 149–160. Basel: Springer.

El Fadl, Khaled Abou. 2016. The Epistemology of Truth in Modern Islam. In *Toward New Democratic Imaginaries – Istanbul Seminars on Islam, Culture and Politics*, ed. Seyla Benhabib and Volker Kaul, 111–124. Basel: Springer.

Hashemi, Nader. 2016. Rethinking Religion and Political Legitimacy Across the Islam-West Divide. In *Toward New Democratic Imaginaries – Istanbul Seminars on Islam, Culture and Politics*, ed. Seyla Benhabib and Volker Kaul, 161–169. Basel: Springer.

Kaul, Volker, and Ingrid Salvatore. 2020. *What is Pluralism?* New York/London: Routledge.

Walzer, Michael. 2015a. *The Paradox of Liberation: Secular Revolutions and Religious Counterrevolutions*. New Haven/London: Yale University Press.

———. 2015b. Islamism and the Left: An Exchange between Andrew F. March and Michael Walzer. In *Dissent* (online only). Winter 2015. Downloaded at https://www.dissentmagazine.org/article/islamism-and-left-exchange.

Part III
Identity Politics

Chapter 11
Populism

Abstract We can distinguish between three approaches on how to deal with populism: exclusion and isolation; conscious ignorance; and instrumentalization. Jan-Werner Müller's analysis of populism points in the direction of the first approach, which is generally adopted by liberals. Social democrats, on the other hand, prefer to ignore populism and rather focus on key social issues. Last but not least, the radical left sees in a certain form of populism a powerful instrument for realizing social claims. The aim of this paper is to review the different approaches to populism and to point out their limitations and weaknesses. Whereas left-wing populism risks to be no less nationalistic than right-wing populism, liberalism and social democracy may not address people's true concerns that bolster the populists' ranks. Liberalism does not recognize that people might have needs other than reasons and social democracy has a too-reduced concept of needs that does not take into account questions of identity.

Keywords Populism · Pluralism · Liberalism · Nationalism · Identity · Social democracy · Radical left · Ernesto Laclau

At present, in Western democracies one can identify more or less three approaches on how to deal with populism: exclusion and isolation; conscious ignorance; and instrumentalization. Jan-Werner Müller's analysis of populism points in the direction of the first approach, which is what liberals generally adopt. Social democrats, on the other hand, prefer to ignore populism; they rather focus on key social issues. Moreover, the radical left views in a certain form of populism a powerful instrument for realizing social claims. Ernesto Laclau's theory of populism is representative of this approach.

I assume that all three of these approaches criticize certain totalitarian forms of populism. Even if it is not easy to determine what exactly a totalitarian populism is, one can still say that these three approaches try to avoid the so-called right-wing populism and its extremist and radical identity politics regarding nation, religion, or race.

The following sections examine the three approaches and points out their limitations and weaknesses.

11.1 The Liberal Approach to Populism: Exclusion and Isolation

After the parliamentary election in Germany in 2017 and the clear electoral success of the right-wing populist party Alternative for Germany (AfD), a campaign ran on Facebook where users asked AfD voters to deprive them of friendship. I assume that there were similar campaigns in Austria after the parliamentary election in October 2017 and the even more pronounced success of the Freedom Party of Austria (FPÖ). Of course, communication in social networks is often instinctive, reflexive, spontaneous, and quite informal, but it says something about our basic attitudes.

And these state that whatever may be the explanation of populism—and it is doubtful whether there can be any explanation for it at all—there can be in any case no justification for it. This is also the thesis of Müller's influential treatise on populism. Müller makes clear that explanatory factors may be a sufficient, but by no means a necessary condition for populism. Müller discusses two explanatory patterns of populism: class struggle and socio-psychological factors, such as fear, frustration, anger, and resentment. While it is undeniable that in particular lower-income and low-educated classes are running over to the populists, Karin Priester, according to Müller, has shown in her recent research on populism[1] that upper classes are equally attracted to the populist selfish worldviews. Populist parties have grown into true people's parties, especially in Austria and France.

Also social-psychological explanations are, in Müller's view, not sufficient. Emotions are not 'just' emotions: they are based upon certain ideas and beliefs. There are *reasons* for emotions, and the reasons that populists bring forth are not justified. The social envy of the lower strata, in the sense of the notion of *ressentiment* theorized by Nietzsche, makes a self-determined lifestyle impossible. And even the impression that the country has been removed from the control of the citizens, does not correspond to the facts. Müller, therefore, concludes that socio-psychological approaches 'conflate the content of a set of political beliefs with the socioeconomic positions and psychological states of its supporters'.[2] Paradoxically, policies based on social-psychological theories and oriented towards prevention of

---

[1] Müller, *What Is Populism?* p. 31.
[2] Müller, *What Is Populism?* p. 36.

11.1 The Liberal Approach to Populism: Exclusion and Isolation

anxiety can only confirm the impression that the proclaimed 'people' of the populists always had: namely, that the elites are indeed out of touch with the country, since they simply do not take seriously the common man and his views. And that is why they lack any democratic legitimacy.

Müller's understanding of populism therefore goes in a completely different direction: 'The core claim of populism is thus a moralized form of antipluralism.'[3] Populists do not simply express needs, whether justified or not. Populists have 'a particular *moralistic imagination of politics*',[4] according to which the nation has an essential moral identity that only they represent and defend. The nationalism of the populists is not further reducible, but an autonomous product of the imaginary of the populists.

That is, if we want to refute populism we must take its claims and ideas seriously, and not simply ignore them and dismiss them as trivial. We have to deal with populism at the level of ideas and show that nationalism in itself is not justified, because it does not take into account the pluralism of modern societies. Müller refers here to the strategy of John Rawls as expounded in *Political Liberalism*. We have the political obligation to accept reasonable forms of pluralism in our societies, because within a certain range pluralism itself is the result of the use of our reason. Müller's proposal for dealing with populism is therefore not the total exclusion and vilification, as it regularly takes place in France with regard to the National Front, now known as National Rally. His advice is to seek confrontation, that is, discussion, intellectual exchange, and so on, with populism within the deliberative structures of our democracy and demonstrate, point by point, the limits of the populist discourse.

But the bottom line here is not whether we follow the Republican model of exclusion or the deliberative model of inclusion. Republicanism, discourse ethics, as well as liberalism repeatedly lead with regard to populism to the same result, namely, the principled and categorical rejection of the populist argument and which of course has as a consequence the de-facto exclusion of the populists. Each of these three political models is based on universalization claims that no populist argument can ever fulfil. On the contrary, populism is based on a particularistic view of the world, that of nationalism. Müller is well aware that pure argumentation will most likely not convince populists.[5] And what happens then? Does Müller have another way out than portraying populists as unreasonable simpletons? The result of such a categorical exclusion is clearly fatal for any democracy and pours more oil into fire. In this respect I fully agree with Müller.

---

[3] Müller, *What Is Populism?* p. 42.
[4] Müller, *What Is Populism?* p. 41; italics in the original.
[5] Müller, *What Is Populism?* p. 158.

11.2 The Socialist Approach to Populism

The socialist thesis is that populism is not a problem of values and their justification, but can be explained in a relatively simple way. Socialists claim that populism is the result of social injustice, inequality, and unsatisfied basic needs—no more, no less.

First, it is important to clarify that although the entire left has this thesis in common, it is nevertheless divided over how to deal with populism. Surprising as it may sound, populism has a large following among some of the left—not the so-called right-wing populism à la Le Pen, Wilders, or Orbán, but the left-wing populism of Podemos or Syriza in Europe and Bernie Sanders and Evo Morales in America. Classical social democrats, on the other hand, strongly criticize every form of populism. However, in contrast to liberals, they deny any form of confrontation with the populists, insisting that populism should simply be ignored. The following section briefly shows that a socialist position is incompatible with left-wing populism, and why, nevertheless, social-democratic politics may miss the core of the problem.

11.2.1 The Instrumentalization Thesis

Certain more radical left-wing groups actively and enthusiastically support the global spread of left-wing populism, which they, in contrast to Müller, clearly and sharply differentiate from right-wing populism. While right-wing populism is based on false national myths and chauvinisms, left-wing populism is based solely on social claims. And this is exactly the thesis of Ernesto Laclau in *On Populist Reason*,[6] who, along with Chantal Mouffe,[7] is the mastermind of left-wing populism. According to them, only someone theoretically as naive as Müller could conceptually equate left-wing populism with right-wing populism. And after all, it seems to be quite obvious that populists such as Le Pen and Mélenchon are both politically and culturally on opposite sides.

Laclau insists that unsatisfied social demands can only be expressed in the form of populism. His argument is that unfulfilled social claims necessarily lead to identity politics. In this sense, Laclau fully agrees with Müller that anti-pluralism is the constitutive feature of populism. The big difference is that for Müller anti-pluralism is a pathology of politics, whereas for Laclau the only possible politics is the development of hegemonic claims. But is not Müller right when he equates right-wing populism and left-wing populism? Both are forms of identity politics, and if we fill Laclau's abstract treatise of identity with concrete political content, we see that both right-wing and left-wing populism defend a form of nationalism. Ça va sans dire in the case of right-wing populism, as Trump's slogan 'America first' shows, but also all left-wing populist parties, advocate a protectionist economic policy that clearly

---

[6] Laclau, *On Populist Reason*, p. 73.
[7] Mouffe, *For a Left Populism*.

has national features. Both forms of populism attack free trade agreements and freedom of movement treaties, and the national working class has clear precedence over the workers of other nations.

But Laclau would shake his head in disbelief when trying to equalize left-wing populism with right-wing populism. Do we not recognize the ontologically completely different foundations of the two populisms? Right-wing populists presuppose the nation as *given*. Left populists make it their task to *construct* the people. They do not start from a more or less obscure spirit of the nation, which somehow unites all those who belong to it and from which moral obligations to the nation can be deduced.[8] Left-wing populists assume nothing but certain social claims, that Laclau defines as democratic claims, and construct the nation only on that basis. The nation of right-wing populists has a metaphysical, essential character; the people of the left-wing populists, on the other hand, is entirely contingent depending on the random construction of social claims.

This is not the right place to discuss why unsatisfied social entitlements inevitably have populism as a consequence. I just want to show that the construction of the people on the basis of social claims must presuppose the nation or the people as much as right-wing populism does, and that Müller is right in this respect that both populisms do not express social claims, but national values. And although Laclau's conception of populism is based on the linguistic-philosophical theory of poststructuralism, his basic thesis that social justice is closely related to nationalism is shared by many other socialist thinkers, most notably Michael Walzer and David Miller,[9] and who with respect to the notion of the nation face similar problems as Laclau.

Let us suppose then that, as Laclau claims, different unsatisfied social demands contribute because of a certain political logic to the 'constitution of a global political subject', the people, or the nation. The people, according to Laclau, are then no longer just the composition of individual demands of the population, but establishes itself the identification of the citizens with each other. Laclau goes on to say that 'although the link was originally ancillary to the demands, it now reacts over them and, through an inversion of the relationship, starts behaving as their ground. Without this operation of inversion, there would be no populism.'[10] That is, where hitherto the group was formed by certain similarities of the social claims of the single individuals, it is now the group from which the social demands of the individual are derived and no longer the individuals themselves who produce the demands.

But what is the content of the group (people, nation) that establishes the identity of individuals with each other? Due to the fact that from an ontological point of view there is nothing else than certain social claims that initially form the group, the group can have no other content than the social claims themselves. In this sense, the group identity is constructed without preconditions. According to Laclau a certain

---

[8] For a defence of national obligations, see Sandel, *Justice*.
[9] Walzer, *Spheres of Justice*, and Miller, *On Nationality*.
[10] Laclau, *On Populist Reason*, p. 93.

social claim, 'a singular element', has to transform itself into the nation, since 'we are not dealing with a conceptual operation of finding an abstract common feature underlying all social grievances, but with a performative operation constituting the chain as such'.[11] But in order to do justice to the universal claim of the nation, the singular social claim must give up any particularistic content, so that all other social claims can be absorbed in it. 'The popular identity functions as a tendentially empty signifier'[12] in the sense that it has no special properties. But although, because of the diversity of social claims, the people cannot adopt a positive but only a negative character,[13] they must somehow create an identity and bring the differences into unity. And this happens when a particular social demand achieves 'the positive reverse of a situation experienced as "deficient being"',[14] enabling it to represent and embody the whole—a totality that is clearly 'purely mythical'[15] and therefore always has to remain contestable.

Laclau is more than aware of the tensions between the claim to totality of the people (equivalence) and its inherent difference, and holds in this regard that equivalence and difference are constitutive of each other, while 'neither is entirely able to eliminate the other'.[16] Although the people can weaken the particularisms and level them somewhat out, the reason for its emergence lies precisely in those very particularistic social claims and therefore the people can never completely nullify them.

> If the empty signifier is going to operate as a point of identification for all the links in the chain, it must actually represent them. It cannot become entirely autonomous from them.... Autonomization of the totalizing moment beyond a certain point destroys the 'people' by eliminating the representative character of that totality.[17]

'An equivalence which was total would cease to be equivalence and collapse into mere identity. There would no longer be a chain, but a homogeneous, undifferentiated mass.'[18] On the other hand, however, the empty signifier constitutes this totality, 'thus adding a qualitatively new dimension'.[19]

Laclau vehemently rejects the suspicion that the populism he conceives can take on a totalitarian character, insisting that it is 'the very condition for the construction of a collective will, which, in many cases, can be profoundly democratic'.[20] While it is generally possible that the people takes on an ethnic character, social claims mostly go beyond specific ethnic identities,[21] and 'in contemporary societies we do

---

[11] Laclau, *On Populist Reason*, p. 97.
[12] Laclau, *On Populist Reason*, p. 96.
[13] Laclau, *On Populist Reason*, p. 96.
[14] Laclau, *On Populist Reason*, p. 116.
[15] Laclau, *On Populist Reason*, p. 116.
[16] Laclau, *On Populist Reason*, p. 120.
[17] Laclau, *On Populist Reason*, p. 162.
[18] Laclau, *On Populist Reason*, p. 200.
[19] Laclau, *On Populist Reason*, p. 162.
[20] Laclau, *On Populist Reason*, p. 166.
[21] Laclau, *On Populist Reason*, p. 198.

not have simply juxtaposition of separate cultural ethnic groups; we also have multiple selves, people constituting their identities in a plurality of subject positions'.[22]

However, in my view, the problem of Laclau's theory is not that it cannot *in principle* rule out and prevent identitarian nationalism, be it of ethnic, racist, or religious nature. The real problem is that it presupposes a nationalist identity as much as right-wing populism. Laclau cannot maintain the tension between identity and difference. Either populism is ultimately reducible to social claims, or it is the basis of these claims. We cannot have both, as Laclau would like to.

The moment when the people becomes more than the accumulation of various social demands and assumes this identity-forming character, which can no longer be reduced to the individual demands and, as Laclau writes, 'add[s] a qualitatively new dimension',[23] social demands either become superfluous or are constituted by the people themselves. If populism is to establish an identity between the different social demands, this requires that it disregards individual social demands, which, as we know, have nothing in common, and invokes common values. Otherwise, populism could never establish an identity among individuals.

That the people itself goes back to a hegemonic social claim does not change this fact. In order to become the basis of identification for all other claims, the demand must 'empty itself', to put it in Laclau's words, of its particular social character, and yet still convey content, even if this only implies 'the positive reverse of a situation experienced as "deficient being"'.[24] And Laclau does not quite casually refer to the role of the myth here. What else could justify the myth than the common history of individuals making social demands? In this sense, Laclau's theory cannot do without 'the image of a pre-given totality',[25] be it of ethnic, racial, or religious origin. And it is not by chance that left-wing populists are nationalists whose demands are not exactly of a 'global' or 'universal' dimension, as Laclau would have liked.[26]

11.2.2 The Ignorance Thesis

Ultimately, Müller is right in claiming that both right-wing and left-wing populism refer to an idea of the nation that is given and not constructed, and are in this sense indistinguishable from each other. In addition, Müller is quite right when he concludes that left-wing populism is nothing but 'redundant if the point is simply to offer a credible left-wing alternative or a reinvented Social Democracy'.[27] Populism sets national values, and social demands are entirely dependent on the respective

---

[22] Laclau, *On Populist Reason*, p. 199.
[23] Laclau, *On Populist Reason*, p. 162.
[24] Laclau, *On Populist Reason*, p. 116.
[25] Laclau, *On Populist Reason*, p. 162.
[26] Laclau, *On Populist Reason*, p. 198.
[27] Müller, *What Is Populism?* p. 184.

understanding of national values. Populism makes social claims lose their independent justification and thus their value. Therefore, social entitlements must be expressed only at the level of needs and not in the form of identity.

From this social democrats draw the conclusion that they have to deal exclusively with social demands and not with populism itself. In the eyes of the social democrats, populism is nothing more than a pale shadow of unsatisfied social claims, an 'ideology'. Where populism, according to Laclau, creates new values that no longer have as basis the individual social claims, populism for social democrats is the direct causal consequence of frustrated social demands and can be completely reduced to them. Even if populism pretends to defend its own values and ideas, these are only instrumental and veiled social demands. For this reason, populism as such must be ignored and the social question must continue to form the centre of social democratic politics.

However, social democracy faces the problem that populists, as outlined in Müller's and Laclaus's theories, actually defend the *nation* and not banal claims. From their own point of view, populists are first and foremost concerned with national values and only on this basis with social demands. When Trump wants to suspend free trade agreements to protect the white working class, he does not do so because he believes their social claims are somehow justified. Mexicans are on average still significantly poorer than the poorest Americans. It is the nation that commits us to solidarity.[28] When German AfD supporters scream 'Foreigners out', they first defend the nation and not jobs.

As a result, socialist, institutional approaches not only question our deepest modern self-understanding, according to which self-knowledge is possible only from the first-person perspective, but also the very foundations of democracy. Müller brings this clearly to the point: institutional theories fail 'to take ordinary people at their word, preferring instead to prescribe political therapy as a cure for fearful and resentful citizens'.[29]

While this might be right, it is not a sufficient argument against social democracy. All causal approaches have to deal with the problem of self-knowledge and there is no shortage of proposals in this regard.[30] As Rawls's *A Theory of Justice* shows, social democrats have no problem with democracy as long as the institutional framework is right. The real question is whether populism can actually be traced back to social claims alone.

Take the issue of immigration: it poses real challenges to society that are, at least prima facie, only partly economic in nature. If it is true that in particular the lower classes cannot be indifferent to the costs of immigration, it is nonetheless the identity of the immigrants that raises the most serious questions. Most of the refugees currently entering Europe are from the so-called Muslim-majority countries. As a matter of mere historical accident, Islam has been widely instrumentalized

---

[28] See Sandel, *Justice*.
[29] Müller, *What Is Populism?* p. 184.
[30] Davidson, 'First Person Authority'.

politically in those societies contributing to radicalization processes of Muslim societies. This means that many refugees really have a different, more traditional value system that tends to be alien to the standards of liberal democracies. Accordingly, Europe's fear with regard to questions of integration is more than understandable, in particular against the background of integration failures of the last decades. How are we going to avoid the parallel societies characterizing the first waves of immigration to Europe in the 1960s? How should we go about certain tendencies violating individual rights, in particular those of women? How do we deal with extremist views?

These are all hard issues that social democracy traditionally ignores and tries to avoid. It is all but clear if identity can actually be reduced to the social question. And simply insisting on the fact that identities are hybrid and multiple and do not provide a basis for justification, as liberals use to do, underestimates and tends to ignore problems of culture and religion. We cannot pursue this analysis here any further, but since national identity is at the heart of the populist project, it has become urgent to clarify the nature of identity.

11.3 Conclusion

The aim of this paper has been to review the different approaches to populism that are currently discussed. Whereas left-wing populism risks to be no less nationalistic than right-wing populism, liberalism and social democracy may not address people's true concerns that bolster the populists' ranks. Liberalism does not recognize that people might have needs other than reasons and social democracy most probably has a much reduced concept of needs that does not take into account questions of identity. The question of identity remains central to populism and we have to look for an approach that is able to address it. What is going to be the exact nature of this approach and to what extent it is different from multiculturalism, on the one hand, and nationalism, on the other, is subject to future research.

References

Davidson, Donald. 1984. First Person Authority. *Dialectica* 38 (2–3): 101–111
Laclau, Ernesto. 2005. *On Populist Reason*. London: Verso Books.
Mouffe, Chantal. 2018. *For a Left Populism*. London: Verso Books.
Miller, David. 1995. *On Nationality*. Oxford: Clarendon Press.
Müller, Jan-Werner. 2016. *What is Populism?* Philadelphia: University of Pennsylvania Press.
Sandel, Michael. 2010. *Justice: What's the Right Thing to Do?* New York: Farrar, Straus and Giroux.
Walzer, Michael. 1984. *Spheres of Justice: A Defense of Pluralism and Equality*. New York: Basic Books.

Chapter 12
Postsecularism

Abstract This chapter discusses Jürgen Habermas', Tariq Ramadan's and Michael Walzer's approaches to religion and politics, analyzing in particular the identity politics of the Muslim communities in Europe. All the three thinkers concede religion to play a fundamental role in society and stress the political importance of religion. But how far should religious identity politics go? Habermas and Ramadan, despite their different philosophical backgrounds, fundamentally agree that religious groups, despite their identity claims, have to eventually embrace the principles of liberal democracies from *within* their distinctive religious perspective. Walzer, on the other hand, argues that the state alone can regulate and put a limit on identity politics.

Keywords Jürgen Habermas · Tariq Ramadan · Michael Walzer · Postsecularism · Separation of state and church · Religion · Politics · Modus vivendi · Tolerance · Citizenship · Discourse ethics · Learning processes · Multiculturalism · Politics of identity · Legal pluralism · Postintegration · Koranic literalism · Sharia · European Islam

In contemporary political philosophy, Jürgen Habermas, Tariq Ramadan and Michael Walzer most prominently intervened on the relationship between politics and religion and introduced a trend that has come to be known as postsecularism. I will summarize here their accounts of postsecularism and make their positions critically engage with each other.

The point of departure of the debate on postsecularism is the fact or at least the general perception of a strong revival of religions and religious feelings in contemporary Western societies and in particular among the new Muslim citizens of recent immigration. New religious claims, social and cultural conflicts as well as serious problems of integration brought us to the question if we not have to overhaul our deepest convictions about the relationship between state, politics and religion. These initial political observations and sociological analyses of our societies in terms of postsecularism resulted soon in reflections on the philosophical foundations of our political order, and it is from this angle that Habermas, Ramadan and Walzer made their points in the current debate on religion and politics. In their respective proposals, they were concerned with both the answer Western liberal democracies should give to the religious challenge and the form religious reactions should take in the liberal democratic context.

Habermas, Ramadan and Walzer stress the political importance of religion and quite agree about secularism and where to draw the line between politics and religion in the postsecular context of liberal democracies. Yet, they disagree about the moral and political conditions necessary to make this line to be accepted and respected. This is due to the fact that they differ in their philosophical understanding of politics.

At first, it strikes surprising that philosophers should engage with the current postsecular political context as a proper philosophical challenge. Shouldn't philosophers ask questions that are independent from space and time? Shouldn't they leave behind the here and now of political turmoil and reason about the relationship of state and religion in general, context-free terms? In short, shouldn't philosophers try to provide universal answers to fundamental questions that go beyond the particular age they live in? It is the historical approach to political philosophy of the respective authors which gives postsecularism its particular philosophical relevance. Universal principles have to be reiterated and grounded historically; they cannot be abstracted from history, but must be situated in the congestions of history. However, Habermas, Ramadan and Walzer disagree about what type of universalism has to be anchored in history and consequently have to approach social reality from different angles and theoretical perspectives.

For Habermas, liberal democracy has a universal foundation; according to Ramadan, only the precepts of Islam have universal status; and Walzer retains a very minimal form of tolerance to be of universal value. How can these different universal values be enacted historically? Habermas roots the principles of liberal democracy in the formation of political communities, Ramadan contextualizes the universalism of Islam and Walzer locates the possibility of mutual respect in political regimes of toleration. Accordingly varies the formulation of their postsecular questions. Habermas asks "how we [should] see ourselves as members of a postsecular society and what [we] must reciprocally expect from one another in order to ensure that in firmly entrenched nation states, social relations remain civil despite the growth of a plurality of cultures and religious worldviews."[1] Ramadan wants to

---

[1] Quotations are from a paper Jürgen Habermas presented at Istanbul Seminars 2008. It was first published in German as "Die Dialektik der Säkularisierung," in *Blätter für deutsche und internationale Politik* 4, 2008, pp. 33–46. Page references here in the text refer to the German article, whereas quotations are taken from the English version Habermas read out in Istanbul and which is published online under the title "A 'post-secular' society – what does that mean?," in *Reset DOC*, https://www.resetdoc.org/story/a-post-secular-society-what-does-that-mean/ (accessed: January 27, 2020). The above quotation is from page 39.

know how Islam can become a Western religion.[2] And the question Walzer sets out himself to answer is "how liberal democrats [should] accommodate orthodox religions (...), and what the limits of (...) accommodation [are]."[3]

It is clear that these questions must lead to different answers of how to deal with religion in politics. Whereas Habermas and Ramadan are concerned with the political integration of religion in civil society and leave it essentially to the democratic and deliberative process of will formation to draw the precise lines between politics and religion,[4] Walzer defends the liberal democratic state as a bulwark against the domination by religions and a political space with civic character that "forces the groups to tolerate (or to act as if they tolerate) one another."[5] Where Habermas and Ramadan want to go beyond a mere *modus vivendi* and require citizens to recognize each other as political equals, Walzer explicitly rejects anything more than a *modus vivendi*. First believe in the possibility of an internal reform of orthodox religions that makes it possible for religious citizens to accept liberal democratic principles, latter thinks that only external forces such as the coercive power of the liberal state and state education can contribute to more liberal forms of religions.

Despite the obvious philosophical differences between Habermas and Ramadan, they come more or less to the same conclusions concerning politics in the postsecular age, yet Walzer stands in a certain opposition to both of them. In what follows, I will point out the respective conceptions of postsecular political justice and political solutions to postsecularism.

But what exactly is postsecularism? Habermas provides a sociological theory of postsecularism. According to him, the postsecular society is not a matter of objective social reality, but of public perception and individual subjectivity. The traditional secularization hypothesis states a close linkage between the modernization of society and the secularization of the population. If this causality still holds in our contemporary societies, it does not imply that "religion loses influence and relevance either in the political arena and the culture of a society or in the personal conduct of life."[6] Religions retain public importance in societies that are largely secularized. Therefore "the description of modern societies as 'postsecular' refers to a change in consciousness" that Habermas attributes to the perception of global

---

[2] I rely on my notes and an audio recording of Tariq Ramadan's lecture "European Muslims and the Postintegration Process" at Istanbul Seminars 2009, June 2. In addition, I relate to his monograph *Islam e libertà*, Einaudi, Turin 2008 (French: *Face à nos peurs. Le choix de la confiance*, Tawhid, Lyon 2008), in which he summarizes his political thought and extends the idea of post-integration. The translation of the quotes is mine.

[3] This quotation of Michael Walzer is taken from an unpublished transcription of his intervention at the roundtable "Rethinking Secularism across the Islam-West Divide" at Istanbul Seminars 2009, June 3. In my summary of Walzer's position on state and religion, I also relate to his "Drawing the Line: Religion and Politics," in M. Walzer, *Thinking Politically*, edited by David Miller, Yale University Press, New Haven & London 2007.

[4] J. Habermas, "Dialektik der Säkularisierung,"op. cit., pp. 40–41.

[5] M. Walzer, "Drawing the Line: Religion and Politics," in M. Walzer, *Thinking Politically*, op. cit., p. 160.

[6] J. Habermas, "Dialektik der Säkularisierung,"op. cit., p. 36.

conflicts hinging on religious strife, the increasing need of orientation in pluralist societies and the formation of multicultural postcolonial immigrant societies.[7]

Why does this renewed politicality of religions rock the foundations of political justice? In the analysis of Habermas, postsecularism compromises the historically grown political communities of Western societies. Postsecularism challenges the self-understanding of these political communities. As long as societies were secularized and political communities had a secular identity, citizens could recognize each other as "member[s] of an inclusive community of citizens with equal rights."[8] Citizens shared a common political identity that provided the basis of political equality and equal citizenship. Postsecularism complicates considerably the mutual identification among citizens.

Habermas criticizes the political theories of secularism and multiculturalism as being inadequate in our postecular times. Secularism bans religion from the public sphere and pushes it back to the private domain. On the contrary, multiculturalism opens the public sphere to the 'politics of identity' and defends legal pluralism and collective cultural rights. However, both foreclose the possibility of an inclusive postsecular political community and distort the balance between shared citizenship and cultural difference.[9]

But why is inclusiveness of the political community and construction of a political identity so important and the great challenge of postsecularism? According to Habermas, a liberal democratic state is not only an association of individuals with rights and obligations, but is essentially based upon an inclusive political community and political culture.[10] It would be wrong to consider a liberal democracy a political formation without shared citizenship and a common political identity, a political model where "the opposing subcultures (…) each nest (…) in niches of their own and subsequently remain (…) foreign *to one another in society*."[11] This *modus vivendi* not only proved historically to be insufficient, but is also politically unstable: The "constitutional state is only able to guarantee its citizens equal freedom of religion under the proviso that they no longer barricade themselves within their religious communities and seal themselves off from one another."[12] Citizens are expected to tolerate each other, although they consider certain worldviews and habits of their fellow citizens wrong and do not like them. And communities are expected not to impede their members to develop plural affiliations and assume the identity of the political community next to the particular communitarian identity.

How is it possible that citizens of a liberal democratic state tolerate and mutually recognize each other as political equals, "concede one another the right to those

---

[7] Ibid., pp. 36–37.
[8] Ibid., p. 40.
[9] Ibid., pp. 41–44.
[10] Ibid., 40.
[11] Ibid., p. 39.
[12] Ibid..

convictions, practices and ways of living that they themselves reject"[13] and that communities cede the monopoly of political and social power over their members? This is the postsecular question reformulated in a political context that is characterized by the reciprocal closure of present Western political communities to foreign minority communities and religious subcultures to a state which does not belong to them.

Habermas gives it a threefold answer. "[In the] constitutional state (...) all subcultures, whether religious or not, are expected to free their individual members from their embrace so that these citizens can *mutually* recognize one another in civil society as members of *one and the same* political community. As democratic citizens they give themselves laws which grant them the right, as private citizens, to preserve their identity in the context of their own particular culture and worldview."[14] The institutional design of liberal democracies facilitates the development of a political community of equals, in which citizens tolerate and recognize each other not despite but precisely because of who they are: "The universalist project of the political Enlightenment by no means contradicts the particularist sensibilities of a correctly conceived multiculturalism."[15] The respect for religious particularities enhances the liberal and democratic transformation of communities.

But of course, "'tolerance' is (...) not only a question of enacting and applying laws; it must be practiced in everyday life."[16] "Because a democratic order cannot simply be *imposed* on its authors, the constitutional state confronts its citizens with the demanding expectations of an ethics of citizenship that reaches beyond mere obedience to the law."[17] "A change in mentality cannot be prescribed, nor can it be politically manipulated or pushed through by law; it is at best the result of a learning process."[18] And "learning processes can be fostered, but not morally or legally stipulated."[19] The normative expectations that rule an inclusive civil society require a complementary learning process on the religious but also on the secular side: "(...) Secular citizens in civil society and the political public sphere must be able to meet their religious fellow citizens as equals"[20] and avoid to "adopt a polemical stance toward religious doctrines that maintain a public influence despite the fact that their claims cannot be scientifically justified."[21]

An ethics of citizenship and learning processes help to shape the political community of postsecular liberal democracies. Yet, in case of religious citizens a mere ethics of citizenship might not do the whole work. What happens if one's religious

---

[13] Ibid., p. 40.
[14] Ibid., p. 39.
[15] Ibid.
[16] Ibid., p. 40.
[17] Ibid., p. 44.
[18] Ibid., p. 45.
[19] Ibid.
[20] Ibid., p. 46.
[21] Ibid., p. 44.

norms contradict the ethics of toleration and individual rights, what happens in case of a conflict of conscience? Can a pious Muslim accept nakedness in public or Muslim women unveiled? Habermas' solution to this problem is identitarian and religious in nature: "Religious citizens and communities (...) are expected to appropriate the secular legitimation of constitutional principles under the premises of their own faith. (...) It is the religious communities that will themselves decide whether they can recognize in a reformed faith [compatible with liberalism] their 'true faith.'"[22]

In conclusion, the success of liberal democracies depends in the Habermasian conception partly on the religions themselves and their metaphysical worldviews. As long as religions do not accept the liberal democratic order to be in accordance with their own creed and adjust only superficially to the constitutional order, liberal democracies lack a normative foundation which is essential to their very conception. And we "would revert to the level of a mere *modus vivendi* – and would thus relinquish the very basis of mutual recognition which is constitutive for shared citizenship."[23]

Yet, do all religions have such a liberal core which allows the toleration of dissenters? Is Islam compatible with the principles of liberal democracies, just to mention the currently most explosive question in Western democracies? Habermas truly believes that this is the case, writing that "the insight is also growing in the Islamic world that today an historical-hermeneutic approach to the Koran's doctrine is required."[24]

Tariq Ramadan has constructed his life project around the question of the reconcilability of Islam and Western liberalism. How can Muslims accept a country in which the religious morality is in fact not respected? Are Western countries not the "house of war" (dar al-harb), in which Muslims are in minority and only legally tolerated before they can return to the "house of Islam" (dar al-islam)? Ramadan engages on the level of Islamic theology and law in order to provide Muslims with a foundation of their faith that allows them to develop an authentic sense of belonging and to fully integrate in Europe and the West.

As a theologian, Ramadan has no doubts about the universal dimension of Islam.[25] However, "shari'a is not a 'system' nor a 'closed body of laws,' but the 'path of faithfulness towards the objectives of Islam' (protection of life, dignity, justice, equality, peace, nature, etc.)."[26] Insofar as the legislation of Western democracies corresponds to those norms of shari'a, Ramadan claims that "they are [*his*] *shari'a* applied in [*his*] society, even though latter is not of Muslim majority."[27] As a consequence, Europe is not the "house of war", but the "house of testimony" (dar

---

[22] Ibid., pp. 44–45.
[23] Ibid., p. 46.
[24] Ibid., p. 44.
[25] T. Ramadan, *Islam e Libertà*, op. cit., p. 79.
[26] Ibid., p. 87.
[27] Ibid., pp. 87–88.

ash-shahada).²⁸ A well-understood Islam does not stand in opposition to Western liberal democracies.

Ramadan pleads for an acculturated conception of Islam – a European Islam –, that distinguishes between the spiritual and cultural community. There is one religious Islam, but various cultures of Islam such as the African, Arabic, Asian and now European Islam. In Islam "the fundamental principles ('acquida) and ritual practices ('ibadat) do not change, but it is important to engage in critical reading and reasoning (ijtihad) in order to adapt religious observance to the mutations and diversities of the social contexts. (…) Faithfulness does not subsist without evolution."²⁹ "The so-called European Islam is an Islam that respects the creed, practices and common principles while appropriating the diverse Occidental and European cultures."³⁰

Yet, isn't a European Islam a far-fetched dream contrasted by the actual cultural isolation of Muslim communities and Koranic literalism among theologians who refuse a contextualized reading of Islam? Ramadan's answer is a clear 'No:' Muslim citizens have no longer identitarian and religious problems with European societies. Ramadan affirms that Islam is a Western religion, a religion of the West; Muslims respect the law, adopt the nationality and participate in the social, political and cultural life of their host countries. The majority of Muslims feels at home in the West and is loyal to their new countries. European Muslims already live with the multiple identities of their religious, cultural and political community and do not feel constrained to choose among them. "Some still make traditionalist discourses, but in practice the major part of the 'ulama, leaders and common Muslims admit explicitly, or in silence, that the new European context has to be taken into account and adequate solutions has to be found to face the new challenges."³¹

It is only in the perception of long-time European citizens that Muslims continue to live in isolated communities and parallel societies and are unwilling to enter in a common political community. The true obstacle to the realization of political justice is the non-recognition of Muslims as political equals in their religious particularity. Ramadan's political conception of postsecularism is therefore very akin to that of Habermas: "Public consciousness in Europe (…) still has to adjust itself to the continued existence of religious communities."³² His political solution is likewise the inclusive political community, which needs to be achieved in a so called two-way process (what Habermas calls a complementary learning process), which involves both old and new citizens in Europe. This process will lead to a new sense and narrative of the 'We,' that supplements the formal legal dimension of citizenship and adds the ethical concept of recognition to it. In this regard, Ramadan contrasts the idea of postintegration with the traditional concept of linguistic, social, legal, cul-

---

²⁸ Ibid., p. 78.
²⁹ Ibid., p. 73.
³⁰ Ibid., p. 67.
³¹ Ibid., p. 72.
³² J. Habermas, „Dialektik der Säkularisierung,"op. cit., p. 36.

tural and religious integration. The notion of postintegration stands for the creation of a common political identity which replaces the "perception of two separate entities – 'we' and 'them' –, of a society that 'receives' and of citizens being still a bit 'immigrant by origin,' which are to be 'received.'"³³

As Habermas, Ramadan insists on the concept of equal citizenship and refuses legal parallel systems and specific laws for Muslims in the domains of education and civil law. Instead, he pleads for a common legal system and the equal treatment of Muslims.³⁴ Existing laws should not be changed in order to discriminate Muslims, as this was the case with the headscarf ban in state schools in France, nor should they be interpreted against legally legitimate claims of Muslims, such as the demand to build mosques visible from afar. According to Ramadan, "the separation between church and state does not aim at the disappearance of religions, but at their coexistence as equals in a plural (and more or less neutral) public space."³⁵ European secularization and laicism are historically compatible with the public engagement and visibility of religions.

Despite undeniable affinities concerning integration policies in general, Ramadan's position on secularism appears more ambiguous and different from that of Habermas. Habermas states clearly that "in a constitutional state, all norms that can be legally implemented must be formulated and *publicly justified* in a language that all the citizens understand. (…) The 'separation of church and state' calls for a filter between these two spheres – a filter through which only 'translated,' i.e., secular, contributions may pass from the confused din of voices in the public sphere into the formal agendas of state institutions."³⁶ Habermas' conception of secularism is based upon the inalienable constitutional principles of liberal rule of law and democracy, which exclude that "the government could become the executive arm of a religious majority that imposes its will on the opposition."³⁷ Ramadan has no such independent commitment to liberal democracy, at least insofar as he argues philosophically and politically from within Islamic theology and jurisprudence. Therefore we cannot avoid to ask him if the neutrality of the state is a principle firmly grounded in the Koran, or if in Islam the legitimacy of the neutral state is a matter of political convenience depending upon Muslims actually being in minority? Is liberalism constitutive of Islam or is a liberal Islam a provisional political and cultural compromise for European Muslims?³⁸

Should Ramadan opt for a more Machiavellian interpretation of liberal democracy, he would rather come closer to Michael Walzer's than Habermas' position,

---

³³ T. Ramadan, *Islam e Libertà*, op. cit., p. 100.

³⁴ Ibid., p. 80.

³⁵ Ibid., p. 54.

³⁶ J. Habermas, „Dialektik der Säkularisierung,"op. cit., p. 45.

³⁷ Ibid..

³⁸ In this regard, Ramadan writes that "European Muslims have understood that secularization and laicism (…) guarantee religious pluralism and protect their rights" (ibid., p. 79), which leaves the interpretation open in both directions.

although Walzer certainly refuses on principle the creation of an Islamic Republic.[39] But Walzer believes "that there is an essential conflict between all orthodox religions and liberal democratic politics."[40] Contrary to Habermas and the Ramadan of the theory of postintegration, Walzer rejects the moral talk of civic ethics, recognition and learning processes that could attenuate that conflict; for the simple reason that "religious absolutism is one possible democratic political language."[41] In fact, religion provides effective reasons for participation in the political process, is a source of political excitement and "engages people in a politics of large causes."[42] Moreover, "religion (…) is an associative force that can serve, and has served historically, to strengthen moral solidarity and political attachment"[43] and might underlie the creation of strong welfare institutions. In short, orthodox religions have their own moral justification in a democracy.[44]

Islamic "protagonists have exactly the same right to join the competition, to mobilize their followers, to appeal to their passions and convictions"[45] as other citizens and communities have. Democratic society is an antagonistic field of opposing groups and forces that legitimately seek political victory appealing to religious ideas and "mobiliz[ing] whatever passion they can mobilize."[46] "Democratic politics can and should be permissive in this regard;"[47] the imperative of inclusiveness might risk to turn politics in a "prosaic, spiritless affair, (…) sophisticated, cautious and pragmatic in its style" and deprive it of "significant and sustained popular participation." Latter can only be motivated by "a vision of the good life and the good society"[48] – "tension is a good thing, natural to any democratic society."[49]

Yet, doesn't a liberal democracy deprive itself of its own foundation under these very premises? What happens if some religious group becomes stronger than others? Do we have to accept a Torah state or holy commonwealth? For Walzer, this is not a political option, since any attempt of religions to use state power to establish and guarantee the permanence of their political rule would be inconsistent with certain minimal conditions for peaceful coexistence. Therefore politics and the coercive use of the state have to be strictly separated and protected from religions. The political limits to religions "are not set by the abstract principle of separation

---

[39] M. Walzer, "Drawing the Line: Religion and Politics," op. cit., p. 159.

[40] M. Walzer, *Roundtable Intervention at Istanbul Seminars 2009*, op. cit..

[41] M. Walzer, "Drawing the Line: Religion and Politics," op. cit., p. 155.

[42] Ibid. p. 156. See also pp. 153–156.

[43] Ibid., p. 157.

[44] Also Habermas sustains that religion provides "scarce resources for the generation of meanings and the shaping of identities" (J. Habermas, „Dialektik der Säkularisierung,"op. cit., p. 46). Yet, his theory of democracy does not justify religious fundamentalism.

[45] M. Walzer, "Drawing the Line: Religion and Politics," op. cit., p. 160.

[46] Ibid., p. 163.

[47] Ibid..

[48] Ibid., p. 153.

[49] Ibid., p. 164.

but by the concrete needs of the regime of toleration."[50] However, all that the separation between state and church requires is that "the engaged citizens, religious and secular, be prevented *in exactly the same way* from achieving anything than total victory."[51] The public space is not a neutral ground, but a civil or secular space that has to be guarded against finality.

How can we assure that politics and religion remain separated in this minimal sense? How can we avoid that orthodox religions capture the liberal-democratic state,[52] if they legitimately can and maybe should try to do so? Walzer's clear answer is that the state has to engage itself in a conflict or battle with religions in its own defense, when the separationist lines are challenged. Obviously this is a risky strategy, but "separationists will also struggle to reduce them, to limit the political effectiveness of zealotry by strengthening the intellectual and institutional bulwarks of a democratic culture."[53]

The liberal democratic state "can and do[es] use coercive power to sustain this politics and to reproduce the political culture upon which it depends: this is the point of public education."[54] And Walzer hopes that a liberal education focusing on the meaning and values of democratic self-determination will radically transform orthodox communities: "Orthodox believers can challenge democratic values and practices, ideologically or theologically, but they can't protect their children from the transforming effects of an egalitarian, secular, and liberal education." In conclusion, Walzer affirms that "democratic states should work to liberalize and democratize the religious and ethnic groups that live inside the state, and they can use their coercive power to do that – though always within liberal or constitutional limitations on the use of coercion."

Liberal politics or state neutrality is not supposed to be voluntarily accepted by all citizens, but has to be either imposed or make itself accepted exercising external force upon the citizens' personal identities and changing externally their subjective motivational sets. "Democratic politics (...) modifie[s] the force of religious (...) commitments and so open[s] the way for a politics that begins in passion but ends in compromise."[55] Walzer and Habermas come here to a similar conclusion, though for quite opposite reasons; even if in Habermas' postsecular theory itself it is unclear if at the end of the day fundamentalist religious citizens not have to be forced as well

---

[50] Ibid., p. 161.

[51] Ibid., p. 160.

[52] Liberal democracies are not the only political regime of toleration (Michael Walzer, *On Toleration*, Yale University Press, New Haven & London 1997), but the one in which postsecularism has to be confronted in Western societies today.

[53] M. Walzer, "Drawing the Line: Religion and Politics," op. cit., p. 152.

[54] All quotes in this paragraph from M. Walzer, *Roundtable Intervention at Istanbul Seminars 2009*, op. cit..

[55] M. Walzer, "Drawing the Line: Religion and Politics," op. cit., p. 164.

to give in and the justification of liberalism can be really independent of external reasons and rely entirely on the citizens' internal reasons.[56]

Paradoxically, Walzer, who grants religious identities to play a much greater role in politics, ends up in the here and now of Western societies with a very resolute and uncompromising theory of postsecularism little sensitive to communitarian particularities. This might be the result of conceiving state-society relations in terms of war that needs to have the state or politics as winner – although the victory will always be only temporary, "peace-for-the-moment."[57]

We have seen different conceptions of the relationship between politics and religion. For various reasons, all three philosophers agree if not upon a principled separation of state and church then at least upon a principled separation of coercive state power from religious ideology and exclude on principle the imposition of one religion over others through state power (although a question mark hangs over Ramadan's position). All three are however very sensitive to postsecularism and its political challenge and defend therefore a very soft version of secularism. Religions are certainly not to be banned from the public sphere. Habermas, Ramadan and Walzer steer between the Scylla of religious totalitarianism and the Charybdis of ideological laicism. Habermas and Ramadan propose civil society as the solution to postsecularism; Walzer tackles postsecularism with the instruments of pure politics.

In conclusion, we can say that where Habermas and Ramadan think the postsecular society, Walzer conceives postsecular politics.

References

Habermas, Jürgen. 2008a. A 'Post-Secular' Society – What does that Mean? *Reset DOC*, https://www.resetdoc.org/story/a-post-secular-society-what-does-that-mean/. Accessed 27 Jan 2020.
———. 2008b. Die Dialektik der Säkularisierung. *Blätter für deutsche und internationale Politik*. 4: 33–46.
Ramadan, Tariq. 2008. *Islam e libertà*. Turin: Einaudi.
Walzer, Michael. 1997. *On Toleration*. New Haven/London: Yale University Press.
———. 2007. In *Thinking Politically*, ed. David Miller. New Haven/London: Yale University Press.
Williams, Bernard. 1982. *Moral Luck*. Cambridge: Cambridge University Press.

---

[56] I refer here to the discussion of Bernard Williams, "Internal and External Reasons," in B. Williams, *Moral Luck*, Cambridge University Press, Cambridge 1982, pp. 101–114. In the external reason statement the truth of the sentence "A has a reason to φ" does not depend upon the agent's actual motivations and commitments; it is no contradiction to say that the agent has a reason for action, even though she has no motive or disposition whatsoever to act upon that very reason. The contrary is true of internal reason statements.
[57] M. Walzer, "Drawing the Line: Religion and Politics," op. cit., p. 164.

Chapter 13
Postcolonialism

Abstract Most of contemporary postcolonial philosophers believe postcolonial self-constitution to be 'multiple' or 'hybrid'. Aim of this chapter is to refute the postmodern strains in postcolonial studies and to show that, on the contrary, postcolonial self-constitution is centered around strong identities. Analyzing postcolonial self-constitution in terms of identitarian hybridity is wrong, insofar as this incorrectly ignores the fundamental evaluative aspects of agency in self-constitution. It is the confrontation with and the rejection of colonialism that can be considered as the source of postcolonial self-constitution. Colonialism was built upon intellectual, cultural and moral differences among races, and in many respects the dignity of persons and their claims for recognition make (post-)colonial self-constitution a matter of strong identity. It are the collective identities of race, ethnicity, religion and nationalism which constitute the postcolonial self. The essay will conclude with the question if strong postcolonial identity can be considered as a foundation of autonomy.

Keywords Postcolonialism · Colonialism · Autonomy · Self-constitution · Identity · Hybridity · Multiple identities · Alterity · Race · Racism · Frantz Fanon · Kwame Anthony Appiah · Homi Bhabha · Gayatri Spivak · Achille Mbembe · Albert Memmi

Most of contemporary postcolonial philosophers believe postcolonial self-constitution to be 'multiple' or 'hybrid'. Aim of this chapter is to refute the postmodern strains in postcolonial studies and to show that, on the contrary, postcolonial self-constitution is centered around strong identities. Analyzing postcolonial self-constitution in terms of identitarian hybridity is wrong, insofar as this incorrectly ignores the fundamental evaluative aspects of agency in self-constitution. It is the confrontation with and the rejection of colonialism that can be considered as the source of postcolonial self-constitution. Colonialism was built upon intellectual, cultural and moral differences among races, and in many respects the dignity of persons and their claims for recognition make (post-)colonial self-constitution a matter of strong identity. It are the collective identities of race, ethnicity, religion and nationalism which constitute the postcolonial self. The essay will conclude with the question if strong postcolonial identity can be considered as a foundation of autonomy.

In this essay I would like to discuss the core issue in postcolonial studies: the conception of *identity*. I want to show why there are many good reasons that postcolonial studies developed around the questions of identity, while maintaining that it is impossible to stipulate postcolonial identity as a postmodern paradigm that celebrates hybridity and multiplicity of identity, and hence a weak conception of identity. On the contrary, I want to argue that if postcolonialism is all about substantial difference,[1] this is due to the fact that postcolonial identity is essentialist and strong. Hence, postcolonial theory must hold a particular strong conception of identity.

Postcolonial studies as such are of very recent development, closely linked to literary criticism and the will in Western academia to give a voice to those people whose cultures and cultural productions have been dominated, subjugated and denied for almost the entire last half of the second Millennium.[2] In fact, literature is widely considered as offering one of the most important ways and spaces to express forms of culture and the emotions, beliefs, concepts and ideas linked to them.[3] *Postcolonialism is first of all about confrontation with and disclosure of any sort of colonialism, whereas colonialism is defined as a deliberate imposition of a way of life by one community on an other community.* Postcolonial studies became defined as "the study of the totality of 'texts' (in the largest sense of 'text') that participate in hegemonizing other cultures and the study of texts that write back to correct or undo Western hegemony."[4] Postcolonialism is about forms of *autonomy* after colonialism.

What I am interested in here is not so much the deconstructive work done by postcolonial theorists to unravel ethnocentrism[5] and all sort of colonial forms of

---

[1] „Nothing is more orthodox in the postcolonial domain than an insistence on the multiple, particular, heterogeneous nature of contexts and subject-positions." P. Hallward, *Absolutely Postcolonial. Writing between the Singular and the Specific*, Manchester University Press, Manchester 2001, p. 21.

[2] R.j.c. Young, *White Mythologies*. Routledge, London 2004, pp. 1–32.

[3] See in particular B. Ashcroft, G. Griffiths, H. Tiffin, *The Empire Writes Back. Theory and Practice in Post-Colonial Literatures*, Routledge, London 1989.

[4] Definition out of G.M. Gugelberger (1994), *Postcolonial Cultural Studies*, in Michael Groden & Martin Kreiswirth (eds.), *The John Hopkins Guide to Literary and Criticism Theory*, John Hopkin University Press, Baltimore (MD), p. 582.

[5] The central question here is how can history be opened up for difference, see R.j.c. Young, *White Mythologies*, Routledge, London 2004 and in particular R. Guha, ed., *Subaltern Studies: Writings on South Asian History and Society*, I-VI, Oxford University Press, New Dehli 1982–1989. Seminal studies on the ethnocentric character of many of our concepts – such as historicism, development, modernity and human rights for example – are the following: D. Chakrabarty, *Provincializing Europe. Postcolonial Thought and Historical Difference*. Princeton University Press, Princeton 2000, on the plurality of the normative horizons specific to our existence;

irrationalities, phobias, compulsions, ignorance and dominance, in short to disclose the contingent arrangement of values and social identifications through colonial categories and representations,⁶ but the way and form confrontation with colonialism or, more precise, (post-)colonial agency is conceived of in postcolonial studies. I do not discuss so much why colonialism is wrong, but how individuals constitute themselves under the (post-)colonial condition. To begin with, *(post-)colonial agency is conceived of in terms of cultural identity in postcolonial theory*. Why?

As D.A. Masolo maintains, it is for good reasons that one of the dominant themes of postcolonial theory is the issue of identity; the justification lies in the very heart of the historical occurrence of colonialism.⁷ And so says Frantz Fanon: the problem of colonization is not only comprised by the intersection of objective and historical conditions, but also by the attitudes men developed facing these conditions.⁸ Colonialism must be seen as a major *condition for self-constitution in the (post-) colonies* which has *implications for the self-constitution of the (post-)colonized*. Identities in the postcolony became constructed or developed as a response to the colonial condition.

The great interrogation in postcolonial theory concerns the question if we have to conceptualize postcolonial identity as weak or as strong. On the one hand, there are postmodern philosophers who maintain that we only can conceive of postcolonial identity in weak terms, on the other hand, there are more 'modern' philosophers who hold that we should consider postcolonial identity in the strongest 'essentialist' expressions. Who is right, and who is wrong?

My proposition is that the postmodern camp gets it wrong, because it gives an unsatisfying account of how self-constitution takes place under the colonial condition. All the talk about postcolonial hybridity, pastiche or bricolage mistakenly ignores the fundamental evaluative aspects of agency, judgments and emotions and misunderstands self-constitution under the colonial condition to be a mechanical and rather ironic act. We have to agree with 'modern' philosophers that we must

---

G.C. Spivak, *A Critique of Post-Colonial Reason: Toward a History of the Vanishing Present*, Harvard University Press, Cambridge, Mass., 1999, on the European cultural presuppositions in philosophical descriptions and prescriptions; H.K. Bhabha, "'Race', Time and the Revision of Modernity", in B. Moore-Gilbert, G. Stanton, W. Maley, eds., *Postcolonial Criticism*, Longman, London/New York 1997, on the insufficient account of the legacies of colonialism in the conceptualization of modernity and postmodernism.

⁶ The most well-known study in this direction is E.W. Said's *Orientalism*, Penguin Books, London 1991, in which he shows how the formation of knowledge and discourses in the West created stereotypes of *the Orient*. R.j.c. Young, *Colonial Desire: Hybridity in Theory, Culture, and Race*, Routledge, London 1995, examines the historical genealogy of terms, such as hybridity, culture, and race. D. Scott, *Refashioning Futures: Criticism after Postcoloniality*, Princeton University Press, Princeton 1999, focuses on uncovering a history of the deep structures of modernity and how these epistemic forms entered into colonial and postcolonial societies.

⁷ D.A. Masolo, "African Philosophy and the Postcolonial. Some Misleading Abstractions about Identity", in E. Eze, ed., *Postcolonial African Philosophy. A Critical Reader*, Blackwell, Oxford 1997, pp. 283–300.

⁸ F. Fanon, "Du prétendu complexe de dépendance du colonisé", in F. Fanon, *Peau noire, masques blancs*, Éditions du Seuil, Paris 1952, p. 68.

conceive postcolonial identity in strong terms, insofar as it is *the confrontation with and the rejection of colonialism* that has decisive implications for postcolonial self-constitution and can be considered its source. It is the *dignity* of persons and their claims for recognition that make (post-)colonial self-constitution a matter of strong identity. My idea is that we must conceptualize postcolonial identity as strong for *empirical reasons*, which are psychological and political. This is not to say that a postcolonial philosopher has to like strong identities or to approve of them. It means only that when she talks of ***postcolonial*** identity, she must talk as a matter of fact about strong identities, insofar as the *post* in postcolonialism signifies the need to see the contemporary condition *as over and against* an anterior set of practices and discourses and not merely as a definition of a chronological moment and geographical space within which something called postcolonialism can occur.[9] The *post* in postcolonialism challenges colonialism and its legitimating narratives in the name of its suffering victims, it is not an ally but an antagonist of postmodernism.[10]

What I would like to demonstrate in this essay is the idea that strong postcolonial identity is the effect of a psychological reaction to colonial humiliations and deprivations. In my view, the 'real' postcolonial question follows as a result of this conclusion and is concerned with the interrogation on the relationship between identity and personal autonomy. Hence, the postcolonial question would be the following: Is a strong postcolonial identity really the source of autonomy?

13.1 Racism and Colonialism

Colonial racism must be considered as a major source of contemporary postcolonial identity issues. We cannot understand such diverse 'identity-laden' situations and events as the riots in the French *banlieues*,[11] the anti-Occidental outbursts in large parts of the Muslim world, the 'color-conscious' impact of the hurricane *Katarina* in New Orleans, Michael Jackson's deliberate change of skin color and the genocide of the Tutsi by the *Hutupower* in Rwanda 1994 without taking into consideration the impact of racial politics on self-constitution during (post-)colonialism.

In order to understand the constitutive character of racial discourses I will first analyze the very concept of race and then see, what economic, political and social practices became justified by racial ideas in the colonies. Next, I will line out the implications for postcolonial self-constitution and discuss with the help of major

---

[9] See on this definition of postcolonialism K.A. Appiah, "The Postcolonial and the Postmodern", in K.A. Appiah, *In my Father's House. Africa in the Philosophy of Culture*. Oxford University Press, Oxford 1992, p. 155.

[10] Ibid., p. 155.

[11] "But in these hours it is in particular inevitable to read a regurgitation of history in the fires of the suburbs: the colonial history of which the young Algerian pyromaniacs are the troubled children or grandchildren." B. Valli, "Come ai tempi dell'Algeria", *la Repubblica*, november 8, 2005, p. 21.

13.1 Racism and Colonialism

postcolonial approaches why postcolonial self-constitution must be centered around strong identities.

The concept of race gained popularity with the discovery of the New World and the economic interests that Europeans had there.[12] Racial classifications are inherently modern[13]; the concept of race stipulated as a scientific truth determined international relations for a long period of modernity. In order to develop all criterial beliefs that characterized the concept of race I will follow the method of K. Anthony Appiah, and I am going to explore the ideas of intellectual elites on racial difference in the period from the eighteenth to the nineteenth century, the high time of colonialism.[14] Most examples treat the question of difference of black people. This is due to the fact that black people were considered the 'lowest' among human beings and so racial ideas ferment the clearest in relation to them. However, since Edward W. Said's "Orientalism" it should be clear that racial classifications were equally applied to all the 'brown' and 'yellow' people.

We might start with an assessment of three accounts by three of the most famous political philosophers. D. Hume: "I am apt to suspect the Negroes to be naturally inferior to the Whites. There scarcely ever was a civilized nation of that complexion, nor even any individual eminent in action or speculation."[15] I. Kant: "This man was

---

[12] "I have no doubt that racial theories grew up, in part, as rationalizations for mistreating blacks, Jews, Chinese, and various others." K.A. Appiah, "Race, Culture and Identity: Misunderstood Connections", in K.A. Appiah, A. Gutmann, *Color Conscious: the Political Morality of Race*, Princeton University Press, Princeton 1998, p. 82. "Racism first develops with colonization." M. Foucault, *Society must be Defended*, Penguin Books, London 2004, p. 257. That the concept of race as a discourse of truth was indeed linked to the form of political power and its interests is very well documented in H. Arendt's *Elemente und Ursprünge totalitärer Herrschaft*, Europäische Verlagsanstalt, Frankfurt a. M. 1958, pp. 193–243, and in particular pp. 246–49. The concept of race turned out to become the main political ideology of the colonizers when the territorial limitation of the European nation-state turned out to impede the continuous expansion of industrial production, economic transactions and financial speculations.

On the relationship between discourses of truth and forms of power in colonialism Arendt makes another extremely interesting remark in form of an analogy: If theories on the end of the world had corresponded as much as ideologies of progress to the political atmosphere of the nineteenth century, theories of de Maistre and Schelling, according to which wild tribes and barbaric peoples are the relics of great civilizations, would have determined the political rationale. Ibid., p. 248.

[13] In a comparison with other historic conceptions of cultural and historical differences between peoples Appiah shows for example that Greeks and Romans accounted for differences as determined by environment and Jews as a matter of the theological consequence of covenants with ancestors. See K.A. Appiah, "The Invention of Africa", in K.A. Appiah, *In my Father's House*, op. cit., pp. 10–12.

[14] I draw here essentially on the method he uses in his essay "Race, Culture and Identity: Misunderstood Connections" in K.A. Appiah, A. Gutmann, *Color Conscious*, op. cit., pp. 41–42 in order to give an account of the historic meaning of a word such as race.

[15] He continues: "No ingenious manufacturers amongst them, no arts, no sciences. On the other hand, the most rude and barbarous amongst the Whites, such as the ancient Germans, the present Tartars, have still something eminent about them...Such a uniform and constant difference could not happen (…) if nature had not made original distinctions betwixt these breeds of men (…)."

black from head to toe, a clear proof that what he said was stupid."[16] Also J.J. Rousseau echoed Hume's argument that blacks were mentally inferior by nature.[17] In short, "in imagination they are dull, tasteless, and anomalous."[18] According to these philosophers there is something inherently characteristic about the group of people of black skin color that puts them apart from other groups of peoples: their intellectual capacities, their faculty to reason is inferior with regard to other groups, whereas the point of reference, it becomes very clear in Hume, is the group of people of white skin color. We have found here the first criterial belief that framed the concept of race: People of different skin color have different *intellectual capacities to reason* and can therefore be classified in a hierarchical scheme. It is famously Kant who in his essay "On the Varieties of the Different Races of Man" draws a hierarchical chart on the different races and arranges them around the stem genus of the white-brunette race. The logical consequence of this belief is that there is no hope that a black person can ever achieve the intellectual status of a white person. The faculty to reason is set in the black group far more inferior than in the white group, no education can make these two groups ever equal in intellectual capacity.

There is another difference of great importance that goes along with skin color that made up the second criterial belief defining the concept of race, the substantial difference in *aesthetics* and *culture*. Blacks are not only of inferior beauty, but "they secret less by the kidnies, and more by the glands of the skin, which gives them a very strong and disagreeable odour."[19] Furthermore, they have no elementary notions of art, music, poetry and 'ethical' religion.[20] The logical consequence of the aesthetic and cultural differences is that people of different skin colors can never participate in the a same community, as the aesthetic differences will impede any form of social interaction and sexual intercourse.

Last but not least, skin color also plays a preponderate role in the different development of *morals*, which constitutes the third criterial belief. A moderate version of this belief: "They are more adventuresome. They are more ardent after their female; but love seems with them to be more an eager desire, than a tender delicate mixture of sentiment and sensation. Their griefs are transient."[21] The moral character of blacks has following properties: bravery, lustfulness, crudeness of feeling and shal-

---

Quoted in E. Eze, Introduction, in his *Postcolonial African Philosophy*, op. cit., p. 7, from D. Hume's essay *Of National Characters*.

[16] Ibid., p. 7.

[17] See J. Comaroff, J.L. Comaroff, *Of Revelation and Revolution, Volume 1: Christianity, Colonialism, and Consciousness in South Africa*, University of Chicago Press, Chicago 1991, p. 88.

[18] T. Jefferson quoted in K.A. Appiah, "Race, Culture, Identity", in K.A. Appiah, A. Gutmann's, *Color Conscious*, op. cit., p. 45.

[19] T. Jefferson quoted ibid., p. 44.

[20] G.W.F. Hegel, *Lectures on the Philosophy of World History. Introduction: Reason in History*, trans. H.B. Nisbet, Cambridge University Press, Cambridge 1975, pp. 173–90.

[21] T. Jefferson quoted in K.A. Appiah, "Race, Culture, Identity", in K.A. Appiah, A. Gutmann's, *Color Conscious*, op. cit. pp. 44–45.

lowness. Orientals are said to be "much given to fulsome flattery, intrigue, cunning" and are "inveterate liars, they are lethargic and suspicious".[22] The radical version of black morality: „The Negro is an example of animal man in all his savagery and lawlessness; (…) to comprehend him correctly, we must abstract from all reverence and morality, and from everything which we call feeling; (…) nothing consonant with humanity is to be found in his character."[23]

In this concept of race it is skin color that divides our human species into groups, and the intellectual, aesthetic, cultural and moral character that is correlated to the color of the skin makes these groups inherently different and mutually exclusive. Given that skin color determines personal characteristics, it is in fact nature, the predetermined, fixed and unchangeable biological constitution that makes one what one is and who one is, that makes up one's *identity*. Now we can define a concept of race: "There are heritable characteristics, possessed by members of our species, which allow us to divide them into a small set of races, in such a way that all the members of these races share certain traits and tendencies with each other that they do not share with members of any other race."[24] Different races live "in a different but thoroughly organized world of their own national, cultural, and epistemological boundaries and principles of internal coherence."[25]

Having outlined the criterial beliefs that shaped the concept of race we can see how the actual practices of *colonialism, economic exploitation* and *slavery* are related to the particular idea of racial identities. As Said argues we do not have to consider these phenomena as an indication of a particular viciousness but rather as an indication how streamlined and effective a general doctrine of cultural and racial essences had become.[26]

Achille Mbembe summarizes colonial racism in the following appropriate drastic words: "As an animal, he/she was even totally alien to me. His/her manner of seeing the world, his/her manner of being, was not mine. In him/her, it was impossible to discern any power of transcendence. Encapsulated in himself or herself, he/she was a bundle of drives, but not of capacities." And Mbembe finally formulates the political consequences: "In such circumstances, the only possible relationship with him/her was one of violence and domination."[27] Given the 'low human development' and 'cruelty of sentiments' among persons of color white men supposed to have a right to enslave colored people and raise income on the latter's person. As physical force was the only value white people could discern, the colored person became a tool at the disposal of the white person. The body of colored person became assimilated to other 'useful' things in the process of production.[28]

---

[22] E.W. Said, *Orientalism*, Penguin Books, London 1991, pp. 38–9.

[23] G.W.F. Hegel, *Lectures on the Philosophy of World History*, op. cit., p. 177.

[24] K.A. Appiah, "The Invention of Africa" in K.A. Appiah, *In my Father's House*, op. cit., p. 13.

[25] E.W. Said, *Orientalism*, op. cit., p. 40.

[26] Ibid., p. 36.

[27] A. Mbembe, *On the Postcolony*, Berkeley University Press, Los Angeles 2001, p. 26.

[28] Ibid, p. 27.

Not only slavery and economic exploitation but also political domination became legitimated by racial differences.[29] Given the superiority of white men in any respect colonization was conceived of as a duty, a civilizing mission relieving the colored populations of the grossest of their failures and bring them the benefits of white men.[30] Summing up all the intellectual, cultural and moral shortcomings colored people were supposed to be deprived of the faculty of self-government and hence prone to be governed by those who could at least educate them in this direction.[31]

It should have become clear by now that colonialism was considered justified *because of* the identity of the colonizeds. Different races became colonized, deprived of their cultures, values and originality, deemed inferior and being removed from their own history on the basis of their intellectual, cultural and moral identities. Identity is central to colonial violence and deprivation. Given that differences in identity are the justification of colonialism, identity must logically play a central role in the confrontation with colonialism.

13.2 Weak Postcolonial Identity

The first argument on the role of identity in the (post-)colony stems from Mbembe's account of "The Aesthetics of Vulgarity" in the postcolony[32]: Given the form of (post-)colonial power, self-constitution must take place around multiple identities. Mbembe's argument does not start from the point that (post-)colonial power is gripped on the identity of the colonizeds, but from the mere character of (post-)colonial power that he describes in terms of "excess of abuse" and "tyranny". Mbembe's fundamental argument is that although (post-)colonial power is tyranni-

---

[29] From 1815 to 1914 direct colonial dominion expanded from about 35 percent of the earth's surface to about 85 percent of it. E.W. Said, *Orientalism*, op. cit., p. 41.

[30] Ibid., p. 33.

[31] That is J.S. Mill's famous justification for colonialism: "For the same reason we may leave out of consideration those backward states of society in which the race itself may be considered as in its nonage. The early difficulties in the way to spontaneous progress are so great that there is seldom any choice of means for overcoming them; and a ruler full of the spirit of improvement is warranted in the use of any expedients that will attain and end perhaps otherwise unattainable. Despotism is a legitimate mode of government in dealing with barbarians, provided the end be their improvement and the means justified by actually effecting that end. Liberty, as a principle, has no application to any state of things anterior to the time when mankind have become capable of being improved by free and equal discussion. Until then, there is nothing for them but implicit obedience to an Akbar or a Charlemagne, if they are so fortunate as to find one." J.S. Mill, *On Liberty*, Penguin Books, London 1974 (1859), p. 69.

[32] See A. Mbembe, "The Aesthetics of Vulgarity" in his *On the Postcolony*, op. cit., pp. 102–141. I will deal here with Mbembe's account of self-constitution in the postcolony. According to Mbembe, there is a great continuity between the colony and the postcolony. "But how does one get from the colony to 'what comes after'? Is there any difference – and, if so, of what sort – between what happened during the colony and 'what comes after'? (…) This is a false question (…) since changing time is however not really possible (….)." pp. 196–197.

cal, postcolonial relations of power must be read beyond the binary categories, such as "resistance vs. passivity, autonomy vs. subjection."[33] (Post-)colonial power is neither resisted nor put up with but continually, if circumspectly, deflated – "people bridle, trick, and (…) toy with power instead of confronting it directly."[34] Multiple identities enable the individual to adhere to the constituted autocratic norms without having to be committed to them and to maintain the possibility of a critical stance towards (post-)colonial norms. According to Mbembe, a multiplication of identity consents to the postcolonizeds the possibility to escape tyranny and deceive autocratic power – "the subject is reaffirming that this power is incontestable – precisely the better to play with it and modify it whenever possible."[35] Multiplication of identities should be read as an individual strategy that allows some sort of freedom in contexts of great constraints. And hence, the postcolony is a "plurality of spheres" in which the postcolonial individual "has had to learn to continuously bargain" and mobilize "not just a single 'identity', but several fluid identities."[36] It is this possibility of assuming multiple identities and engaging in ambiguous and modifiable practices that makes postcolonial relations not only relations of conviviality but also of powerlessness.

Mbembe holds, that the postcolonial condition is such that it requires the individual to multiply its identities. However, it seems that the individual only multiplies its identity, because the (post-)colonial condition does not allow it to be or to live as it would actually would like to live. In Mbembe's framework one could say that the individual has some true identity and some further identities, which it does not endorse at all but mobilizes in order to 'survive' the grips of (post-)colonial power. We can suppose that whenever it deems the possibility, the individual will stop playing 'identity games' and endorse fully the identity it feels committed to. In contrast to what Mbembe says, the postcolonial individual does less internalise the "authoritarian epistemology" than to put up with it bare of other possibilities. If we keep in mind that identity implies *identification with* or a form of commitment and valuation,[37] Mbembe cannot proof that postcolonial self-constitution takes place around multiple identities. What he describes are mere individual strategies of 'muddling through' rather than multiple identities. In fact, Mbembe's account gives us no information at all how the individuals constitute themselves under the postcolonial condition, except for the fact that they develop a talent for play and a sense of fun. We can only imagine that the reason for their laughing is related to their self-understanding. But latter does not become explicit in Mbembe.

---

[33] Ibid, p. 103.

[34] A. Mbembe, "Provisional Notes on the Postcolony", *Public Culture* 5, 1, 1992, p. 22.

[35] A. Mbembe, *On the Postcolony*, op. cit., p. 129.

[36] A. Mbembe, "Provisional Notes on the Postcolony", *Public Culture*, op. cit., p. 5.

[37] See for a definition of identity and identification A. Bilgrami, "Identity and Identification: Philosophical Aspects", *International Encyclopedia of the Social and Behavioral Sciences* (IESBS) 2001, pp. 7148–7154. "A first stab at answering it might be to say that someone identifies with a certain characteristic, if she **values** it."

It is Homi Bhabha who worked out a theory on why the (post-)colonial self-constitution must turn around weak or 'hybrid' identity taking into account aspects of identification and the importance of culture and identity in the arrangements of (post-)colonialism. Bhabha's understanding of identity is based on a *poststructuralist reading of culture*, and how individuals must relate towards or *must identify with* culture from an *external point of view of a third person* and not necessarily from *the internal point of the person itself*. Bhabha locates three conditions for a process of identification: First, to exist means to enter into being through a relationship with 'alterity'. Second, the place of identification is itself a place of division. Third, identification is not the confirmation of a fixed identity but the production of an image of identity and the transformation of the individual through the appropriation of this image.[38] Bhabha develops a new *general* theory to analyze objectively *the ambivalent role culture must play in the self-constitution* and explains then the features and role of identity in postcolonial self-constitution.

Bhabha maintains not only that postcolonial self-constitution is weak, but also, very similar to Mbembe, that it is just the hybridity of (post-)colonial identity that provides a real space for resistance. In fact, due to his constructivist approach the two questions, why (post-)colonial identity is hybrid and weak and why hybrid identity does give rise to an autonomous space in the (post-)colony, come down to one question on how (post-)colonial self-constitution does proceed. Unlike in Mbembe (post-)colonial hybrid identity is not the result of a deliberate choice but of colonial cultural representations and the colonial project. Bhabha derives from a general *necessity of identification* in any cultural context the necessity of representation of the colonized individual in the colonial 'Other place'. Therefore (post-)colonial identity must be logically hybrid and ambivalent.

Before exposing his argument on hybrid self-constitution, Bhabha shows why colonial identifications do not create strong (post-)colonial identities. Bhabha maintains, similar to what we have illustrated in the first part, that the most significant aspect of colonial discourse consists in its ideological construction of Otherness in form of racial and cultural essences. However, the structure of these stereotypes renders the stereotype itself unable in constructing the identity of the colonized, insofar as the stereotype is necessarily a location of ambivalence. The stereotype, even if it is the form through which perception, identification and representation are channeled, must remain always indeterminate and ambiguous, as it has to be confirmed by a diachronic reality that can never really prove the veracity of the stereotype.[39] As the stereotype denies the possibility of the 'differential game', it straitjackets always any option as either/or and faces the problem of representing the individuals in all the significant and psychic relations. The stereotype is fixed to a certain representation and requires total identification. Nonetheless, for that a stereotype persists it needs consent. The positioning of the colonized individual is

---

[38] See H.K. Bhabha, *The Location of Culture*, Routledge, London 1994, pp. 44–45.

[39] H.K. Bhabha, „The Question of the Other: Stereotype, Discrimination and the Discourse of Colonialism" in H. Bhabha, *The Location of Culture*, op. cit., pp. 66–84.

problematic for the stereotype, to the point that the individual must identify itself with a stereotype that is at the same time alienating and potentially offensive to her. The visibility of the racial/ethnic/colonial Other is on the one hand a point of identification ("Look, a Negro") and on the other hand a conflict-laden location, since the objectivity of the stereotype represents the Other but must be simultaneously constituted by this Other. In this sense, the stereotype has no real force in constructing a racial identity of the colonized. Hence, the stereotype cannot be a source for (post-)colonial identity: there is no reason why the colonized should identify with the stereotype and become caught up in their racial identity. In Bhabha's terms, the colonized can always refuse to return the colonizer's gaze.

The point Bhabha makes here is very important. Postcolonial self-constitution is not *determined* by colonial stereotypes and racial categories. Major theorist hold that there is a very close relation between identification and identity, and that social categories determine the way people actually constitute themselves. According to Appiah,

> "once labels are applied to people, ideas about people who fit the label come to have social and psychological effects. In particular, these ideas shape the ways people conceive of themselves and their projects. So the labels operate to mold what we may call identification, the process through which individuals shape their projects – including their plans for their own lives and their conceptions of the good life – by reference to available labels, available identities. (…) It seems right to call this 'identification' because the label plays a role in shaping the way the agent makes decisions about how to conduct a life, in the process of the construction of one's identity."[40]

On this view, we can observe strong racial or ethnic identities in the postcolonies *because of* the racial and ethnic categories introduced by colonialism. This analysis of the reasons for strong postcolonial identities is false, as people just do not have any reasons to identify with insulting stereotypes. In contrast to what Ian Hacking maintains, postcolonial people are not made up by colonial classifications.[41]

If we understood that colonial stereotypes as such do not generate strong identities, we can now pass over to Bhabha's explanation of the hybrid forms of postcolonial self-constitution. If we understand hybridity in terms of 'in-between', why should the colonized identify with aspects of colonial power, if she has no reason, as we have just seen, to identify with colonial stereotypes? For Bhabha, the hybridity of identity does not go back to *evaluative* or *psychological* forms of identification of the colonized, but to the social and political *structures* of colonial identification and governance that delineate the space for (post-)colonial agency. Up to now, we have used the word identification synonymous to some form of valuation or endorsement. However, Bhabha defines identification more general as "to be for an Other",

---

[40] K.A. Appiah, *The Ethics of Identity*, Princeton University Press, Princeton 2005, p. 66.

[41] I. Hacking, "Making up People", in I. Hacking, *Historical Ontology*, Harvard University Press, Cambridge, Mass., 2002; see specifically for the postcolonial context A. Stoler, *Carnal Knowledge and Imperial Power: Race and the Intimate in Colonial Rule*, University of California Press, Berkeley 2002.

and the necessity of "being for an Other" entails the representation of the individual in the "differentiating order of otherness".[42]

Bhabha's argument works like this: There are given structures – colonial identification and governance constitute the "differentiating order of otherness" – which must be considered as the foundation or cornerstone of (post-)colonial self-constitution, and the way the colonizeds are situated in-between colonial identifications and the colonial project of civilizing produces their irreducible hybrid identity, autonomous space and resistance. Bhabha's thesis on hybridity becomes clearer when he shows how the colonized actually *must* 'play' with colonial stereotypes confronting colonialism.

The colonial strategy to consolidate power works by inducing the colonized to imitate the forms and values of the dominant culture. This requires the colonized to cross or shift the Manichean boundaries between colonizers and colonizeds. The colonized gains forms of freedom through taking on a 'white mask' and returning the difference that constitutes the image of colonial identification. That is why Bhabha proposes that in Fanon's "Black Skin, White Masks" colonial identity is ambivalent rather than psychologically and phenemonologically fixed.

The option of multiplication of identity shifts makes colonial individuals an incalculable object that are difficult to place by the colonizers. They trouble and finally suspend the colonial authority, insofar as the colonial strategy of civilizing depends upon a system of differences and requires the colonizeds to remain at least partially different and potentially hostile. Colonial power becomes deferred by 'mimicry' and 'sly civility' of the colonizeds.[43] And hence, colonial power is immanently liable to destabilization through 'identity games' of the colonizeds. As Bhabha suggests, this 'liminal' moment of identification *produces* a subversive strategy, a process of iterative unpicking and relocating.[44]

The important point in Bhabha's theory is that the colonizeds must constitute themselves through interaction with the colonial identification and colonialism without necessarily valuing neither of both.

Bhabha can uphold such a point, only if he rigorously separates identification and generally self-constitution from all evaluative aspects of agency, in particular from judgments and emotions. As a consequence, for Bhabha identification becomes either an 'ironic' act of 'mimicry' and 'sly civility' or a 'mechanic', almost

---

[42] H. Bhabha, *The Location of Culture*, op. cit., p. 45.

[43] We can find two essays in Bhabha entirely dedicated to colonial resistance: „Of Mimicry and Human Beings: the Ambivalence of Colonial Discourse"and "Sly Civility" in H. Bhabha, *The Location of Culture*, op. cit., pp. 85–92 and 93–101. The 'menacing' potential of mimicry and sly civility is constituted by its double perspective, which through the disclosure of the ambivalence of the colonial discourse simultaneously breaks up its authority. Mimicry is also "the name for the strategic reversal of the process of domination…that turns the gaze of the discriminated back upon the eye of power." Bhabha quoted in B. Moore-Gilbert, G. Stanton, W. Maley, eds., *Postcolonial Criticism*, op. cit., p. 35.

[44] H.K. Bhabha, „In a Spirit of Calm Violence", in G. Prakash, ed., *After Colonialism: Imperial Histories and Postcolonial Displacements*, Princeton University Press, Princeton 1995, pp. 326–343.

'automatic' process independent from the will of the individual. In the first interpretation, identification in terms of irony is an act of agency without including however the notion of valuation. In the second interpretation, the social structure, providing the material for identification, constitutes a dialectical moment in an individual's identity, although the individual might never be aware of it. The colonizeds do not value colonialism, however they are objectively *determined* to identify with it, as it happens that they live within a *cultural structure*, and that necessarily demands identification in terms of "being for an Other", whatever this 'Other' might represent. However, excluding the evaluative notion of agency from identification, Bhabha cannot provide an explanation of (post-)colonial self-constitution.

We might say that Bahbha's point on objective features of cultural identity represents an effort to revise the 'illusion of identity' in the colonial context without having any explanatory power though. To say that (post-)colonial identification must be hybrid because of the structural design of the colonial context does not imply that an individual *actually* constitutes herself along these lines. For Bhabha there is no contradiction to say that the colonizeds despised colonialism and equally identified with it. And hence, Bhabha does not explain, but *'deconstructs'* (post-)colonial self-constitution from a *poststructuralist* point of view. In the poststructuralist reading, self-constitution must proceed through appropriation of or 'identification' with cultural signs, which all bear the marks of 'indeterminacy' and 'Otherness'.[45] But in order to **explain** (post-)colonial self-constitution and how it manifests in social practices, we have to take into account the judgments and emotions of the (post-)colonizeds (which by the way make that their civility is 'sly' and not 'authentic') and cannot simply state that they are 'unfounded' or 'unreal' because of their reference to 'underdeterminate' cultural signs.

In my opinion, Bhabha's efforts, to give a plausible explanation of the empirical reasons for which postcolonial self-constitution must be hybrid, is based on a one-sided, barely discursive reading of colonialism which does not take into account the practices of subjugation and exploitation that became justified with the racial discourses. If it is clear that a stereotype can be *refused* in social relations and cannot fix an identity, why can't we ask what were the judgments and emotional reactions of the colonizeds with regards to the violent colonial practice and *violations of values which were taken to be central to the identity of the colonizeds*? We can ask how the colonizeds saw from their *own perspective* the justification of the colonial project and the denial of being equal human beings *in the name of* their identity. It is imaginable that they had something to say on their own destiny as the "Wretched of the Earth" and *proper reasons to resist colonialism*. Even granted the fact that at the origin of the collapse of colonialism were not the reasons for which the colonizeds actually resisted it, but rather some involuntary 'identity games', these reasons nevertheless played a non-negligible role in the way the colonizeds became to understand and constitute themselves.

---

[45] On the quality or features of signs in poststructural theory see R. Barthes, *Empire of Signs*, Hill and Wang, New York 1983.

I hope to have demonstrated that both, Mbembe and Bhabha, misread *empirical* postcolonial self-constitution as multiple or hybrid, because the first does not take into account the evaluative stance in self-constitution and the second wrongly thinks to be able to do without it. An explanation of self-constitution must be closely related to agency and the reasons for which individuals identify with and do certain things. The *evaluative* dimension of *identification with* lacks in Mbembe's and Bhabha's account of (post-)colonial self-constitution.

My thesis is that the colonizeds rejected colonialism in the same manner as the stereotypes, and that the proper reasons for which the colonizeds had to oppose colonialism were rooted in and motivated by their dignity. However, we cannot conclude with Bhabha that the dignity with which colonial stereotypes were rejected contributed to weak (post-)colonial identities. Quite on the contrary, if the dignity of the colonizeds helped *negatively* to reject the stereotypes, it also demanded *positively* for recognition, and hence made (post-)colonial self-constitution turn around rather strong identities. Let us now analyze the relationship between dignity, recognition and (post-)colonial identity.

13.3 Strong Postcolonial Identity

The history of anti-colonial grass-root movements shows that the largest part of the colonizeds lived with the impression of being subjugated and exploited, and that it is actually the rejection of colonialism and inferiority, in short their dignity that constituted and motivated their resistance. I think we can find in Fanon's "Black Skin, White Masks" the best account to what degree the colonizeds perceived colonial practice as an atrocious violation of values and their integrity. Through his psychoanalytic analysis and personal accounts of the colonial situation, Fanon illustrates how the colonizeds experienced the colonial encounter and their dreams of an all-reversing revolution[46]:

> ""Look at the nigger!…Mama, a Negro!…Hell, he's getting mad…. Take no notice, sir, he does not know that you are as civilized as we…." My body was given back to me sprawled out, distorted, recolored, clad in mourning in that white winter day. The Negro is an animal, the Negro is bad, the Negro is mean, the Negro is ugly. "Look how handsome that Negro is!…" "Kiss the handsome Negro's ass, madame!" Shame flooded her face. At last I was set free from my ruminations."[47]

In my view, this deliberate confrontation with colonialism and its classifications, the simple non-acceptance of colonialism because of one's own dignity, is the real source for (post-)colonial self-constitution.

---

[46] F. Fanon, "Du prétendu complexe de dépendance du colonisé" in F. Fanon, *Peau noire, masques blancs*, op. cit., pp. 80–86.

[47] F. Fanon, "L'expérience vécue du Noir", in F. Fanon, *Peau noire, masques blancs*, op. cit., pp. 91–92, ["The fact of blackness", in L.M. Alcoff, E. Mendieta, eds., *Identities*, op. cit., p. 63–64].

Before further specifying (post-)colonial self-constitution one must ask the legitimate question why there is essentially only one source for (post-)colonial self-constitution. There are a number of factors that make it difficult to define or assess what can or are to be the meaning and implications of a long period of domination of one society by another, factors such as length, quality and intensity of the domination, as well as experience of specific groups and individuals – and there are always reasons for which different individuals and groups experience historical episodes differently at different levels.[48] Many authors have shown the fact that colonialism lasted principally because of the straight collaboration between the colonists and an elite among the colonizeds, a sort of class alliance between foreign capital and a local comprador elite as dependency theorists put it[49] or forms of extraversion as postmodern theorists hold.[50] This shows that in a colonized society people did not suffer equally under colonialism and some even became better off and were probably also attracted by colonial lifestyle. Therefore it is a legitimate question to ask if we can generalize the source for (post-)colonial self-constitution.

We should not confound the different individual strategies of accommodation with and maybe attraction to colonialism with self-constitution under the colonial condition. The colonial condition means first of all a hierarchy among men that cannot be changed through individual strategies. The fact of natural inferiority can be accommodated, but not rationally and emotionally accepted, so that each colonized in whatever situation she found herself and however attracted she was to colonial lifestyle was confronted with her ascribed identity when dealing with the colonizers. So, even if, as Appiah maintains, most of the colonizeds in the rural areas could ignore the formal colonial system, "the increasingly deeper penetrations of an alien modernity"[51] during (post-)colonialism exposed them to the colonial ascriptions. It is this confrontation with the proper inferiority and the commands of the proper dignity to reject it and strive for equality that constitute the (post-)colonial self.

Another critique of postcolonial generalizations and reductionism comes from A. McClintock, who criticizes generally postcolonial studies for their "panoptic tendency to view the globe through generic abstractions void of political nuance."[52] According to her, political differences between cultures are subordinated to their temporal distance from European colonialism without taking into account that postcolonialism is unevenly developed globally and that most of the former colonized countries cannot be said to share a single common condition, the postcolonial condition. She contests that cultures are primarily preoccupied with their erstwhile

---

[48] D.A. Masolo, "African Philosophy and the Postcolonial", in Eze, ed., *Postcolonial African Philosophy*, op. cit., pp. pp. 283–300.

[49] A. Hoogvelt, *Globalization and the Postcolonial World. The New Political Economy of Development*, Palgrave, London 2001, pp. 37–43.

[50] J.F. Bayart, "Africa in the World: A History of Extraversion", in *African Affairs*, 99(395), 2000, pp. 217–267.

[51] K.A. Appiah, "The Invention of Africa", in K.A. Appiah, *In my Father's House*, op. cit., p. 9.

[52] A. McClintock, *Imperial Leather. Race, Gender and Sexuality in the Colonial Contest*, Routledge, London 1995, p. 11.

contact with European colonialism, and that men and women live postcoloniality in the same way and share the same singular postcolonial condition. There are other processes of cultural mutation and discontinuities important for (post-)colonial self-constitution which exceed the colonial racial discourse, and historical effects of the colonial project are not predetermined.

It seems to me very clear that if postcolonialism is understood in sociohistorical terms as the analysis of whatever economic, political or social aspects that resulted from colonialism, there is surely not one single source for (post-)colonial self-constitution; from this sociohistorical point of view, the postcolonial self constructs itself through a variety of (post-)colonial sources. However, we can legitimately reduce *postcolonialism* to the way in which the colonial set of practices and discourses is confronted with and judged from the perspective of the colonizeds and to the impact it had on self-constitution, in order to allow for the dimension of *agency* which does not feature in the sociological understanding of postcolonialism.[53] This *postcolonial* self-understanding must not necessarily play any more a concrete political role in the specific contexts of the former colonized countries, the *postcolonial condition* can have become superseded by various features which make that it does not play a further role. If we take further into account that colonial racism and the alleged knowledge about Africans, Orientals, etc., and their distinctive essential character, culture and traditions made it that these races were governed almost everywhere nearly the same,[54] then we can legitimately generalize the pattern of confrontation with colonialism and its impact on postcolonial self-constitution. In what terms should we conceive then of postcolonial self-constitution?

Frantz Fanon, when he analyzes the relationship between black and white people, contrary to what Bhabha says, does not consider 'identitarian games' and hybridity as a real possibility for postcolonial self-constitution. He holds that the cultural interstice within which the colonizeds lived cannot provide proper forms for (post-)colonial self-constitution as long as there prevail exploitative relationships of domination and annihilation.

For Fanon the *psychology of the colonizeds* is deeply shaped by the *complex of inferiority and dependency* developed during colonialism.[55] There are two effects of this complex on postcolonial self-constitution: one is acceptance of the stigma of colored people by the colonizeds and recognition of white supremacy, the other is refutation of the identitarian stigma and affirmation of equality among identities. The *first effect* of the complex of inferiority is that black people develop the desire to put on a 'white mask' in the attempt to achieve recognition of their humanity, develop the desire to be identified as white in order to become equal to the

---

[53] Moreover, any other causal definition of postcolonialism that integrates also the structural consequences of colonialism on postcolonial culture, economy and politics faces the problem of *infinite regress*.

[54] E.W. Said, *Orientalism*, op. cit., pp. 37–38.

[55] F. Fanon, *Peau noire, masques blancs*, op. cit., p. 19.

colonizers and enjoy all their rights and benefices.⁵⁶ And hence, postcolonial self-constitution takes place in the interstices of black and white culture and seems to be indeed hybrid. However, there are two problems with such an account of hybrid identity. First, according to Fanon the reasons for the development of this type of hybrid identity do not lie in the Bhabhian forms of ironic detour of colonial dominance through 'mimicry', but in psychopathologic aberrations of the colonizeds. Second, we have seen above that efforts of assimilation do not end up in recognition on the part of the colonizers, insofar as hybrid identity can never be equal to white identity. And so, it seems that those colonizeds who aspire white identity must lay down any other form of identity and can by definition not hold a hybrid identity. After all, this impossibility makes the question of why black people are supposed to be inferior to remain acute.

The *second effect* of the complex of inferiority of the colonizeds, according to Fanon, is to take up the question of inferiority and to show that identities cannot be hierarchized but must be considered to be of equal value, to show that there are no reasons to be discriminated because of one's identity. I propose that this is the way postcolonial self-constitution proceeds. The confrontation with colonialism must pass through a reconsideration of the identity of the colonizeds. This irreducible dimension of identity in postcolonial self-constitution is essentially due to the justification of colonial power with the identity of the colonizeds and the psychological reaction to colonialism motivated by dignity. It is Fanon himself who best expressed this:

> "What! When it was I who had every reason to hate, to despise, I was rejected? When I should have been begged, implored, I was denied the slightest recognition? I resolved, since it was impossible for me to get away from an inborn complex, to assert myself as BLACK MAN. Since the other hesitated to recognize me, there remained only one solution: to make myself known."⁵⁷

For Fanon it is a fact of psychology that after colonization Blacks want to demonstrate at any price to Whites the wealth of their thought and equal power of their intellect.

If somebody is discriminated because of its alleged identity, one can either show that identity in general does not provide reasons for discrimination or show that there is nothing in one's identity that gives reason for discrimination, that one's identity deserves equal recognition as the identity of others. One strategy is to script positively the features of identity, to affirm the positive value of identity, another strategy would be to refute altogether that different identities justify different treatment – that there is something special about being Black, Arabic, Native, Muslim or Hindu that justifies discrimination – and to appeal to shared values of the humanity. In this interpretation "the basis for that [postcolonial] project (…) is based (…) in

---

⁵⁶ See in particular F. Fanon's essay on „La femme de couleur et le Blanc" and "L'homme de couleur et la Blanche" in F. Fanon, *Peau noire, masques blancs*, op. cit., pp. 15–35 and 35–53. See also A. Memmi, *The Colonizer and the Colonized*, Earthscan Publications, London 1990, pp. 186–193.

⁵⁷ F. Fanon, "L'expérience vécue du Noir", in F. Fanon, *Peau noire, masques blancs*, op. cit., pp. 92–93, ["The fact of blackness", in L.M. Alcoff, E. Mendieta, eds., *Identities*, op. cit., p. 64].

an appeal to a certain simple respect for human suffering, a fundamental revolt against the endless misery of the last thirty years."[58]

The great problem with the universalistic strategy is that a specific non-identitarian, objective morality shared by the entire humanity was probably first formulated during European Enlightenment and then given a cultural reinterpretation by Europeans, so that some aspects, in particular the Enlightenment understanding of Reason, could be used politically under the guise of the 'civilizing mission' and the 'burden of the white man' as a justification for colonialism. Hence, if, as Fanon states, Enlightenment has been reduced by imperialism to the figure of the settler-colonial white man, a postcolonial appeal to non-identitarian values was psychologically, but also politically not very attractive. It is this point that Fanon wants to make, when he says that the way the colonial world was put into question by the colonizers could not engender a rational response by the colonizeds, and that postcolonial self-constitution could not be centered around a universal discourse, but must adopt the road of an absolute affirmation of originality.[59] It is also for this reason that Fanon justified violence in the anticolonial struggle. Or as Albert Memmi holds, when the colonizeds asked for recognition, they could not do this in the name of universal values common to all men; they had been excluded from universality both in word and in fact.[60] "In this context, insisting on the right to live a dignified life will not be enough. It will not even be enough to require that one be treated with equal dignity despite being black: for that will require a concession that being black counts naturally or to some degree against one's dignity. And so one will end up asking to be respected *as a black*."[61]

A great part of postcolonial self-constitution is the restoration of those values that have been denied by colonialism. *The postcolonial question is about cultural values and recognition after the colonial experience.* Trying to understand the colonial condition from the view of the first person and taking into account that *individuals do reject to see their own beliefs and values they feel committed to as inferior or worthless* and *are generally willing to affirm them* shows why postcolonial identity is empirically essential rather than differential.

Partha Chatterjee illustrates well the identitarian moment that opposition to the colonial regime in colonial India brought forth.[62] His point is that nationalism in the colonies began before becoming a political movement, that the nation was already sovereign while the state was still colonial. According to Chatterjee, Indians divided the world of social institutions and practices into the material and spiritual domain. The material aspect was the domain of the colonial state and its administration in

---

[58] K.A. Appiah, "The Postcolonial and the Postmodern", in K.A. Appiah, *In my Father's House*, op. cit., p. 151.

[59] F. Fanon, *Les damnés de la terre*, Maspero, Paris 1979, p. 10.

[60] A. Memmi, *The Colonizer and the Colonized*, op. cit., p. 198.

[61] K.A. Appiah, "Race, Culture, Identity", in K.A. Appiah, A. Gutman, *Color Conscious*, op. cit., p. 98.

[62] P. Chatterjee, *The Nation and its Fragments. Colonial and Postcolonial Histories*. Princeton University Press, Princeton 1993.

which difference was not a viable criterion, the spiritual aspect was the inner domain bearing the marks of cultural identity and the desire to construct an aesthetic form recognizably different from the Western model. Nationalism had to choose its site of autonomy from a position of subordination to a colonial regime that had on its side universalistic justificatory resources and, hence, could not be indifferent to distinctions between language, religion and caste in the public sphere. It is the communitarian element that determines postcolonial self-constitution in order to reverse the intellectual, cultural and moral colonial disqualifications, in order to defend against what G.C. Spivak called the colonial 'epistemic violence'.

The consequences that arise from postcolonial self-constitution are that cultural identity is particularly important in postcolonialism. In postcolonialism, emphasis is laid on the people's culture and their own knowledge systems as well as the utilization of local resources against the import of Western models into environments in which they are considered unsustainable; emphasis is laid on the specific dynamics of individual societies that operate in their own particular times. However, the question remains open if cultural identity can be truly the source for postcolonial autonomy. There are three answers given by postcolonial theorists to the question how serious we must *morally* take postcolonial self-constitution around strong identities: one answer is to take it morally very serious, another answer is to give it strategic and temporary moral importance, and the last answer is to dismiss postcolonial self-constitution as morally untenable. I will briefly line out these three positions.

13.4 Postcolonialism and Morality

If Fanon understands perfectly well that the colonial context pushes the colonizeds to affirm some sort of identity, according to him this does not provide any reasons to believe in the irreducible reality of races, ethnies or religions. *The psychological reaction to the colonial condition is not a viable moral fundament for postcolonial self-constitution*. Autonomy for Fanon means to go beyond the historical facts of colonial discrimination and to affirm that there are no human races.[63] Hence, he defends nationalism as a political and not cultural project. The nation substantiates "its existence in the fight which the people wage against the forces of occupation."[64] This morally totally unqualified political project of the postcolonial nation led many postcolonial theorists to take serious the empirical reality of the way the postcolonial self got constituted and to draw a political project upon this postcolonial self-understanding.

According to the different historical trajectories of colonized societies and the different cultural sources available for identification in the struggle against

---

[63] F. Fanon, *Peau noire, masques blancs*, op. cit., pp. 181–188.
[64] Fanon, "On National Culture", in P. Williams, L. Chrisman, eds., *Colonial Discourse and Postcolonial Theory. A Reader*, Columbia University Press, New York 1994, p. 41.

colonialism, postcolonial theorists theorized an array of postcolonial racial, religious and cultural identities as the moral basis for a postcolonial political project. We find the most important moral expressions of postcolonial identitarian self-constitution in *Negritude, Nativism, Islamism* but also *Hinduism*, and in particular *Nationalism*. Amilcar Cabral synthesizes the political objectives for the postcolonies as follows: "*development of a popular culture* and of all positive indigenous cultural values; *development of a national culture* based upon the history and the achievements of the struggle itself; constant promotion of the political and moral awareness of the people (of all social groups) as well as *patriotism*."[65]

I would like to illustrate the moral consequences that are drawn from postcolonial self-constitution by way of an example in postcolonial theory: *Negritude*. Given the fact of the estrangement and discrimination of the 'self' under colonialism "negritude is the awarness of being black, the simple acknowledgement of a fact which implies the acceptance of it, a taking charge of one's identity as a black man, of one's history and culture."[66] From the fact of racial discrimination is derived a moral principle based upon racial features, black skin color, that affirms the existence of an African personality that is constituted by "*the sum of the cultural values of the black world*".[67] Characteristics of negritude are a specific black moral law and a black society.

It is the moral understanding of racial identity that provides autonomy to black people. In order to realize themselves they must develop not as individuals but as the black race, "striving together for the accomplishment of certain more or less vividly conceived ideals of life."[68] It is this moral basis of the black race, and not the mere psychological dimension of unity brought forth by colonialism and racial discrimination that enables solidarity among black people and helps them to achieve liberation and economic strength.[69]

---

[65] A. Cabral, "National Liberation and Culture", in P. Williams, L. Chrisman, eds., *Colonial Discourse and Postcolonial Theory*, op. cit., p. 64.

[66] A. Césaire quoted in B. Moore-Gilbert, G. Stanton, W. Maley, eds., *Postcolonial Criticism*, op. cit., p. 7.

[67] L.S. Senghor, "Negritude: A Humanism of the Twentieth Century", in P. Williams, L. Chrisman, eds., *Colonial Discourse and Postcolonial Theory*, op. cit., p. 30.

[68] W.E.B. Du Bois, "The Conservation of Races", in L.M. Alcoff, E. Mendietta, eds., *Identities*, op. cit., p. 44.

[69] Similar argumentation we can find in **Nativism** and **Islamism**.

We can find nativist essentialism in O.J. Chinweizu, I. Madubuike, *Toward the Decolonisation of African Literature*, Routledge, London 1985, who prescribes that a true African art must reflect and transcribe the immediate reality of African life and must be consistent with 'tradition'. Ngugi wa Thiongo, *Decolonising the Mind: The Politics of Language in African Literature*, Heinemann, Portsmouth 1986, holds that African writers should express themselves in indigenous languages.

Absolutist Islamism, that roughly started with the rise of the Muslim Brotherhood in Egypt in the 1930ies, must be read in the same way as negritude as a revaluation of values that were deemed inferior and worthless during colonialism. See A. Bilgrami "What is a Muslim?" in K.A. Appiah, H.L. Gates, eds., *Identities*, op. cit., pp. 198–219, and G. Kepel, *Jihad: The Trail of Political Islam*, Belknap Press, Cambridge, Mass., 2002. In most colonies in North Africa, the Middle-East and Central and South Asia Islam was always a major source for social and cultural life, and much of

13.4 Postcolonialism and Morality

Other philosophers, among which Appiah and Amy Gutmann,[70] defend in the line of Jean-Paul Sartre a so-called "Antiracist Racism", a necessary step in a dialectical progression to the final unity and the abolition of differences of race.[71] These philosophers do not believe that postcolonial self-constitution creates substantial moral values, but hold that in order to achieve true autonomy postcolonial self-constitution must be considered as *temporarily* morally valuable. For Sartre, for example, postcolonial self-constitution around a strong black identity keeps its moral significance as long as the ideal of human brotherhood has not become a practical possibility. Although, according to Sartre, there is no essence of blackness, a racial context can prescribe color consciousness as a situational moral engagement. The morality of communitarian identities is functional and persists as long as communitarianism helps to achieve other moral goods such as civic equality and to overcome injustices. Identity claims may be historically and strategically necessary for members of oppressed groups as a means of rallying together, providing mutual support and fighting unjust treatment.

If many postcolonial philosophers endorse the idea that one should draw positive moral consequences from the way postcolonial self-constitution proceeds and affirm communitarian or racial identities, other theorists draw negative moral consequences and maintain that *postcolonial* self-constitution should deprive the individual of its right to agency. Both agree upon how postcolonial self-constitution proceeds, but draw opposite moral consequences from this empirical fact. The first say that postcolonial identity provides autonomy, the second say that postcolonial identity and autonomy are mutually exclusive. According to Gayatri Spivak every actual identity is a wound, and she claims, similar to Fanon, that identitarian claims centered around nationalism or some sort of fundamentalism are merely therapeutical to heal the wounds of 'epistemic violence'. It is her thesis that colonialism and patriarchism have eroded the space for autonomy to such a degree that there remains no more room from which the postcolonial individual 'can speak'. For Spivak the postcolonial individual is nothing more than a subject-effect:

> A subject-effect can be briefly plotted as follows: that which seems to operate as a subject may be part of an immense discontinuous network ('text' in the general sense) of strands that may be termed politics, ideology, economics, history, sexuality, language, and so on (…). Different knottings and configurations of these strands, determined by heterogenous

---

colonialism "devoted all its forces to killing the Islamic spirit". Consequently, it became considered as the great source of postcolonial dignity and autonomy in the face of the "Crusader spirit" and cultural hostility that motivated modern imperialism. See for this reading of Islamism the founder of the Muslim Brotherhood Sayyid Quotb's "Social Justice in Islam", in W.E. Shepard, *Sayyid Quotb and Islamic Activism*, Brill, Leiden 1996, chap. 8, 60, p. 282.

[70] K.A. Appiah, A. Gutmann, *Color Conscious*, op. cit.

[71] J.P. Sartre, "Orphée Noire", in L.S. Senghor, ed., *Anthologie de la nouvelle poésie nègre et malgache de langue française*, Presses Universitaires de France (PUF), Paris 1992, but also J.P. Sartre, *Colonialism and Neocolonialism*, Routledge, London 2001.

determinations which are themselves dependent upon myriad circumstances, produce the effect of an operating subject.[72]

Any sort of agency is impossible because of the production, inscription and manipulation of subject-effects: "There is no space from which the sexed subaltern subject can speak."[73]

13.5 What Postcolonial Project?

If we could find good arguments based upon a conception of dignity in favour of our thesis, namely that a *proper postcolonial* identity must be considered rather strong than hybrid and weak, we did not settle the question, if postcolonial self-constitution is to be considered as a source of autonomy or not. It seems obvious that postcolonial identities are constructed and developed against colonialism, that they spring out of a psychological reaction against the justification of colonial rule on grounds of a theory of hierarchy of identities, but this does not provide us with an answer to the question, if postcolonial identity has a normative ground. We know that there are strong postcolonial identities, we know that postcolonial identity is a politcally very sensitive issue, but we do not know what *should be* their political relevance. And this seems for me to be the *proper postcolonial question* that lies behind many of the interrogations in postcolonial theory.

Can the communitarian model be the solution to the postcolonial mystery of political justice? Or should it be only a temporary instrumental answer? Or must we rather teach, according to the strategy of Spivak, autonomy to the postcolonial individuals and how to separate themselves from their identity? Should we fight postcolonial identites, merely tolerate them, or do we have to recognize them?

I propose that a response to the postcolonial question requires a throurough formal understanding of the relationship between identity and autonomy.

References

Alcoff, Linda, and Eduardo Mendieta, eds. 2003. *Identities*. Oxford: Blackwell.
Appiah, Kwame Anthony. 1992. *In my Father's House. Africa in the Philosophy of Culture*. Oxford: Oxford University Press.
———. 2005. *The Ethics of Identity*. Princeton: Princeton University Press.
Appiah, Kwame Anthony, and Amy Gutmann. 1998. *Color Conscious: The Political Morality of Race*, 1998. Princeton: Princeton University Press.

---

[72] G.C. Spivak quoted in P. Hallward, *Absolutely Postcolonial. Writing between the Singular and the Specific*, op. cit., p. 28.
[73] G.C. Spivak, „Can the Subaltern Speak?", in P. Williams, L. Chrisman, eds., *Colonial Discourse and Postcolonial Theory*, op. cit., pp. 102, 103.

References

Arendt, Hannah. 1958. *Elemente und Ursprünge totalitärer Herrschaft*. Frankfurt: Europäische Verlagsanstalt.
Ashcroft, Bill, Gareth Griffiths, and Helen Tiffin. 1989. *The Empire Writes Back. Theory and Practice in Post-Colonial Literatures*, 1989. London: Routledge.
Barthes, Roland. 1983. *Empire of Signs*. New York: Hill and Wang.
Bayart, Jean-François. 2000. Africa in the World: A History of Extraversion. *African Affairs* 99 (395): 217–267.
Bhabha, Homi. 1994. *The Location of Culture*. London: Routledge.
———. 1997. Race', Time and the Revision of Modernity. In *Postcolonial Criticism*, ed. B. Moore-Gilbert, G. Stanton, and W. Maley. London/New York: Longman.
Bilgrami, Akeel. 2001. Identity and Identification: Philosophical Aspects. *International Encyclopedia of the Social and Behavioral Sciences* (IESBS). pp. 7148–7154.
Chakrabarty, Dipesh. 2000. *Provincializing Europe. Postcolonial thought and Historical Difference*. Princeton: Princeton University Press.
Chatterjee, Partha. 1993. *The Nation and its Fragments. Colonial and Postcolonial Histories*. Princeton: Princeton University Press.
Chinweizu, Jemie, and Ihechukwu Madubuike. 1985. *Toward the Decolonisation of African Literature*. London: Routledge.
Comaroff, John, and J.L. Comaroff. 1991. *Of Revelation and Revolution, Volume 1: Christianity, Colonialism, and Consciousness in South Africa*. Chicago: University of Chicago Press.
Eze, Emmanuel, ed. 1997. *Postcolonial African philosophy. A Critical Reader*. Oxford: Blackwell.
Fanon, Frantz. 1952. *Peau noire, masques blancs*. Paris: Éditions du Seuil.
———. 1979. *Les damnés de la terre*. Paris: Maspero.
Foucault, Michel. 2004. *Society must be Defended*. London: Penguin Books.
Gugelberger, Georg. 1994. Postcolonial Cultural Studies. In *The John Hopkins Guide to Literary and Criticism Theory*, ed. Michael Groden and Martin Kreiswirth. Baltimore: John Hopkin University Press.
Guha, Ranajit, ed. 1982–1989. *Subaltern Studies: Writings on South Asian History and Society*. Vol. I–VI. New Delhi: Oxford University Press.
Hacking, Ian. 2002. *Historical Ontology*. Cambridge, MA: Harvard University Press.
Hallward, Peter. 2001. *Absolutely Postcolonial. Writing between the Singular and the Specific*. Manchester: Manchester University Press.
Hegel, Georg. 1975. *Lectures on the Philosophy of World History. Introduction: Reason in History*. Trans. H.B. Nisbet. Cambridge: Cambridge University Press.
Hoogvelt, Ankie. 2001. *Globalization and the Postcolonial World. The New Political Economy of Development*. London: Palgrave.
Kepel, Gilles. 2002. *Jihad: The Trail of Political Islam*. Cambridge, MA: Belknap Press.
Masolo, Dismas (1997), "African Philosophy and the Postcolonial. Some Misleading Abstractions about Identity", in E. Eze, ed., Postcolonial African philosophy. A critical reader, Blackwell, Oxford 1997, pp. 283–300.
Mbembe, Achille. 1992. Provisional Notes on the Postcolony. *Public Culture* 5 (1): 3–37.
——— 2001. *On the Postcolony*. Los Angeles: Berkeley University Press.
McClintock, Anne. 1995. *Imperial Leather. Race, Gender and Sexuality in the Colonial Contest*. London: Routledge.
Memmi, Albert. 1990. *The Colonizer and the Colonized*. London: Earthscan Publications.
Mill, John Stuart. 1974. *On Liberty*. London: Penguin Books.
Prakash, Gyan, ed. 1995. *After Colonialism: Imperial Histories and Postcolonial Displacements*. Princeton: Princeton University Press.
Said, Edward. 1991. *Orientalism*. London: Penguin Books.
Sartre, Jean-Paul. 2001. *Colonialism and Neocolonialism*. London: Routledge.
Scott, David. 1999. *Refashioning Futures: Criticism after Postcoloniality*. Princeton: Princeton University Press.

Senghor, Leopold, ed. 1992. *Anthologie de la nouvelle poésie nègre et malgache de langue française*. Paris: Presses Universitaires de France (PUF).
Shepard, William. 1996. *Sayyid Quotb and Islamic Activism*. Leiden: Brill.
Spivak, Gayatri C. 1999. *A Critique of Post-Colonial Reason: Toward a History of the Vanishing Present*. Cambridge: Harvard University Press.
Stoler, Ann. 2002. *Carnal Knowledge and Imperial Power: Race and the Intimate in Colonial Rule*. Berkeley: University of California Press.
Thiongo, Ngugi wa. 1986. *Decolonising the Mind: The Politics of Language in African Literature*. Portsmouth: Heinemann.
Williams, Patrick, and Laura Chrisman, eds. 1994. *Colonial Discourse and Postcolonial Theory. A Reader*. New York: Columbia University Press.
Young, Robert. 1995. *Colonial Desire: Hybridity in Theory, Culture, and Race*. London: Routledge.
———. 2004. *White Mythologies*. London: Routledge.

Chapter 14
Communalism in Sub-Saharan Africa: The Reintegration of Child Soldiers

Abstract The use of child soldiers is one of the most morally disturbing forms of human rights violations. Yet, children often *join voluntarily* armed groups and *refuse* to leave behind their military role, once they are offered a life more similar to that of a 'normal' child. Given the dramatic failure of Disarmament, Demobilization and Reintegration (DDR) programs treating child soldiers as victims, the recently formulated "Integrated DDR Standards" of the United Nations (UN) recommend, in an effort to consider their agency, psychosocial instead of psychotherapeutic approaches to reintegration. Psychosocial approaches judge the child soldiers' identity as obstacle to reintegration and propose child soldiers' participation in cultural practices of civil society to redress and 'heal' their identity. I argue that psychosocial-oriented DDR programs are not only theoretically incoherent but also practically wrong, since they do not take into account the proper reasons for which child soldiers volunteer and come to identify with the army. As a result, they push child soldiers back to a cultural and social context that once constituted the 'root causes' of their becoming soldiers. Children endorse soldiering, insofar as warfare provides them with means of emancipation from poverty and social exclusion as well as with some sense of dignity. Therefore, successful reintegration of child soldiers is intrinsically linked to the promotion of their personal autonomy.

Keywords Agency · Child soldiers · Children's rights · Cultural identity · Disarmament · Demobilization and reintegration (DDR) programs · Personal autonomy

One of the most peculiar characteristics of international politics since the end of the Cold War is the massive recruitment of children[1] as soldiers. We can identify three

---

[1] I use the term 'children' indiscriminately for all individuals between 0 and 18 years. I do not distinguish further between small children and youngsters as psychologists sometimes do (see Erik H. Erikson, *Identity: Youth and Crisis*, New York, W.W. Norton 2004). The reason for this is not that any current positive legislation makes such a difference, but that such a distinction in fact risks to misconstrue the *reasons* for which children become soldiers, emphasizing a specific youth iden-

major structural reasons[2] – *demography*, *warfare* and *technology* – explaining this sudden and unprecedented rise[3] in the employment of child soldiers. If we consider the demographic summary indicators of former colonized areas of the world, we are particularly struck by the fact that the population under 18 makes up almost half of the total population of postcolonial countries.[4] Moreover, many of these countries turned into weak or failed states with scarce institutional capacities after the end of the East-West bloc confrontation and geopolitics. This led to 'new' forms of civil war[5] functioning around informal criminalized economies that blurred for the most part the distinction between combatants and civilians.[6] The demographic constellation with the unusually high proportion of young people in the total population entailed that children became actively involved in the war.[7] Moreover, technical development of light arms very much facilitated the use of weapons. Today, children as young as 8 years can learn to employ, without great difficulty, modern lightweight semi-automatic weapons.

---

tity that could explain the increasing insecurity and violence in a society (see Samuel Huntington, *The Clash of Civilizations and the Remaking of World Order*, New York, Simon & Schuster 1996 and Robert Kaplan, "The Coming Anarchy: How scarcity, crime, overpopulation, tribalism, and disease are rapidly destroying the social fabric of our planet," *The Atlantic Monthly*, February 1994). This point will become clearer in section two and three of this essay.

[2] I call them structural reasons, because they do not explain the motivation of children for engaging in war. These reasons are not subjective or motivating reasons, insofar as they do not answer the question of why children choose to fight. They are necessary reasons for the rise in the number of child soldiers, however they are not sufficient reasons for explaining the motives of children to become soldiers.

[3] Since the time of the Spartan and Roman Empires children were always used as soldiers. Recent historic examples of children being used in warfare are the Hitler youth and Vietnam youths engaging in suicide missions against American soldiers (see The United Nations Children's Fund (UNICEF), *The State of the World's Children 2005. Childhood Under Threat*, New York, UNICEF 2004, p. 3).

[4] The statistics: Whereas in the industrialized world children's share of the total population is no more than 20 per cent, in Sub-Saharan Africa children make up well over 50 per cent of the total population, in the Middle East and North Africa a little bit less than 50 per cent and in South Asia, Latin America and the Caribbean around 40 per cent of the totality.

[5] From 1990 to 2003, there were 59 different major armed conflicts in 48 locations and only four of these involved war between nations. Of the six wars and 29 severe crises in 2006, only one war and two severe crises were transnational (see *Conflict Barometer 2006*, Heidelberg Institute for International Conflict Research (HHIK) (https://hiik.de/conflict-barometer/bisherige-ausgaben/?lang=en, accessed on March 20, 2020)

[6] Mary Kaldor, *New and Old Wars. Organized Violence in a Global Era*, Stanford, Stanford University Press 1999. Some analysts deny the distinction between politically-oriented 'old' wars and criminal or ethnic-oriented 'new' wars, without purpose and a breakdown in the rules of warfare, in order to stress the social injustices that are at the origin of many of the postcolonial wars (Stathis Kalyvas, "'New' And 'Old' Civil Wars: A Valid Distinction?" *World Politics* 54 (1), 2001, pp. 99–118).

[7] An estimated 90 per cent of global conflict-related deaths since 1990 have been civilians, and 80 per cent of these have been of women and children (see UNICEF, *The State of World's Children 2005*, op. cit., p. 40).

About 10% of the world's fighting forces are under the age of 18.[8] In 2006, the United Nations (UN) estimated that more than 300,000 children are taking an active part in armed conflict in government armed forces, government militias and in a range of armed opposition groups. The most significant use of child soldiers is in Africa, where up to 100,000 children, were estimated to be involved in armed conflict in mid-2004. However, children are also engaged in warfare in various Asian countries and in parts of Latin America as well as the Middle East.[9] In the last three decades, millions of children under 18 have been killed and over ten million seriously injured or permanently disabled by armed conflict.[10]

At first sight, few issues look more indisputable than that of child soldiers. As one of the journalists of the *Time Magazine* puts it "even in an age when it's hard to get people to agree even on what they disagree about, nobody lobbies for sending children into battle, and the people who put them there serve as the kind of villains any storyteller would love."[11] In a sense, child soldiers are the *perfect victims*; almost everybody does recognize the fact of children are going to war as a deep and a very much disturbing anomaly. It seems therefore unsurprising that child soldiers have become lately a pop-cultural trope that appear regularly in novels, movies, magazines and on TV.[12] Starbucks, the world's leading coffeehouse chain, has chosen to feature the memoirs of a former boy soldier in its 6000 stores in 2006.[13]

However, taking a closer look on child soldiers, one can observe some highly astonishing and unexpected details. In general, child soldiers do not want to leave the armed groups, even when they are offered the possibility to do so. Paradoxically, most of today's child soldiers *join voluntarily* some armed group[14] and must be

---

[8] Jimmie Briggs, *Innocents Losts*, New York, Basic Books 2005, p. 150.

[9] The countries that currently use child soldiers are the following: Afghanistan, Angola, Burundi, Central African Republic, Chad, Colombia, Democratic Republic of Congo, Guinea, Haiti, India, Indonesia, Iran, Iraq, Israel/Palestine, Ivory Coast, Lebanon, Liberia, Myanmar, Nepal, Philippines, Republic of Congo, Russia, Rwanda, Sierra Leone, Somalia, Sri Lanka, Sudan, Uganda, Yemen (see "Enfants soldats: 58 États s'engagent," *Libération*, February 6, 2007, source UNICEF (https://www.liberation.fr/planete/2007/02/06/enfants-soldats-58-etats-s-engagent_12655, accessed on March 20, 2020).

[10] Briggs, *Innocents Losts*, op. cit., p. xii.

[11] "Pop Culture finds Lost Boys," *Time Magazine*, February 2, 2007 (http://content.time.com/time/magazine/article/0,9171,1584807,00.html, accessed on March 20, 2020).

[12] Child soldiers feature prominently in the Hollywood blockbusters "Blood Diamond" and "Hotel Rwanda." With his publication of "A Long Way Gone. Memoirs of a Boy Soldier" at the beginning of this year, the former child soldier Ishmael Beah is about to become a "literary-humanitarian equivalent of a rock star" ("Pop Culture finds Lost Boys," *Time Magazine*, op. cit.). After becoming the figurehead of many international organisations and NGOs in their campaigns against the use of child soldiers, Beah, currently going on a 10-city book tour sponsored by Starbucks, is a highly demanded guest in all sorts of TV shows.

[13] In the first 3 weeks, over 65,000 copies of the book were sold. Since weeks, Beah's book is on the New York Times Best-seller List.

[14] Against the common expectation, the majority of the child soldiers do in fact enlist 'voluntarily:' "New research reveals that there is an important element of volunteerism" in the decision of young people to join the armed forces (United Nations Development Program (UNDP), *Youth and Violent*

forced to leave these groups, whenever the UN and non-governmental organizations (NGOs) negotiate their release with the goal to offer these children something more similar to a 'normal' childhood. As a matter of fact, many of the disarmament, demobilization and reintegration (DDR) programs for child soldiers fail, because most of the kids drastically refuse to be treated as 'kids' and nursed as traumatized victims of war[15] and simply escape the Interim Care Centers (ICCs) in order to either rejoin the armed groups or start life on the streets among their peers. This reality does confront us with several serious questions. Are our horror-stricken and scandalized reactions to the use of child soldiers based upon erroneous moral fundamentals? Are we fundamentally wrong about trying to prevent and protect children from engaging in warfare? Does reintegration fail, because the programs and therapies NGOs offer are too strongly individually based and do not take into consideration the cultural dimension of conflict and reintegration? Or, do we probably misconceive the role identity plays for a child?

According to me, the interesting question about child soldiers is not so much if, after all, our widespread intuitions that children are victims of war are wrong, but why we cannot treat them as victims, even if it is undeniably the case that they are victims. In this essay, I will address the fundamental question of how child soldiers *are to* be treated in a perspective of disarmament, demobilization and reintegration.

Due to the many failures of DDR programs, the fact that we cannot victimize child soldiers has been in the meantime partly recognized by organizations working on the ground. It is held that the reason for which we cannot focus primarily on children as victims is the fact that children function within cultural and communitarian systems.[16] Given the child soldiers' identity as warriors and their resulting social stigmatization, "demobilization procedures should be established to facilitate their rupture with military identity" and help child soldiers to develop a new, 'civilian' identity.[17] Taking into account the 'identity' aspect of healing and reintegration,

---

Conflict: Society and Development in Crisis?, New York, UNDP 2006, p. 19). See also Child Soldiers International, former Coalition to Stop the Use of Child Soldiers, (https://web.archive.org/web/20161014232943/https://www.child-soldiers.org/, accessed on March 20, 2020); Rachel Brett & Irma Specht, *Young Soldiers. Why They Choose to Fight*, Boulder/Geneva, Lynne Rienner/ILO 2004; Krijn Peters & Paul Richards, "Why we Fight: Voices of Under-Age Youth Combatants in Sierra Leone," *Africa* 68, 1998, pp. 183–210.

[15] "Former child soldiers in Liberia resented being labelled 'war affected'" (Beth Verhey, "Child Soldiers: Preventing, Demobilizing and Reintegrating," *Africa Region Working Paper Series* 23, November 2001, p. 11).

[16] Alcinda Honwana was the first to formulate this thesis in *Okusiakala ondalo yokalye: Let us light a new fire. Local Knowledge in the Post-War Healing and Reintegration Of War-Affected Children in Angola*, Consultancy Report for Christian Children's Fund, November 1998 (http://citeseerx.ist.psu.edu/viewdoc/download?doi=10.1.1.618.7261&rep=rep1&type=pdf, accessed on April 20, 2020) and "Negotiating Post-War Identities. Child soldiers in Mozambique and Angola," *CODESRIA Bulletin* 1–2, 1999, pp. 4–13. See also her *Child Soldiers in Africa*, Philadelphia, University of Pennsylvania Press 2007.

[17] Verhey, *Child Soldiers*, op. cit., pp. 11 and 17.

DDR programs shifted gradually from passive individual-based to participatory community-based assistance.[18] Most recently, youth detainees in U.S. detention facilities in Iraq must undergo religious training programs taught by moderate Muslim clerks before being released.[19]

However, if we refer to the agency of child soldiers in terms of *practical* identity,[20] it remains not only a puzzle about why child soldiers should ever assume a civilian identity, but above all, we loose out on the reasons for which children endorse soldiering. They become committed soldiers neither because they identify with some war heroes such as Rambo – they are not born to be wild – nor due to manipulation, but because they try to escape the inhuman conditions of absolute poverty, abandonment and hopelessness. Very often, oppressive communities and families are part of the problem and cannot count as a solution to the phenomenon of child soldiers.[21] Well-being, and not identity, accounts for the reasons children have to become soldiers.

Therefore, I will defend the claim that the true reason why child soldiers hate to be nursed as 'patients' is not a specific *practical* form of personal identity, but a sense of *dignity* that, in turn, *gives rise* to their personal identity. Insofar as war constitutes for many of them the only possibility to some form of independence and personal autonomy under the socio-economic and political circumstances they grow up, child soldiers construct themselves over a period of time an identity of a soldier and identify with their role in the military. Despite the reality of manipulation, exploitation and genuine grievances, soldiering reinstitutes a form of dignity to the children that does not allow them to be treated as victims of their circumstances. As long as child soldiers do not perceive any future perspective or any other adequate means through which they can satisfy their needs and construct themselves an alternative identity, they clearly will prefer warfare to any other civilian activity. In their mind, they are 'figures of success,' and DDR programs, if they do not want to be counterproductive and even harmful, have to face this reality. They have to deal neither with victims nor with demons, but with kids and youngsters 'who made it' and who have come to occupy a central position in public life.[22]

In the first section, I illustrate the challenge of agency that DDR programs, for children, must face. In the second and third section, I analyze different conceptions of child soldiers' agency and refute community-based DDR programs in favor of

---

[18] See the UN *Integrated Disarmament, Demobilization and Reintegration Standards (IDDRS)*, Children and DDR, 5.30 (https://unddr.org/uploads/documents/IDDRS%205.30%20Children%20 and%20DDR.pdf, *accessed on March 20, 2020*).

[19] "U.S. Working to Reshape Iraqi Detainees," *Washington Post*, September 19, 2007, p. A01.

[20] 'Practical identity' means that the identity of a person does provide her reasons for action.

[21] Myriam Denov, *Is the Culture Always Right? The Dangers of Reproducing Gender Stereotypes and Inequalities in Psychosocial Interventions for War-Affected Children*, London: Coalition to Stop the Use of Child Soldiers 2007; Atle Dyregrov, Leila Gupta, Rolf Gjestad & Magne Raundalen, "Is the Culture Always Right?," *Traumatology* 8 (3), 2002, pp. 135–145.

[22] Filip de Boeck & Marie-Françoise Plissart, *Kinshasa. Tales of the Invisible City*, Ghent, Ludion 2004, pp. 184–188.

autonomy-based DDR concepts. Based upon these reflections, I will give in the conclusion a concrete example of how DDR programs could successfully reintegrate child soldiers.

14.1 Child Soldiers as Victims

When we face the topic of child soldiers, we generally have following reaction; we cry "scandal," "barbarism," "criminals." Our intuitive, outrageous reaction has become integrated in the corpus of international law that now bans the involvement of children under 18 in armed conflict.[23] Graça Machel's report on the "Impact of Armed Conflict on Children" to the UN General Assembly in 1996 provided the first comprehensive assessment of the multiple ways in which children's rights are violated in the context of armed conflict. Child soldiers are to be considered *a priori* as being "*kidnapped* by a paramilitary group and *compelled* to bear arms or *forced into* sexual slavery" and not enjoying a proper childhood.[24] However *voluntarily* a child might join armed groups, children do not have the intellectual and psychological capacity, by reason of their mental immaturity, to take such a decision and to be a soldier.[25] Studies, for example, show that children have an underdeveloped death concept, in the sense, that children are not yet conscious of their own mortality.[26] As a result, young children do not fully perceive the dangers of the battlefield and take undue risk, carrying out most hazardous operations.[27] It is said that they perceive war as if it were a game. Child soldiers are victims in the truest sense of the word.

---

[23] Over the last decade three major clauses have been introduced into international law that ban the use of child soldiers. The most important legal standard relating to child soldiers is the *Optional Protocol to the Convention on the Rights of the Child on the involvement of children in armed conflict* that entered into force in 2002 and sets 18 as the minimum age for direct participation in hostilities, for recruitment into armed groups, and for compulsory recruitment by governments. The *Rome Statute of the International Criminal Court* of 1998 defines as war crimes "conscripting or enlisting children under the age of 15 years into armed forces or groups or using them to participate actively in hostilities" (Article 8(2)(e)(vii)). The *ILO Worst Forms of Child Labour Convention 182*, coming into force in 2000, commits each ratifying state to "take immediate and effective measures to secure the prohibition and elimination of the worst forms of child labour as a matter of urgency." For a complete list of the main regional and international legal standards relating to child soldiers see http://www.operationspaix.net/DATA/DOCUMENT/6360~v~The_International_Legal_Framework_for_the_Protection_of_Children_in_Armed_Conflict.pdf, accessed on March 20, 2020).

[24] UNICEF, *State of the World's Children 2005*, op. cit., p. 3 [emphasis mine].

[25] See Rachel Brett & Margaret McCallin, *Children: the Invisible Soldiers*, Stockholm, Swedish Save the Children 1996; Guy Goodwin-Gill & Ilene Cohn, *Child Soldiers: the Role of Children in Armed Conflicts*, Oxford, Clarendon Press 1994; Human Rights Watch/Africa Human Rights Watch Children's Rights Project, *Easy Prey: Child Soldiers in Liberia*, New York, Human Rights Watch 1994.

[26] Peter W. Singer, *Children at War*, Westminster, Knopf 2005, pp. 80–81.

[27] See Ahmadou Kourouma, *Allah n'est pas obligé*, Paris, Seuil 2000.

14.1 Child Soldiers as Victims

Consequently, as the international community recently confirmed in the "Paris Commitments" in February 2007, children who committed war crimes or crimes against humanity are to be treated not as alleged perpetrators, but as victims of the violation of international law taking into account their status as children.[28]

Emphasizing the victim-aspects of child soldiers stands in stark contrast with observations and experiences from the battlefield. In the battlefield, child soldiers are often the most brutal perpetrators, nothing in their behavior indicates their victimhood. On the contrary, far from self pitying, child soldiers *enjoy* their military life and develop 'Kalashnikov-lifestyles:'[29] "For fun, [they] wear female dresses, high heeled shoes, wigs, pirate rags, *happy horror*. They patrol the streets, as if they go at a masked ball."[30] Once a soldier, the joy children take in torturing and exterminating the enemy can be chilling. The film "Blood Diamond" shows the eagerness with which child soldiers of the "Revolutionary United Front" (RUF) in Sierra Leone would ask victims whether they wanted "short sleeves or long sleeves," and would cut the victim's arms off at the wrist or upper arm according to the victim's request. "We were shouting, we were happy, we were clapping."[31] The RUF fighters became notorious for maiming and killing by chopping off the arms, breasts, hands, legs, tongues, and heads of their victims. One RUF fighter reports that …

> when we caught *kamajors* [progovernment militia], we would mutilate them by parts and display them in the streets. When villagers refused to clear out of an area, we would strip them naked and burn them to death. Sometimes we used plastic and sometimes a tire. (…) I saw a pregnant woman split open to see what the baby's sex was. (…) Two officers, '05' and 'Savage,' argued over it and made a bet. Savage's boys opened the woman. It was a girl.[32]

In the memoirs of her life as a child soldier, China Keitetsi writes that most kids had "a kind of lust for killing and torturing. They could even smile when having made a rare killing, as they competed to earn nicknames, such as Commando, Rambo and Suicide."[33] „Kadogo[34] have the reputation to be reckless, invincible, terrible and

---

[28] *"Paris Commitments" to protect children from unlawful recruitment or use by armed forces or by armed groups*, (https://www.unicef.org/protection/files/Paris_Principles_EN.pdf). The "Paris Commitments" are the result of an 18-month process to review the "Cape Town Principles and Best Practice on the prevention of recruitment of children into the armed forces and on demobilization and social reintegration of child soldiers in Africa," adopted by non-governmental organizations at a conference in Cape Town in 1997.

[29] William Reno, *Warlord Politics and African States*, London, Lynne Rienner 1998, p. 158; China Keitetsi, *Child Soldier*, London, Souvenir Press 2004, p. 166.

[30] Birgit Virnich & Bartholomäus Grill, Dossier: Krieg der Kinder, *Die Zeit* 36, August 28, 2003, p. 14.

[31] Sierra Leonean child soldier quoted in D. Rosen, *Armies of the Young. Child Soldiers in War and Terrorism*, New Brunswick (NJ), Rutgers University Press 2005, p. 57.

[32] Ibid..

[33] Keitetsi, *Child Soldier*, op. cit., p. 134.

[34] In Swahili, child soldiers are referred to as *kadogos*, meaning 'little ones.'

even invulnerable,"³⁵ they often are the most brutal and merciless harassers, looters and killers. In Mozambique, child soldiers are called *matsangas*, a name associated with violence, terror and indiscriminate killings.³⁶

The fact that child soldiers conceive themselves as tough fighters, rather than as poor war-affected victims, constitutes a serious problem for DDR programs. As Peter W. Singer comments, it is "a sad reality (…) that many child soldiers do not want to leave their new lives. (…) This holds true even among abductees, who at the onset tend to define themselves as victims."³⁷ Surveys show that child soldiers often wish to remain in the army.³⁸ However, the above outlined victimization-thesis implies that DDR programs cannot recognize this reality and respect the wishes of children. According to the victimization-thesis, the fact that child soldiers lack some fundamental characteristics of *autonomous* agency necessitates treating them as heteronomous agents or victims in need of special care and assistance. Insofar as child soldiers do not know what is in their best interest, we have all the reason to disregard their preferences and values and treat them as what they are - "innocents losts." The victimization-thesis justifies and necessitates paternalism: "In fact, since we believe that young people are not in a position to give consent, many things we do to them are perfectly acceptable even when they *explicitly refuse consent*."³⁹

In his memoirs, Ishmael Beah, a former child soldier from Liberia, illustrates vividly the failure of the victimization-thesis to deal effectively with child soldiers. The first problem arises, when child soldiers refuse to be released from their armed group when given the chance to do so. Beah indicates the reason for this reluctance: "I still didn't know exactly what was going on, but I was beginning to get angry and anxious. Why had the lieutenant decided to give us up to these civilians? We thought that we were part of the war until the end."⁴⁰ From the point of view of the victimization-thesis, the issue seems quite clear at hand. These children have suf-

---

³⁵ Alphonse Maindo Monga Ngonga, "Survivre à la guerre des autres," *Politique africaine* 84, 2001, p. 54.

³⁶ Alcinda Honwana, "Innocent & Guilty. Child Soldiers as Interstitial & Tactical Agents," in Alcinda Honwana & Filip de Boeck (eds.), *Makers & Breakers. Children & Youth in Postcolonial Africa*, Oxford, James Currey 2005, p. 34.

³⁷ Singer, *Children at War*, op. cit., p. 89.

³⁸ Kale Kayihura, *Uganda: The Integration of Child Soldiers into the School System*, Paris, Association for the Development of Education in Africa 2000, p. 17.

³⁹ Amy Gutmann, "Children, Paternalism, and Education: A Liberal Argument," *Philosophy and Public Affairs* 9 (4), 1980, p. 339 [emphasis mine]. In the history of Western political thought children unlike women, slaves and 'household dependents' never were believed to have a voice which needs to be heard. Amy Gutmann defends very illustratively this standard position on childhood: "(…) We generally do not consider children – or at least young children – to be rational beings; that is, people *whose present values and preferences demand respect* or whose future values can provide a discernible, independent standard for justifying our present action towards them" (Gutmann, *Children, Paternalism and Education*, op. cit., p. 339 [emphasis mine]).

⁴⁰ Ishmael Beah, "The Making, and Unmaking, of a Child Soldier," *New York Times Magazine*, January 14, 2007 (http://www.nytimes.com/2007/01/14/magazine/14soldier.t.html?ex=1326430800&en=18db63da3854259e&ei=5088&partner=rssnyt&emc=rss, accessed on March 20, 2020).

fered tremendous experiences of violence and death, an experience that has a profound impact upon their personality. Studies show that war-affected children suffer considerable forms of trauma that influences the way they see the world and makes them often respond violently to their social environment.[41] Most cautious studies show that if not the totality of child soldiers are psychologically fully dysfunctional, 10–15% of child soldiers exhibit crippling trauma, depression, or anxiety, and other 40% of child soldiers are at risk of becoming dysfunctional if they do not receive support.[42] Instead, other studies give evidence that as many as 97 percent of child soldiers may go through some form of post-traumatic stress disorder (PTSD),[43] regardless of the time they spent in violence.[44]

Therefore, before reintegrating child soldiers in society, they are supposed to have to be healed of their war trauma and "relearn childhood" in special rehabilitation centers. Yet, what happens if professional caregivers want to "cool them down"[45] and re-educate to be normal children again? Beah tells the story about his sojourn in an Interim Care Center.

> We refused to do anything that we were asked to do, except eat. At the end of every meal, the staff members and nurses came to talk to us about attending the scheduled medical checkups and the one-on-one counseling sessions that we hated at the minihospital that was part of Benin Home. As soon as the live-in staff, mostly men, started telling us what to do, we would throw bowls, spoons, food and benches at them. We would chase them out of the dining hall and beat them.[46]

Of course, one could attribute the aggressive behavior to the severity of their trauma. However, it is not just that the children refuse to be treated clinically, but they generally respond violently to their social environment and demonstrate commonly an orientation towards violent exploitation.[47] Child soldiers are upset of being treated as sick, traumatized and war-affected children, whose wishes and demands can be

---

[41] "There is a general agreement that children can indeed be traumatized by their experiences of armed conflict; that biological symptoms of child trauma, such as arousal and disassociation, are common across different cultures and that children's distress should be recognised" (Linda Dowdney, *Trauma, Resilience and Cultural Healing: How do we move forward?*, 2007, p. 3). See also Julie Guyot, *Suffer the Children: The Psychosocial Rehabilitation of Child Soldiers as a Function of Peace-Building*, 2007, p. 4; Michael Wessells, *Child Soldiers: From Violence to Protection*, Cambridge (Mass.), Harvard University Press 2007.

[42] Michael Wessells, *Trauma, Culture and Community: Getting Beyond Dichotomies*, 2007, p. 3 (http://www.child-soldiers.org/psycho-social/english)

[43] The term PTSD is used to describe the psychological and physical problems which can sometimes follow particular threatening or distressing events.

[44] Ilse Derluyn et al., "Post Traumatic Stress in Former Ugandan Child Soldiers," *The Lancet* 363 (9412), March 13, 2004, pp. 861–863.

[45] UNICEF, *The Disarmament, Demobilization and Reintegration of Children Associated with the Fighting Forces. Lessons Learned in Sierra Leone 1998–2002*, Dakar, UNICEF West and Central Africa Regional Office 2005, p. 20.

[46] Beah, *The Making, and Unmaking, of a Child Soldier*, op. cit..

[47] Beah reports that the demobilized child soldiers at the centre "would fight [each other] for hours for no reason at all" (Ibid.).

refused by adults. "It was infuriating to be told what to do by civilians. Their voices, even when they called us for breakfast, enraged me so much that I would punch the wall, my locker or anything nearby. A few days earlier, we could have decided whether they would live or die."[48] Keitetsi confirms in her memoirs that she believed to be "above any civilian, making [her] to have the final say (…)."[49] Child soldiers live in rehabilitation programs as a form of *humiliation* and *alienation*. They feel dishonored.

Experience proves that child soldiers cannot be treated in terms of heteronomy or victimhood, they cannot be dealt with neither as ordinary children. This is the major lesson of the past 25 years of demobilization and reintegration programs for child soldiers. Rehabilitation-oriented DDR programs relegating child soldiers to special reception centers and offering health and training programs fail to reach child soldiers. In Mozambique, the placement of child soldiers in recuperation centers did not work, and in Sierra Leone, "the majority of the children were fed up of living in centres."[50] Beth Verhey reports that "in Liberia, 89 percent of child soldiers in the 1996–1997 demobilization 'wandered away' from demobilization sites."[51] Consequentially, the lesson learned by UNICEF from the first wave of DDR programs in Sierra Leone was "that rehabilitation was not just about the psychological process of 'de-traumatization' or a process of education or skills training for a new way of life."[52]

Why does the center-solution not foster the reintegration of child soldiers? The standard answer given today is that clinical and psychotherapeutic approaches fail to treat child soldiers as *agents* and stigmatize as well as marginalize them as *patients*. "The emphasis on PTSD has resulted in an approach that does not fully balance individual agency with victimization."[53] It is sustained that stressing pathological outcomes in the context of a medicalized approach, risks an over-emphasis on victimization failing to "recognize the resources, resilience and potential contribution, of many children."[54] Child soldiers want to and need to participate in their own healing and reintegration.

The international community and NGOs slowly moved away from the standard implications of the victimization-thesis with regard to the question of how to treat child soldiers and started to take children's agency more seriously and to value

---

[48] And Beah continues that "one afternoon, after we had chased off several staff members, we placed a bucket over the cook's head and pushed him around the kitchen until he burned his hand on a boiling pot and agreed to put more milk in our tea" (Ibid.).

[49] Keitetsi, *Cild Soldier*, op. cit., p. 146.

[50] UNICEF, *Lessons Learned in Sierra Leone*, op. cit., p. 44; Honwana, *Negotiating Post-War Identities*, op. cit., p. 9.

[51] Verhey, *Child Soldiers*, op. cit., p. 10.

[52] UNICEF, *Lessons Learned in Sierra Leone*, op. cit., p. 22.

[53] Guyot, *Suffer the Children*, op. cit., p. 7.

[54] Ibid..

children's participation and self-expression.⁵⁵ Kofi Annan states in his report on "We, the Children" that "it is now recognized that *children should be involved* in the design and implementation of programs on their behalf, especially demobilization and reintegration processes, and, in general, policies to restore peace and put an end to violations of children's rights."⁵⁶

All the question is what form precisely the participatory design of DDR programs should take. Should DDR programs work out ways of forging new social identities for child soldiers in post-conflict society or should they enhance the autonomy of the young individuals, given the responsibility and independence they often enjoyed in armed groups? In order to answer this question, we need to understand what child soldiers' agency amounts to, or where child soldiers' agency flows from. To do this, we need to indicate the reasons for which child soldiers volunteer and identify as soldiers.

14.2 Child Soldiers as Agents: Communitarian and Psychosocial Approaches

Some authors maintain that humanitarian accounts are wrong to emphasize the inherent vulnerability and dependence of child soldiers and conclude that "ethnographic and historical accounts of young soldiers stress the agency, autonomy, and independence of youth."⁵⁷ Child soldiers "possess individual survival strategies, apply their own intelligence, strategize about situations, enter into relationships, have conversations, or do anything that ordinary soldiers might do."⁵⁸ It is only for political reasons that humanitarian descriptions do not recognize the maturity, competence and rationality of child soldiers: "These forms of explanation tend to work as a kind of emotional bedrock (…),"⁵⁹ that in particular NGOs often need to appeal to in order to justify their work. There is nothing specific about *child* soldiers. Therefore, they need to be treated in the same manner as adult soldiers are.⁶⁰

This position is not only counter-intuitive, but incoherent in itself. It does not hold that every child soldier, in whatever context, has to be universally considered as autonomous. The new paradigm emerging from cultural studies precisely denies that there is one sole, *universal* concept of childhood and stresses the conceptual diversity of childhood. Childhood has to be understood as being always embedded in a cultural, historical, and social context. Childhood and children's agency are a

---

⁵⁵ Kofi Annan's (former Secretary General of the United Nations) report, *We, the Children. Meeting the Promises of the World Summit for Children*, New York, UNICEF 2001, p. 99 [emphasis mine].
⁵⁶ Annan, *We, the Children*, op. cit., p. 85.
⁵⁷ Rosen, *Armies of the Young*, op. cit., p. 134.
⁵⁸ Ibid..
⁵⁹ Mats Utas, *Sweet Battlefields: Youth and the Liberian War*, Uppsala University Dissertations in Cultural Anthropology 1, 2003, p. 8.
⁶⁰ Rosen, *Armies of the Young*, op. cit..

social and cultural construction. Hence, it follows that it depends upon the respective social context, if child soldiers are to be considered as autonomous or not.

From such a perspective, the victimization-thesis fails in practice, insofar as the normative concept it is based upon, is only the result of a specific Western construction or invention of childhood.

> The standard European and northern American interpretations of children and youngsters usually view them as dependent, not fully grown and not yet ready to act in a responsible way. The social space to which children are relegated is that of the family and of school. This conceptualization is so pervasive that children who do not correspond to these definitions are immediately perceived as potential victims in need of help. (…) Viewed from such a western perspective, it is indeed not difficult to document how children are often reduced to victims requiring help due to the political, economic, sociocultural, psychological and sexual violence that pervades the African continent today.[61]

As the argument goes, it is only a matter of cultural preference that we, in Western societies, have developed various forms of protection for children until they reach the age of majority. In non-Western societies, children develop much earlier agency and a sense of responsibility. When young teenagers in Africa, Asia or Latin America feel themselves sufficiently adult for taking the decision to join armed forces,[62] this is in line with and based upon local cultural and social conventions.[63] It is even considered as a social duty of children to become soldiers in order to maintain the family, when circumstances do require this.[64] Child soldiers' agency is constructed by the identity of the children's cultures, and therefore children are not "vulnerable and passive victims, *subjected* to, or 'made and broken,' (…) but (…) active subjects, 'makers and breakers' of that reality."[65]

However, this more or less standard anthropological approach to childhood does not exactly want to defend the thesis that children in war exercise autonomous agency or the agency of adults, as it is conceived of in the respective cultures in which child soldiers grew up.[66] "This was clear from the conversations with elderly Angolans and Mozambicans who saw the violent and terrorizing actions employed by many child soldiers as falling outside what they would consider 'acceptable'

---

[61] de Boeck, *Kinshasa*, op. cit., pp. 181–182.

[62] Krijn Peters & Paul Richards, "Why we Fight: Voices of Under-Age Youth Combatants in Sierra Leone," *Africa* 68, 1998, pp. 183–210.

[63] „In line with more local notions of agency, children and youngsters in such African contexts are often not regarded, nor do they regard themselves, as future or proto adults but as social actors in the present with a marked role and presence at the very heart of the societal context"(de Boeck, *Kinshasa*, op. cit., p. 182).

[64] Filip de Boeck, "Borderland Breccia: The Mutant Hero in the Historical Imagination of a Central-African Diamond Frontier," *Journal of Colonialism and Colonial History* 1 (2), 2000, pp. 1–44; Maindo Monga Ngonga, *Survivre à la guerre des autres*, op. cit..

[65] de Boeck, *Kinshasa*, op. cit., p. 182.

[66] Volker Kaul, "Diamantenhandel und der Krieg in Kongo/Zaire,"*Afrika Spectrum* 42 (1), 2007, pp. 49–71.

responsible adult behavior, even in times of war."[67] The fact that children become increasingly accused of witchcraft in many sub-Saharan African societies, a phenomenon unknown until very recently, demonstrates to what extent cultures, in reality, disapprove the agency and power children exercise in war and criticize it as irresponsible.[68] In many cultures, child soldiers are not considered autonomous, since they did not perform the initiation ritual before turning into a soldier. In fact, the phenomenon of child soldiers dramatically erodes the pillars of many cultures that are based upon patriarchal gerontocratic orders.[69]

If culture is not the source of their agency, how else can we explain that children are happy with their military life and become ferocious soldiers? The major answer we find in the literature today is that child soldiers develop the *practical identity of warriors*. According to this model, child soldiers involved in armed forces gradually loose their previous identity of 'sons' or 'daughters' and are constructed as a "warlike persona."[70] It is reported that as soon as a child joins an armed group, she has to undergo a process of indoctrination and initiation to violence that is designed to bind the children to the group and to make them assume a new identity: "that of merciless killers"[71] or "killing machines."[72] During the initiation process, children are not only subjected to hard physical training and disciplinary sanctions, but are also compelled to take part in ritualised killings and commit atrocities, such as killing a family member or some of their relatives, drinking the blood of their victims or burning their natal neighbourhood. "It seemed to be a very organised strategy of (…) breaking down their defences and memory, and turning them into fighting machines that didn't have a sense of empathy and feeling for the civilian population."[73] Nicknames of alternative personas[74] and war heroes such as Zorro,

---

[67] Honwana, "Innocent & Guilty," op. cit., p. 43. After tracing a continuity between the local understanding of childhood and child soldiering in Sierra Leone, Susan Shepler, however, does not want to "argue that it was *their customs or practices of youth* that led to the worst abuses of child soldiers" (Susan Shepler, "The Social and Cultural Context of Child Soldiering in Sierra Leone," PRIO workshop on *Techniques of Violence in Civil War*, Oslo, August 20–21, 2004, p. 24 [Emphasis mine]).

[68] Filip de Boeck, "Le 'deuxième monde' et les 'enfants-sorciers,'" *Politique africaine* 80, 2000, pp. 37–52.

[69] de Boeck, *Kinshasa*, op. cit., pp. 159–161 and pp. 189–194; Jean-François Bayart, "La problématique de la démocratie en Afrique noire: La Baule…et puis après?," *Politique africaine* 43, 1991, pp. 5–20.

[70] Honwana, *Innocent & Guilty*, op. cit., p. 38. Jiovani Arias, *The Psychosocial Care of Demobilized Child Soldiers in Colombia: Conceptual and Methodological Aspects*, London: Coalition to Stop the Use of Child Soldiers 2005

[71] Honwana, *Negotiating Post-War Identities*, op. cit., p. 8.

[72] Ibid., p. 7.

[73] A Human Rights Watch worker quoted in Singer, *Children at War*, op. cit. p. 75.

[74] Some of the self-styled *noms de guerre* of the RUF fighters in Liberia are the following: Black Jesus, Captain Backblast, Body Naked, Blood, Colonel Bloodshed, Commando around the World, Commander Blood, General Share Blood, General Bloodshed, God Father, Commander Bullet, Captain Cut Hands, Queen Cut Hands, Captain Bonus, Dry Gin, Mohammed Killer Boy, Major Cut Throat, Mr. Die (Rosen, *Armies of the Young*, op. cit., p. 60).

Rambo, Superman, Terminator, Godzilla, and the Power Rangers, various drugs and divers fetishes for protection are supposed to further commit the kids to the common cause and enhance their combative moral and performance.[75]

As one psychologist engaged in rehabilitation of child soldiers confirms, it is maintained that "under certain conditions, practically any child could be changed into a killer."[76] Or, as Honwana notes, psychological pressure, indoctrination, manipulation and dehumanisation "remould their identities."[77] Jiovani Arias observes that child soldiers "evidence difficulty in establishing emotional connections outside of the members of their group – perhaps because the latter have become their closest socio-family referent, or 'substitute' family."[78] In this picture, the newly constructed warrior identity becomes the source of a child soldier's agency.

As a result, if DDR programs want to successfully demobilize and reintegrate child soldiers, they have to address and change their identity of warriors. If children are constructed as fighting machines, how can they be 'deconstructed' in order that they readopt the identity of a 'normal' child and member of civil society? The so-called 'psychosocial'[79] approaches suggest that, insofar as the children's social and political identity as well as social fabric need to be reconstructed, specific 'healing systems' located within the native cultural and social environment of the children have to be enhanced.[80] The official UN DDR standards for children conclude that…

> cultural, religious and traditional rituals can play an important role in the protection and reintegration of girls and boys into their communities, such as traditional healing, cleansing and forgiveness rituals; the development of solidarity mechanisms based on tradition; and the use of proverbs and sayings in sensitization and mediation activities. (…) Reconciliation ceremonies can offer forgiveness for acts committed, allow children to be 'cleansed' of the violence they have suffered, restore cultural links and demonstrate children's involvement in civilian life. Such ceremonies increase the commitment of communities to the children's reintegration process.[81]

International child welfare practice, put together in the UN "Integrated DDR Standards" launched in December 2006,[82] meanwhile consistently concluded that

---

[75] Kourouma, *Allah n'est pas obligé*, op. cit..

[76] Singer, *Children at War*, p. 75.

[77] Honwana, *Innocent & Guilty*, op. cit., p. 41.

[78] Arias, *The Psychosocial Care of Demobilized Child Soldiers*, op. cit., p. 2.

[79] The word 'psychosocial' implies a "dynamic relationship between psychological and social effects, each continually influencing the other" (Verhey, *Child Soldiers*, op. cit., p. 17).

[80] Honwana, *Let us light a new fire*, op. cit., p. 33; Arthur Kleinman, *Patients and Healers in the Context of Culture*, Berkeley, University of California Press 1989.

[81] IDDRS, *Children and DDR*, op. cit., 5.393.

[82] See also the proceedings of the International Conferences on DDR and Stability in Africa in Freetown, Sierra Leone, June 21–23, 2005 (https://www.un.org/press/en/2005/dc2972.doc.htm) and Kinshasa, DRC, June 12–14, 2007, the World Bank's "Multi-Country Demobilization and Reintegration Program" (MDRP) (http://documents.worldbank.org/curated/en/481721468149096857/pdf/564580WP0MDRP110Box349496B01PUBLIC1.pdf, accessed on March 20, 2020) and the "Stockholm Initiative on Disarmament Demobilisation Reintegration" (SIDDR Process) (https://reliefweb.int/sites/reliefweb.int/files/resources/

"psychosocial support should be offered instead of individual therapy to help children"[83] dealing with psychological problems and finding a way back to civil society.[84] Rehabilitation-oriented DDR programs do not suffer, as it is often maintained, from insufficient funding, lack of patience and endurance as well as corruption and inefficiency.[85] It is stressed that even the best-funded facilities cannot compensate for the children's emotional need of family and community ties as well as cultural traditions and values and do not prepare children for social roles and responsibilities in civil society.[86]

There is a striking and conceptually very deep distinction between psychotherapeutic and psychosocial approaches to DDR programs for child soldiers. Whereas psychotherapeutic models distinguish strictly between a child soldier's *rehabilitation* and her *reintegration* in civil society as two distinctive and temporally successive phases,[87] in the psychosocial premise, a child soldier's rehabilitation and her reintegration are identical and collapse into one single phase, which means that a child soldier is *rehabilitated when she is reintegrated*. Or, to put it into Elizabeth Jareg's terms, "'reintegration' eventually becomes indistinguishable from 'rehabilitation' as the child's psychosocial progress is inextricably linked with their once again becoming members of the community."[88] The question is for what reason a process of psychological recuperation becomes synonymous with participation in a cultural and social system. Moreover, if, as we have seen above, child soldiers are said to be constructed as 'war machines,' why should they want to become reintegrated by their community of origin? The answer given by psychosocial approaches to both questions is that child soldiers *suffer from their identity as warriors*, since it afflicts them with their traumatic experiences. In a sense, they recognize to have a 'sick' or 'ill' identity that needs to be healed through the adoption of a new, civil identity.

According to psychosocial approaches, child soldiers refuse trauma-related medical treatment, since it is external to their agency. What child soldiers really are suffering from, is their stigmatization as evil and as 'bandits' by their community. Mental ill-health is provoked by an imbalanced relationship of an individual with

---

ED1EF744FE93A788C1257428003110CB-gvtSweden_feb2006.pdf, accessed on March 20, 2020).

[83] IDDRS, *Children and DDR*, op. cit., 5.30.

[84] Neil Booth, Alison Strang & Michael Wessells, *A World Turned Upside Down: Social Ecological Approaches to Children in War Zones*, West Hartford, Kumarian Press 2006; Verhey, *Child Soldiers*, op. cit., p. 17; Michael Wessells, *Child Soldiers*, op cit., 2007.

[85] Krjin Peters, Paul Richards & Koen Vlassenroot, "What Happens to Youth During and After War. A preliminary review of literature on Africa and an assessment of the debate," *RAWOO Working Paper*, October 2003, p. 16; Alcinda Honwana, *Reintegration of Youth into Society in the Aftermath of War*, 2006, p. 2 (http://www.un.org/esa/socdev/unyin/documents/namibia_honwana.pdf)

[86] Verhey, *Child Soldiers*, op. cit., p. 13.

[87] Singer, *Children at War*, op. cit..

[88] Elizabteh Jareg, *Crossing Bridges and Negotiating Rivers – Rehabilitation and Reintegration of Children, Associated with Armed Forces*, 2005, London: Coalition to Stop the Use of Child Soldiers, pp. 2–3.

her social environment. As Honwana says, ill-health is a cultural idiom and "social construction with its meaning and management shaped by social and cultural understanding."[89] The crucial point of the psychosocial critique is that trauma therapy ignores the *ethical* roots of ill-health as well as reintegration and, thereby, not only not heals the child soldiers trauma but also contributes to further marginalization of the demobilized child soldiers.

In Angola and Mozambique, for example, "many people believe that war-related psychological trauma is directly linked to the anger of the spirits of those killed during the war, and who were not properly buried."[90] It is commonly thought that in order to get rid off the traumatizing spirits, child soldiers must change their identity so that they come to stop transgressing ethical norms. In many sub-Saharan African communities, identity-change involves the child soldier's participation in rituals of ostentatious and public rupture with military identity, rituals that 'cleanse' or 'purify' the child soldier and prepare her to become a member of the community. This is an example of a healing ritual in Mozambique: "The boy, dressed with the dirty clothes he brought from the RENAMO camp, entered the hut and undressed himself. Then fire was set to the hut, and the boy was helped out by an adult relative. The hut, the clothes and everything else that the boy brought from the camp had to be burned."[91]

The question that is not answered by this analysis is why child soldiers, as strongly committed warriors, should be troubled by the spirits of their victims and conceive themselves as having a sick identity. It could be true that the spirits of the victims chase the culprits. However, as long as the child is endorsing soldiering, she cannot care about and has to be even proud of being haunted by the victims' spirits. Being haunted by spirits is part of her identity and is characteristic of her being a good soldier. From the psychosocial perspective, it should rather be maintained that the trauma for child soldiers only begins, when she does not any longer believe to be haunted. Let me explain.

If the psychologies of child soldiers are constituted through their initiation to violence and the symbols of their group, as psychosocial approaches insist upon, child soldiers must come to define themselves through the role they assume within

---

[89] Honwana's position summarized by Dowdney, *Trauma, Resilience and Cultural Healing*, op. cit. p. 1.

[90] Honwana, *Let us Light a New Fire*, op. cit. p. 34. More or less the same beliefs are said to occur in West Africa (see Yawa Ossi Essiomle, *Psychologische Betreuung ehemaliger Kindersoldaten in Westafrika*, Dissertation, Freie Universität Berlin 2005 (https://refubium.fu-berlin.de/handle/fub188/3621, accessed on March 20, 2020).

[91] Honwana, *Negotiating Post-War Identities*, op. cit., p. 10. This is another example of a healing ritual in Angola: "In the past when a young man returned from the war, before getting into the family house he was taken to the river. In the river an elderly person treats him with water and the leaves of a tree called *mululua*. The treatment in the river always takes place at dawn ... in the middle of the river (in the stream), the soldier has to drink medicine – *lulua*, *ngola* and *cassale* – and the liquid extracted from the *mululua* leaves is splashed in the body (…). When he gets out of the river, the soldier cannot look back until he gets to the village" (Honwana, *Let us Light a New Fire*, op. cit., pp. 36–37).

14.2 Child Soldiers as Agents: Communitarian and Psychosocial Approaches

the armed forces and not any longer through their former civilian identities as 'daughters' or 'sons.' Since, as psychosocial approaches further hold, mental illheath is understood by the respective individual as resulting from a failure to fulfil properly her duty, child soldiers suffering from fear and anxiety should consequentially understand these emotions as a failure to be in line with the obligations the role of a soldier is bringing with. In this case, the best thing we can do for the traumatized child is to help her to become a better soldier. From the psychosocial perspective, what we really have to do, if we want to protect child soldiers, is to go into the different military camps and ask the commanders to provide better training to the children or propose to bring in some experienced mercenaries who could help out the children.

In conclusion, the direct consequence of the theoretical foundation of psychosocial approaches should not be civil reintegration but military reinsertion of child soldiers. Unsurprisingly, many have made precisely this conclusion. In Angola, Rwanda and Uganda special military schools were created, since it was thought that child soldiers would refuse and be demoralized by the civilian school system.[92] However, reports on the Uganda experience with these so-called "Kadogo Schools" indicate that "the majority of the 'demobilized' child soldiers ran away, resorted to delinquent behavior, or returned to military life."[93] Following an evaluation, the "Kadogo School" in Rwanda was closed in 1998, since agencies and the government emphasized the need for community-based approaches and family reunification.[94] Children do not like soldiering for its own sake.

Psychosocial approaches counter that child soldiers *actually must* distance themselves from their military identity and judge it as something particularly negative and repulsive. Child soldiers have to come to draw a distinction between *negative* and *positive identities*. Honwana puts forward that "this is clearly seen in the case of the child soldiers who *have to* acknowledge and appease the dead in order to avoid being haunted by them."[95] Yet, if, as we have seen above, the identity of a warrior brings along and sometimes is even defined by the haunting of spirits, latter cannot render the warrior-identity something negative. The negative qualification of an identity cannot come from the identity itself. Psychosocial approaches, therefore, must assume that although child soldiers identify as warriors, they want for some reason to get rid off that identity and adopt a 'positive' identity, "one that links the individual to a past that he/she wishes to maintain."[96]

Supposed that the child soldier remembers pre-war social commitments and identifications, for what reason does she have to consider those civil commitments as 'positive' and her present military commitments as 'negative'? The answer must be that war-making is interpreted by the child soldier as a transgression of

---

[92] Verhey, *Child Soldiers*, op. cit., pp. 12–13.
[93] Ibid., p. 13.
[94] Ibid., p. 16.
[95] Honwana, *Negotiating Post-War Identities*, op. cit., p. 12. [Emphasis mine].
[96] Ibid..

established cultural and social norms of her society. But must the child soldier really be bothered by this transgression? After all, her newly acquired military culture considers civil cultural norms as inadequate. What makes it that civil culture morally trumps military culture? Insofar as identity is the source of agency, and values are culturally and socially constructed, there is no way to determine what is a 'positive' or more 'real' and genuine' identity and what is a 'negative' or 'sick' identity. If child soldiers are the committed soldiers, as they are depicted, they have absolutely no reason to engage in cultural healing and reintegration. As Beah affirms, "in my head my life [as child soldier] was normal,"[97] and so, from their point of view, child soldiers do, contrary to the assumptions of psychosocial approaches, not understand what should be wrong with them being a soldier and are not troubled by their image as 'bandits.' "I threw the Walkman at her and left, putting my fingers in my ears so I couldn't hear her say, 'It is not your fault. (…) You were just a little boy. (…) You'll get through this.'"[98]

If DDR programs address the agency of child soldiers in terms of identity, *making* them participate in some form of cultural healing, they still treat them, even from within the psychosocial perspective itself, as patients and cannot avoid victimization and overcome refusal to reintegration. Moreover, they subscribe to a position in which child soldiers cannot have *proper* reasons for endorsing a military identity independent of manipulation and, therefore, as I will maintain in the next paragraph, they actually do not take into account their agency. Experience confirms that community-based approaches are not very much successful,[99] if child soldiers were not abducted as it was for example the case in Northern Uganda with the "Lord Resistance Army" (LRA).[100]

---

[97] Beah, *The Making, and Unmaking, of a Child Soldier*, op. cit..

[98] Ibid..

[99] The success of psychosocial programs is intricately difficult to evaluate. In the absence of war and conflicting armed groups or where military groups commit to not further recruit child soldiers, it remains often unclear if social reintegration and family reunification succeed because of the child soldiers' volition or due to communal pressure and lack of other opportunities. Therefore, it seems that the real test for the success of psychosocial approaches is, when war is still continuing and child soldiers effectively have the possibility to rejoin the armed groups. Experience from the DRC and Angola shows, however, that even culture-sensitive DDR programs fail in the middle of violent conflict and war, even when the condition for their applicability in form of an intact family and community web are given (see Honwana, *Reintegration of Youth into Society*, op. cit., p. 4; Singer, *Children at War*, op. cit., pp. 189–190; Refugees International Report, *Child Soldiers in the Congo. Business as Usual*, April 1, 2003; DAI, *Independent Evaluation of Special Projects for Child Soldiers in the Democratic Republic of Congo*, Final Report Presented to The World Bank's Multi-country Demobilization and Reintegration Program (MDRP), Contract No. 7137037, February 5, 2007).

[100] Beth Verhey reports that in Uganda children themselves note the importance of cleansing ceremonies so that their communities do not view them as 'contaminated' (Verhey, *Child Soldiers*, op. cit., p. 16):

14.3 Child Soldiers and Emancipation

In the premise of psychosocial as well as psychotherapeutic approaches, the reasons for which children *voluntarily* choose to fight and *identify* as soldiers, become utterly irrelevant for their reintegration. As a result, DDR programs often push child soldiers back into a *cultural and social context* that constituted precisely the reasons for which they became soldiers in the first place.[101] Community-based approaches tend to reproduce gender stereotypes and social inequalities that were often the reason for children's marginalization and frustration.[102] Not to speak about the incapacity of conflict and poverty-stricken communities to redress child protection problems.[103] Cultural healing is often practiced by the same communal authorities, such as traditional healers, church and village leaders, that gave children away to the armed groups and mediated their recruitment.[104] Krjin Peters and Paul Richards, interviewing child soldiers in Sierra Leone, report that "frustrated by the failure of demobilisation to offer a way out (...), several informants promptly re-enlisted (...) after the military *coup* of 25 May 1997."[105]

The main point of the victimization-thesis is that children do not *voluntarily* choose warfare, but that social circumstances *make them choose* soldiering, given their lack of autonomous agency. To put it in different terms, a child would not take up the arms, if the social context would be different. Children choose to become soldiers, *only* because they are *victims* of extreme poverty, insecurity, domestic exploitation and abuse, abandonment, orphanage, bad and unaffordable education systems as well as lack of employment and opportunity, only to mention the main constraining factors. As a result, their agency is defined as "anomalous agency,"[106] "victim's agency,"[107] "agency of the weak," or the "agency of pain."[108] Or, as Rachel Brett and Irma Specht conclude, analyzing interviews with former child soldiers and the reasons they gave for joining armed forces, "their actual descriptions (...)

---

[101] Steven Archibald & Paul Richards, "Conversion to Human Rights? Popular Debate about War and Justice in Central Sierra Leone," *Africa* 72 (3), 2002, pp. 339–367; Myriam Denov, *Is the Culture Always Right?*, op. cit.; Dyregrov et al., *Is the Culture Always Right?*, op. cit.; Krjin Peters, "From Weapons to Wheels: Young Sierra Leonean Ex-Combatants become Motorbike Taxi-Riders," *Peace, Conflict and Development* 10, 2007; Peters & Richards, *Why we Fight*, op. cit..

[102] Paul Richards, "To Fight or to Farm? Agrarian Dimensions of the Mano River Conflicts (Liberia and Sierra Leone)," *African Affairs* 104 (417), 2005, pp. 1–20; Archibald & Richards, *Conversion to Human Rights?*, op. cit..

[103] Beth Verhey, *Going Home. Demobilising and Reintegrating Child Soldiers in the Democratic Republic of Congo*, London, Save the Children 2003, p. 22.

[104] Honwana, *Innocent & Guilty*, op. cit., p. 40.

[105] Peters & Richards, *Why we Fight*, op. cit., p. 187.

[106] Jean Comaroff & John Comaroff, "Reflections on Youth. From the Past to the Postcolony," in Honwana & de Boeck, *Makers & Breakers*, op. cit., pp. 19–30.

[107] Mats Utas, "Agency of Victims. Young Women in the Liberian Civil War," in Honwana & de Boeck, *Makers & Breakers*, op. cit., pp. 53–80.

[108] Title of the second part of Honwana & de Boeck, *Makers & Breakers*, op. cit..

raise serious questions, about how many of them could be classified as volunteers *objectively*."[109] Hence, the effective degree of free choice must be doubted in many cases.[110]

However, as David Rosen correctly maintains, analysing the phenomenon of child soldiers solely in terms of victimhood inevitably leads to their demonization, since from that point of view their joy in soldiering and killing is incomprehensible. "Neither demons nor victims are rational actors."[111] In order to avoid the thesis of victimization or demonization, some recur to a distinction between the 'tactical' and the 'strategic' level of agency. Honwana maintains that the young combatants are deprived of full 'power,' in the sense, that they do not master "the larger picture and the long-term consequences of their actions, in the form of political gain or benefits/profits."[112] Yet, this multi-level conception of agency is precisely the justification of the victimization-thesis. In this picture, the agency of child soldiers inevitably disappears, and they turn into manipulated demons.

In order to understand why children do not perceive themselves as victims of war and instead identify for very specific reasons as soldiers, we have to switch from the third-person perspective to the first-person perspective of the child soldier. From a third-person perspective, social exclusion and marginalization are the reasons for which children choose to go to war. Their victimhood in society, commonly described as "dead society" or referred to as society in multi-crisis,[113] *causes* them to become soldiers. Therefore, the reasons that make children join the army remain always external to their actual subjective motivational set. From this third-person perspective, it is impossible not to consider child soldiers as victims. However, from the first-person perspective, the fact that children perceive themselves as victims of their social environment and the failure of patrimonial politics[114] precisely makes soldiering so attractive to them. It is the very fact of social crisis and poverty that makes children indeed embrace *voluntarily* and *freely* the arms. Because children are socially subjugated, war appears to them as liberation from their social constraints and misery. From their point of view, remaining in civil society is considered as the real involuntary and unfree choice, and not joining the armed forces. "The accounts repeatedly stress that *it makes little sense* to stand down *voluntarily* without any real promise of social reintegration, education or training, or civilian job prospects."[115] Victimhood does not deprive children of endorsing proper reasons as well as seeking ways for emancipation and self-realization.

---

[109] Brett & Specht, *Young Soldiers*, op. cit., p. 109 [my emphasis].

[110] Ibid., p. 5.

[111] Rosen, *Armies of the Young*, op. cit., p. 134.

[112] Honwana, *Innocent & Guilty*, op. cit., p. 50. For a similar position see Caroline Moser & Fiona Clark, *Victims, Perpetrators or Actors. Gender, Armed Conflict and Political Violence*, London, Zed Books 2001.

[113] de Boeck, *Kinshasa*, op. cit., p. 159.

[114] Peters & Richards, *Why we Fight*, op. cit..

[115] Ibid., p. 187 [Emphasis mine].

14.3 Child Soldiers and Emancipation

Given the circumstances, war is an opportunity to reach some form of human dignity. As Birahima, the fictive child soldier in Ahmadou Kourouma's novel "Allah n'est pas obligé", explains: "With the Kalachnikovs, the child soldiers had all they needed. They had money, even American dollars. They had shoes, stripes, radios, small helmets and even cars that are also called 4x4. I shouted Walahé! Walahé! I wanted to leave for Liberia. Immediately. I wanted to become a child soldier, a small soldier. A child soldier or soldier child, that's the same shit. I only had the word small soldier in my mouth. In my bed, when I pooped or did pee-pee, I yelled by myself small soldier, child soldier, soldier child."[116]

Anthropologists show with great clarity the emancipatory potential of war for children against the background of "the sometimes violent rejection of ancestral and parental figures in response to what is understood as their absence, their impotence, or their withdrawal of protection."[117] Street children in Kinshasa, many of which became child soldiers, explain: "At home, eating is an uncertain and difficult thing" and therefore they prefer to "sign a contract with death."[118] As Filip de Boeck analyzes, the street "is also perceived as an almost oneiric space of diversion, possibility and promise, where 'your body belongs to yourself' and you can 'dedouble yourself,' dance, drink, 'dream,' and 'have fun.'"[119] Female child soldiers from the rebel group FRELIMO in Mozambique saw their participation in combat as empowering and liberating and continued to see it this way as adults. They experienced warfare not only as liberating from colonial rule but also from the traditional structures of male dominance. "For these women, revolutionary ideologies played an important role both in (…) helping them create new roles and identities in postcolonial Mozambique."[120]

Warfare does not only provide access to food – "one ate as much as five and some leftovers always remained"[121] – but also fosters self-realization. *Kadogos* in the DRC gained around 100 U.S. dollars monthly, an income that allowed them to live an idiosyncratic interpretation of the modern good life through ostensive consumption of beer, women and consumer goods.[122] China Keitetsi tells us about the pride she felt being able to buy her mother a house after some time in the military and

---

[116] Kourouma, *Allah n'est pas obligé*, op. cit., pp. 43–44. [Translation mine].

[117] Michael Lambek, "Nuriaty, the Saint and the Sultan. Virtuous Subject and Subjective Virtuoso of the Post-Modern Colony," *Anthropology Today* 16 (2), 2000, p. 12.

[118] de Boeck, *Kinshasa*, op. cit., p. 188.

[119] Ibid..

[120] Study of Harry West reported in Rosen, *Armies of the Young*, op. cit., p. 17. Rosen also gives an account of two other studies on female child soldiers of the "Eritrean People's Liberation Front" and "Tigray Peoples Liberation Front" in Ethiopia, in which Virginia Bernal and Angela Veale equally show that war is perceived by many children as a form of access to independence and sexual equality (Ibid., p. 18).

[121] Kourouma, *Allah n'est pas obligé*, op. cit., p. 79; Achille Mbembé, "Pouvoir, violence et accumulation," in Jean-Francois Bayart, Achille Mbembé & Comi Toulabor, *Le politique par le bas en Afrique noire. Contributions à une problématique de la démocratie*, Paris, Karthala 1992, p. 253.

[122] de Boeck, *Kinshasa*, op. cit., p. 42.

returning to her father, who before she became a soldier regularly abused her, as an independent young woman. Celebrating 'Kalashnikov-lifestyles,' *kadogos* become some sort of pop stars and cultural heroes in their society.[123] They are objects of female admiration: "He turns into the hero of young girls, who dream only of one thing: become a *kadogo* herself or marry a *kadogo*."[124] As de Boeck maintains, children and youngsters constitute the site of identity construction in society and "appear as the ultimate focal points of the contemporary Central African imaginary."[125]

DDR programs must take place against the background of the search for personal autonomy. Also child soldiers who perceive themselves as victims all the way long, considering war as a loss of time exposing them to cruel experiences,[126] commit themselves to their military role and will not leave the armed forces until they find a decent alternative for self-realization. Keitetsi, who portrays herself as the victim *par excellence*, started to always dress like a soldier, treated others most brutally, became obsessed with hierarchy and considered civilians as stupid. When she was offered a job as cleaning girl, she went back to the military only after a few days: "I realized that I simply didn't fit into this community, being a small girl with a vast military experience."[127] Moreover, DDR programs need to be aware of forms of solidarity and friendships that developed within the armed forces and that relate child soldiers to their group.

What should DDR programs look like then? I will finish this essay with a very short proposal on this matter.

14.4 The Reintegration of Child Soldiers

DDR programs must address socioeconomic questions taking into account the identity of child soldiers. Family reunification and returning child soldiers back to their communities are often the wrong measures. Often the kids have been abused by their family or lost it completely and so would have to be integrated into families of far relatives, who often are already overburdened with their own kids.[128] Accounts of child soldiers suggest that the perspective of having to return to the native village and becoming involved in farming is not very attractive. Richards argues that children do not so much dislike agricultural activities as they fear their vulnerability to

---

[123] Richard Banégas & Bogumil Jewsiewicki, "Vivre dans la guerre. Imaginaires et pratiques populaires de la violence en RCD," *Politique africaine* 84, 2001, pp. 5–17; Richard Banégas & Jean-Pierre Warnier, "Nouvelles Figures de la réussite et du pouvoir," *Politique africaine* 82, 2001, pp. 5–24; Reno, *Warlord Politics and African States*, op. cit., p. 158.

[124] Maindo Monga Ngonga, *Survivre à la guerre des autres*, op. cit., p. 54.

[125] de Boeck, *Kinshasa*, op. cit., p. 158.

[126] Honwana, *Innocent & Guilty*, op. cit., p. 47.

[127] Keitetsi, *Child Soldier*, op. cit., p. 147.

[128] de Boeck, *Le 'deuxième monde' et les 'enfants-sorciers,'* op. cit..

social exclusion by local elites and gerontocrats.[129] Moreover, in the military these kids gained a certain level of responsibility and economic autonomy and cannot simply be relegated to a position of dependence.

In order to account for the self-understanding of the children, DDR programs should avoid any forms of care and conceive interventions as 'acupunctural.' Ways must be found to attract and promote these kids without intervening paternalistically with their preference-formation. Therefore, reintegration cannot be conceived as a way of re-organizing and re-directing their life. This would amount to treating them as patients rather than agents and deny them participation in their construction of a new personal identity. NGO-projects often fail for exactly this reason. Also, attending some vocational school does not yet fit their way of life and might come for many kids too early, given their lack of professional experience and the insecurity about the future economic development and needs of the country.[130]

The example Peters gives of child soldiers turning into taxi-men in the provincial towns of Sierra Leone points to the right direction. As a bike-rider says, "the war was exciting, but bad. To be a bike-rider is exciting and good."[131] Former comrades joined together and bought a bike, that they use as a taxi in shifts. Moreover, bike-owners formed taxi-men unions in order to protect themselves against the arbitrariness of local elites and corrupt officers. However, taxi-driving is, of course, a limited business.

A viable alternative and autonomy-based, truly participatory approach to social intervention is the award-winning concept of a 'pocketmoney-company' for youngsters, labeled "Teenkom" and designed by the Berlin-based agency ArtSourceLab.[132] Teenkom is a role-game based upon the principles of the market and the peer-group. Employers post a mini-job offer that gets forwarded to those youngsters enrolled in Teenkom that match the requested profile. Teenkom always operates in several competing, autonomous groups, in order to foster 'gang' identification and solidarity among the group members. It is an IT-based system that requires online-registration and the creation of an account for employers and youngsters and forwards automatically job offers by SMS or e-mail. Employers do not know the true identity of the kids, since they operate with specific Teenkom ID-cards and names. Employers and children evaluate each other, and the evaluations flow into the online-profile of both. Teenkom imposes only the rules of the game, otherwise it respects fully the self-organization and the autonomy of its members satisfying their demand for personal responsibility.

As long as there is war, Teenkom-like DDR programs would not force child soldiers to demobilize but offer them temporary enrollment in a Teenkom group. Only once child soldiers are convinced of this alternative to war, measures should be undertaken to protect them from re-enrollment and provide them with free food and

---

[129] Richards, *To Fight or to Farm?*, op. cit..
[130] UNICEF, *Lessons Learned in Sierra Leone*, op. cit., pp. 38–19.
[131] Peters, *From Weapons to Wheels*, op. cit., p. 15.
[132] See www.artsourcelab.net and www.teenkom.de

housing for a period of time. Child soldiers would enjoy a certain economic independence and make diverse professional experiences before re-engaging in an alternative identity construction. This could be sustained through the offer of free formative and educative courses, individual psychotherapies and family tracing. Insofar as Teenkom group-members share a common identity, youngsters could maintain their commitments to their friends and further engage in group solidarity.

The open question is, why child soldiers should be motivated to participate in such programs. The answer is that kids do not, so much, like the war than the fruits of war. And if these fruits can maturate in some alternative way, few kids would prefer war.

References

Annan, Kofi. 2001. *We, the Children. Meeting the Promises of the World Summit for Children.* New York: UNICEF.
Archibald, Steven, and Paul Richards. 2002. Conversion to Human Rights? Popular Debate about War and Justice in Central Sierra Leone. *Africa* 72 (3): 339–367.
Banégas, Richard, and Bogumil Jewsiewicki. 2001. Vivre dans la guerre. Imaginaires et pratiques populaires de la violence en RCD. *Politique africaine* 84: 5–17.
Banégas, Richard, and Jean-Pierre Warnier. 2001. Nouvelles Figures de la réussite et du pouvoir. *Politique africaine* 82: 5–24.
Bayart, Jean-François. 1991. La problématique de la démocratie en Afrique noire: La Baule…et puis après ? *Politique africaine* 43 (1991): 5–20.
Bayart, François, Achille Mbembé, and Comi Toulabor. 1992. *Le politique par le bas en Afrique noire. Contributions à une problématique de la démocratie.* Paris: Karthala.
Beah, Ishmael.2007. *The Making, and Unmaking, of a Child Soldier.* New York Times Magazine, January 14, 2007. http://www.nytimes.com/2007/01/14/magazine/14soldier.t.html?ex=1326430800&en=18db63da3854259e&ei=5088&partner=rssnyt&emc=rss. Accessed on 20 Mar 2020.
Booth, Neil, Alison Strang, and Michael Wessells. 2006. *A World Turned Upside Down: Social Ecological Approaches to Children in War Zones.* West Hartford: Kumarian Press.
Brett, Rachel & Margaret McCallin. 1996. Children: the Invisible Soldiers, Stockholm, Swedish Save the Children.
Brett, Rachel, and Irma Specht. 2004. *Young Soldiers. Why They Choose to Fight.* Boulder/Geneva: Lynne Rienner/ILO.
Briggs, Jimmie. 2005. *Innocents Losts.* New York: Basic Books.
DAI. 2007. *Independent Evaluation of Special Projects for Child Soldiers in the Democratic Republic of Congo*, Final Report Presented to The World Bank's Multi-country Demobilization and Reintegration Program (MDRP), Contract No. 7137037, February 5, 2007.
De Boeck, Filip. 2000a. Borderland Breccia: The Mutant hero in the Historical Imagination of a Central-African Diamond Frontier. *Journal of Colonialism and Colonial History* 1 (2): 1–44.
———. 2000b. Le 'deuxième monde' et les 'enfants-sorciers. *Politique africaine* 80 (2000): 37–52.
De Boeck, Filip, and Marie-Françoise Plissart. 2004. *Kinshasa. Tales of the Invisible City.* Ghent: Ludion.
Denov, Myriam. 2007. *Is the Culture Always Right? The Dangers of Reproducing Gender Stereotypes and Inequalities in Psycho-social Interventions for War-affected Children.* London: Coalition to Stop the Use of Child Soldiers.
Derluyn, Ilse, et al. 2004. Post traumatic stress in former Ugandan child soldiers. *The Lancet* 363 (9412): 861–863.

Dowdney, Linda. 2007. *Trauma, Resilience and Cultural Healing: How Do We Move Forward?* London: Coalition to Stop the Use of Child Soldiers.
Dyregrov, Atle, Leila Gupta, Rolf Gjestad, and Magne Raundalen. 2002. Is the Culture Always Right? *Traumatology* 8 (3): 135–145.
Erikson, Erik. 2004. *Identity: Youth and Crisis*. New York: W.W. Norton.
Essiomle, Yawa Ossi (2005), *Psychologische Betreuung ehemaliger Kindersoldaten in Westafrika*, Dissertation, Freie Universität Berlin 2005. https://refubium.fu-berlin.de/handle/fub188/3621. Accessed on 20 Mar 2020.
Goodwin-Gill, Guy, and Ilene Cohn. 1994. *Child Soldiers: the Role of Children in Armed Conflicts*. Oxford: Clarendon Press.
Gutmann, Amy. 1980. Children, Paternalism, and Education: A Liberal Argument. *Philosophy and Public Affairs* 9 (4): 338–358.
Guyot, Julie. 2007. *Suffer the Children: The Psychosocial Rehabilitation of Child Soldiers as a Function of Peace-Building*. London: Coalition to Stop the Use of Child Soldiers.
Honwana, Alcinda. 1998, *Okusiakala Ondalo Yokalye: Let us Light a New Fire. Local Knowledge in the Post-War Healing and Reintegration Of War-Affected Children in Angola*, Consultancy Report for Christian Children's Fund, November 1998. http://citeseerx.ist.psu.edu/viewdoc/download?doi=10.1.1.618.7261&rep=rep1&type=pdf. Accessed on 20 Apr 2020.
———. 2005. Innocent & Guilty. Child Soldiers as interstitial & tactical agents. In *Makers & Breakers. Children & Youth in Postcolonial Africa*, ed. Alcinda Honwana and Filip de Boeck, 31–52. Oxford: James Currey.
———. 2006. *Reintegration of Youth into society in the aftermath of War*. http://www.un.org/esa/socdev/unyin/documents/namibia_honwana.pdf.
———. 2007a. Negotiating Post-War Identities. Child soldiers in Mozambique and Angola. *CODESRIA Bulletin* 1-2 (1999): 4–13.
———. 2007b. *Child Soldiers in Africa*. Philadelphia: University of Pennsylvania Press.
Honwana, Alcinda, and Filip de Boeck, eds. 2005. *Makers & Breakers. Children & Youth in Postcolonial Africa*. Oxford: James Currey.
Human Rights Watch/Africa Human Rights Watch Children's Rights Project. 1994. *Easy Prey: Child Soldiers in Liberia*. New York: Human Rights Watch.
Huntington, Samuel. 1996. *The Clash of Civilizations and the Remaking of World Order*. New York: Simon & Schuster.
Jareg, Elizabteh. 2005. *Crossing Bridges and Negotiating Rivers – Rehabilitation and Reintegration of Children, Associated with Armed Forces*. London: Coalition to Stop the Use of Child Soldiers.
Jiovani, Arias. 2005. *The Psychosocial Care of Demobilized Child Soldiers in Colombia: Conceptual and Methodological Aspects*. London: Coalition to Stop the Use of Child Soldiers.
Kaldor, Mary. 1999. *New and Old Wars. Organized Violence in a Global Era*. Stanford: Stanford University Press.
Kalyvas, Stathis. 2001. 'New' And 'Old' Civil Wars: A Valid Distinction? *World Politics* 54 (1): 99–118.
Kaplan, Robert. 1994. *The Coming Anarchy: How Scarcity, Crime, Overpopulation, Tribalism, and Disease are Rapidly Destroying the Social Fabric of Our Planet*. The Atlantic Monthly, February 1994.
Kaul, Volker. 2007. Diamantenhandel und der Krieg in Kongo/Zaire. *Afrika Spectrum* 42 (1): 49–71.
Kayihura, Kale. 2000. *Uganda: The Integration of Child Soldiers into the School System*. Paris: Association for the Development of Education in Africa.
Keitetsi, China. 2004. *Child Soldier*. London: Souvenir Press.
Kleinman, Arthur. 1989. *Patients and Healers in the Context of Culture*. Berkeley: University of California Press.
Kourouma, Ahmadou. 2000. *Allah n'est pas obligé*. Paris: Seuil.
Lambek, Michael. 2000. Nuriaty, the Saint and the Sultan. Virtuous Subject and Subjective Virtuoso of the Post-Modern Colony. *Anthropology Today* 16 (2): 7–12.

Maindo Monga Ngonga, Alphonse. 2001. Survivre à la guerre des autres. *Politique africaine* 84: 33–58.
Moser, Caroline, and Fiona Clark. 2001. *Victims, Perpetrators or Actors. Gender, Armed Conflict and Political Violence*. London: Zed Books.
Peters, Krjin. 2007. From Weapons to Wheels: Young Sierra Leonean Ex-Combatants become Motorbike Taxi-Riders. *Peace, Conflict and Development* 10: 2007.
Peters, Krjin, and Paul Richards. 1998. Why we Fight: Voices of Under-Age Youth Combatants in Sierra Leone. *Africa* 68 (2): 183–210.
Peters, Krjin, Paul Richards & Koen Vlassenroot. 2003. What Happens to Youth During and After War. A preliminary review of literature on Africa and an assessment of the debate. *RAWOO Working Paper*, October 2003.
Refugees International Report. 2003. Child Soldiers in the Congo. *Business as Usual*, April 1, 2003.
Reno, William. 1998. *Warlord Politics and African States*. London: Lynne Rienner.
Richards, Paul. 2005. To Fight or to Farm? Agrarian Dimensions of the Mano River Conflicts (Liberia and Sierra Leone). *African Affairs* 104 (417): 1–20.
Rosen, David. 2005. *Armies of the Young. Child Soldiers in War and Terrorism*. New Brunswick: Rutgers University Press.
Shepler, Susan. 2004. *The Social and Cultural Context of Child Soldiering in Sierra Leone. PRIO workshop on Techniques of Violence in Civil War*. Paper presented at the PRIO workshop Techniques of Violence in Civil War, Oslo, Norway, August 20–21, 2004.
Singer, Peter W. 2005. *Children at War*. Westminster: Knopf.
The United Nations Children's Fund (UNICEF). 2004. *The State of the World's Children 2005. Childhood Under Threat*. New York: UNICEF.
UN Integrated Disarmament, Demobilization and Reintegration Standards (IDDRS). 2020. *Children and DDR*, 5.30. https://unddr.org/uploads/documents/IDDRS%205.30%20Children%20and%20DDR.pdf. Accessed on 20 Mar 2020.
UNICEF. 2005. *The disarmament, demobilization and reintegration of children associated with the fighting forces. Lessons learned in Sierra Leone 1998–2002*. Dakar: UNICEF West and Central, Africa Regional Office.
United Nations Development Program (UNDP). 2006. *Youth and Violent Conflict: Society and Development in Crisis?* New York: UNDP.
Utas, Mats. 2003. Sweet Battlefields: Youth and the Liberian War, Uppsala University Dissertations in Cultural Anthropology 1.
Verhey, Beth. 2001. *Child Soldiers: Preventing, Demobilizing and Reintegrating*. Africa Region Working Paper Series 23, November 2001.
———. 2003. *Going Home. Demobilising and Reintegrating Child Soldiers in the Democratic Republic of Congo*. London: Save the Children.
Virnich, Birgit & Bartholomäus Grill. 2003. Dossier: Krieg der Kinder. *Die Zeit* 36, August 28.
Wessells, Michael. 2007. *Child soldiers: From violence to protection*. Cambridge, MA: Harvard University Press.

Chapter 15
Conclusion: For the Time Being: *Modus Vivendi* Liberalism or Political Liberalism?

Abstract The book comes to the conclusion that the compatibility paradigm does not yet provide a valid theory that strikes the right balance between identity and emancipation. The pendulum swings either to the side of Kantian transcendentalism or to that of unfettered communitarianism. Therefore, this conclusion suggests that until we have found a theory of liberalism that manages to accommodate *fully* both identity and emancipation, we need to go back to liberal theories that in the past despite shortcomings have politically fared more successfully than righteous Kantianism. It lines out the governance approach that has its origin in the 'liberal neutrality' paradigm of classic liberalism and today is often referred to as *modus vivendi* liberalism. This concluding chapter puts forth some arguments why, despite its shortcomings, it is preferable to the moralistic approach of practical reason that is at the root of political liberalism.

Keywords Modus vivendi liberalism · Political liberalism · Social contract · Neutrality of the state · Civil wars · Rational choice · Practical reason · General will · Enlightenment · Peace of Westphalia · Thomas Hobbes · John Locke · Jean-Jacques Rousseau · Immanuel Kant

The aim of this book is to pass review, analyze in depth and evaluate critically what we could call the 'compatibility paradigm.' This paradigm consists in all those theories that do not see as classic liberalism and more moderately political liberalism a strong opposition between identity and individual emancipation, but which are convinced that emancipation needs to be envisaged and can be achieved only from *within* the different identities. As I argue, this has become the almost unchallenged point of departure of much of contemporary political and moral theory, once pluralism is seen and recognized as a permanent and not mere contingent feature of our societies.

The book comes however to the conclusion that the compatibility paradigm does not yet provide a valid theory that strikes the right balance between identity and emancipation. The pendulum swings either to the side of Kantian transcendentalism (see Part I of the book) or to that of unfettered communitarianism (see Part II of the book). And this is not without real political problems, as I maintain in the third part of the book. In the face of a strongly moralizing and elitist liberal position proclaiming "Enlightenment Now",[1] populism, majoritarianism, authoritarianism and communalism are on the rise around the globe.

Therefore, I would like to suggest in these concluding remarks that, for the time being, until we have found a theory of liberalism that manages to accommodate *fully* both identity and emancipation, we need to go back to liberal theories that in the past despite shortcomings have politically fared more successfully than righteous Kantianism. And as a matter of fact, the governance approach of liberal egalitarianism, of which the contours are arising in his book, after all separates the questions of emancipation and identity, making emancipation a matter of public policies while restricting identity to civil society and the private sphere. Therefore I line out more in detail the governance approach that has its origin in the 'liberal neutrality' paradigm of classic liberalism and today is often referred to as *modus vivendi* liberalism. I put forth some arguments why, despite its shortcomings, it is preferable to the moralistic approach of practical reason that is at the root of political liberalism.

15.1 *Modus Vivendi* Liberalism

The post-Cold War era is often characterized as one of unprecedented identity conflicts.[2] From the Balkan wars to the ethnic conflicts in Sub-Saharan Africa and Asia to the rise of Islamic fundamentalism, global politics has been confronted with the question of how to accommodate identities and religious and ethnic pluralism. However, identity conflicts are certainly not new in world history. If we take Europe as example, it was devastated for centuries first by religious and then national conflicts, to the point that Europe from the Reformation onwards was the theater of an intense philosophical debate of how to deal with these conflicts. And it is precisely in these adverse circumstances that liberalism, at least liberal political thought, is born. Liberalism from its very on-set, and not just in the wake of globalization, is supposed to be an *answer* to the challenges of identity, that in particular with regard to political Islam are not so different from those of the interreligious wars following the Counter-Reformation.

At first sight, it might seem rather surprising that European thinkers, such as in particular Thomas Hobbes and John Locke, came to consider liberalism as solution to the identity conflicts ravaging the continent. Confessional and communal violence was anything but new at the time, not in other parts of the world, but also not in Europe itself. And never was liberalism, with its emphasis on the individual and its freedom, supposed to be a possible answer to identity conflicts. The way identity

---

[1] Pinker, *Enlightenment Now*.
[2] Kaldor, *New and Old Wars*.

issues were resolved up to then was through a political scheme that in its outlines comes very close to what we call today multiculturalism. The Roman Empire and the Ottoman Empire as well as the Mughal Empire in India all granted extensive autonomy and rights of self-government to the communities present on their territories in order to defuse possible conflicts. The common law of the empire was *neutral* with respect to the conflicting values of the communities and its sole function was to regulate intercommunitarian affairs and to protect communities from mutual interventions. This was the standard recipe for social peace up to Hobbes' days and actually lasted with the Habsburg Empire long into European modernity. And until today, multicultural arrangements and communalism remain the predominant political models in particular in Sub-Saharan Africa and in India. ('Communalism in Sub-Saharan Africa,' in this volume) Why do then Hobbes and the liberals following him contest this multicultural model?

The intuitive answer today is that multiculturalism perhaps achieves social peace, but it does so often at the cost of the individual, its rights and emancipation. Yet, Hobbes in *Leviathan*, as mentioned above, is exclusively interested in putting an end to religious strife and the achievement of social peace. For Hobbes and classic liberals, the problem of multiculturalism is rather that it might result in instability, given that it misconceives the origins of conflict and civil war. In Hobbes' state of nature, a metaphor for the state of England at his lifetime, a "war of all against all," men are at war not because of religious values or truths or communal differences, but for the simple fact that each one is a rational being trying to maximize his or her interests and well-being. In this perspective, religious conflicts are an expression of these conflicting individual interests, not their source. At the surface, religion seems to be the cause of war, but if one scratches just deep enough the real cause comes to the fore: desires, preferences, interests. Religion, in this regard, is more of a false consciousness, so as later Marx makes it more explicit. In Hobbes' analysis, it is the anxiety about the future that makes people incline to adopt religious beliefs.

The idea that conflicts, in the end, are reducible to individual rational choices is a fundamental theorem in contemporary war and peace studies and in the analysis of the ethnic and religious conflicts emerging after the fall of the Berlin Wall.[3] Evaluating a data set of wars during 1960–99, Paul Collier and Anke Hoeffler come to the conclusion that those conflicts have their cause not in 'grievances,' such as, amongst others, ethnic and religious divisions in society, but in 'greed' and can be explained by economic variables alone.[4]

Accordingly, individuals end their conflicts only under the condition that the exit of the state of nature guarantees a greater well-being. Multiculturalism plays here no role, given that it is concerned with group identity and values rather than individual interests. The problem however is that individual interests are divergent and potentially conflicting, as the case of disagreement in religious views demonstrates.

---

[3] Kaul, "Foreword: Contemporary Conflicts, Political Legitimacy and Political Islam;" Kaul, "Diamantenhandel und der Krieg in Kongo/Zaire."
[4] Collier & Hoeffler, "Greed and Grievance in Civil War." See also Berdal & Malone, *Greed & Grievance*.

If the state would favor or advantage, for moral or other reasons, some of those interests at the expense of others, the state of nature would of course continue to persist as a state of war. The only solution available, upon which all individuals can agree and thereby put an end to the state of nature, is a civil state that is thoroughly *neutral* between the different interests, leaving them unaltered, not touching upon them. In this way, individuals can continue to pursue their interests as *freely* as before, but this time with the guarantee provided by the law that the other individuals do not interfere with them. The law and the political obligations to which it gives rise make freedom in the private sphere possible.

To sum up, Hobbes argues that state law needs to be neutral between *individuals* and not groups. In this regard, law needs to protect individual interests and *not* group interests. Yet, this is not the end of religion as we know it, and collective identities more in general. Hobbes, and later Locke and the liberal thinkers following him, never ban any form of religion. On the contrary, the freedom of conscience, guaranteed by the neutrality of the state, protects religions and assures them a firm place in *civil* society, as long as and under the strict condition that they stay *outside* the public sphere and consequently politics. Classic liberalism does not claim that individuals have any moral obligation to repudiate their identities. It does not engage with individual conscience and leaves individuals free to practice their identities and religion in so far as they do not contradict the law. To some extent, classic liberalism remains committed to the medieval doctrine of the 'Two Swords', that separates rigorously between the political and legal realm, on the one hand, and the moral, ethical and religious realm, on the other hand. Law in classic liberalism is not conceived *against* identities, but simply independent of them. The legitimacy of the state requires the separation of the public and the private sphere, politics and religion, law and identity. To put it succinctly, emancipation takes place in the first sphere, whereas identities are practiced within the latter sphere.

This model, that runs like a red thread through the history of liberal thought up to Rawls' *A Theory of Justice* and is today most prominently defended by *modus vivendi* liberalism,[5] seems to be the ultimate solution to identity conflicts, given that it protects as much as multiculturalism the practice of identities, though it does so on an individual and not collective basis, while it maximizes individual interests. It is however interesting to note that despite these first powerful philosophical formulations of liberalism, the political practice that eventually managed to put an end to religious wars in Europe was entirely different and at the same time profoundly illiberal. For centuries, it is the principle of "cuius regio, eius religio" that dominates the politics of European states, with the consequence that the public sphere was anything but neutral and the freedom of the private sphere became seriously violated, despite the various provisions in the Peace Treaties of Westphalia of 1648 that guarantee religious freedoms. Was this just a bad coincidence or are there deeper

---

[5] Ferarra, "How to Accommodate Modus Vivendi Within Normative Political Theory"; Geuss, *Philosophy and Real Politics*; Gray, *Two Faces of Liberalism*; McCabe, *Modus Vivendi Liberalism*; Williams, *In the Beginning Was the Deed*.

structural connections between the original conceptions of classic liberalism and the identity politics that followed in practice?

I would like to suggest that this was not just accidental and that classic liberalism goes along with and actually might give rise to majoritarianism and nation-building processes.[6] Although Hobbes changes drastically the foundations of religious identity making it a mere expression of individual interest, fact is that identity remains a powerful force in the individuals' lives. Individuals have an interest and stake in *their* religion, given that it is functional within their psychological economy. When individuals enter from the state of nature into the civil state, this interest and stake in their identity *persists* and they continue to be rational beings that seek the greatest possible profit. They know that the law generally goes in their favor. Yet they also know, as much as Hobbes' Fool, that it would be even more convenient if the state makes their interests and conceptions of the good its own, whenever the probability of resistance and opposition from those citizens that in this way get marginalized and excluded is very low or negligible. And it is clear that the more powerful and glorious a religion is, the more it is able to provide real protection for an uncertain future. When power relations between the different interest groups are unequal, the Hobbesian liberal state has no *moral* resources to protect the neutrality of the state and consequently minorities. One could bring forth that under counterfactual circumstances, such as under a veil of ignorance, it would not be convenient to break the law.[7] Yet in the real world and real politics that argument is simply wrong. If there is a substantial majority, it is *of course* its interest that the state represents it. Accordingly, even if classic liberalism does not formally endorse the principle of "cuius regio, eius religio," it does not have a sufficiently powerful justification of the neutrality of the state that could counter and run against it.

Historically, *nolens volens* liberalism prepares the ground for nationalism, that gains force precisely at the moment at which in the Peace of Westphalia the sovereignty of the state, that is its independence from external and above all internal influences and interests, as formulated by Hobbes, becomes the foundational principle of international relations.[8] It is in the end the ensuing politics of nation-building that helps to overcome the identity conflicts in civil society.

Rawls argues in *A Theory of Justice* that through the principles of justice and in particular the difference principle "justice as fairness and goodness as rationality are congruent."[9] Although the Rawlsian principles of justice certainly make political obligations more rational than they are in Hobbes' *Leviathan*, Sebastiano Maffettone shows to what extent even such a more elaborated position is problematic. He claims that "there are no guarantees – even assuming that every citizen in a well-ordered

---

[6] Kymlicka, *Politics in the Vernacular*.
[7] Salvatore, "Counterfactuals."
[8] Smith,"Nationalism in Early Modern Europe."
[9] Rawls, *A Theory of Justice*, p. 450.

society has a sense of justice – that the same principles of justice will be rational for all citizens to follow."[10]

15.2 Political Liberalism

The 'liberal neutrality' approach, according to which the state recognizes equally identities in the private sphere and civil society and emancipation is conceived in terms of maximization of individual interests, has limited conceptual sources to put an end to identity conflicts and in the end risks to give rise to majoritarianism and to move conflicts form the religious to the national level, as it occurred in what Eric Hobsbawm calld the long nineteenth century.[11] It was first Rousseau and then Kant who understood the inherent instability of this model, with the first arguing that "man is born free and everywhere he is in chains"[12] and the second complaining "man's self-incurred immaturity."[13]

Rousseau in his *Discourse on Inequality* shows to what extent the passage form the state of nature to the civil state does not reign in and moderate the pursuit of individual interests, but actually accentuates it. It is only in civil society that men develop the sense of *amour propre* and with it the very idea of interests that go beyond mere self-preservation. Civil society is the original locus that instills selfishness and vanity into individuals and therefore enables, allows for and gives rise to relations of domination – just the contrary to what Hobbes believes. As a result, collective identities such as in particular class, gender and religion form only within civil society and are social inventions in order to create distinction, and with it, domination. Rousseau is very explicit in maintaining that identity conflicts are the product and result of civil society, due to a liberal social contract whose unique rationale is the protection of particular individual interests. In a liberal state, identity conflicts become transformed from proper group conflicts into individual conflicts that use group identities for the purpose of domination and political lobbying. Rousseau maintains that despotism is the logical, but also pathological result of this unfettered individualism.

Rousseau's solution is not the return to the multicultural arrangements of premodernity. Rousseau could have concluded that individualism failed and that a political and social order needs to be grounded in given and available collective identities, able to control individuals' rational interests. Rousseau could have invoked the authority of religion in order to rein in selfishness and vanity, endorsing the principle "cuius regio, eius religio" that was prevalent in Europe at his time.

---

[10] Maffettone, *Rawls*, p. 255.
[11] Hobsbawm, *Nations and Nationalism Since 1780*.
[12] Rousseau, *Of the Social Contract*, p. 41.
[13] Kant, *'What is Enlightenment?'*, p. 1.

Rousseau rejects identity politics, not because collective identities do not actually have power over us. As Kant shows in his famous answer to the question "What is Enlightenment?", the contrary is actually true. "Enlightenment is man's emergence from his self-incurred immaturity. Immaturity is the inability to use one's understanding without guidance from another."[14] Far too often do we follow social conventions about how people ought to conduct themselves. Far too often do we follow social scripts or narratives about how people of a certain type ought to conduct themselves. Rousseau does not refute collective identities for their lack of motivational force, but because they violate our *dignity*. As beings endowed with reason, we have the power to give ourselves our own rules, we do not depend upon others for knowing what we have to do. Collective identities risk to actually oppress individuals, keeping them heteronomous rather than promoting their autonomy. This is why Rousseau thinks that building a political order upon collective identities and an already established social order is inherently unstable. Collective identities are not contrary to our interest, as Hobbes claims, but contrary to our morality.

Accordingly, Rousseau proposes a reformulation of the social contract that has a *moral* and not only rational, interest-based foundation. In order to avoid the despotic Leviathan and the dynamics of social domination in the civil state, individuals must be able to govern themselves according to principles they can freely accept and to put their particular, rational interests aside in political and social matters. The question to which Rousseau seeks an answer is therefore the following: "How is a method of associating to be found which will defend and protect – using the power of all – the person and property of each member and still enable each member of the group to obey only himself and to remain as free as before?"[15] And this is Rousseau's solution: "Each of us puts his person and all his power in common under the supreme direction of the general will."[16] Individuals are supposed to have a general will next to their particular will and it is the general will upon which they act in all matters concerning them as *citizens*.

It remains however the question why the general will could not embrace voluntarily social identities or be itself their source. Why could not our reason come to the conclusion that identities after all have their justification and even contain the truth? Why could not the general will correspond to the will of the nation or the values of any other identity group? Why according to Rousseau citizenship cannot be reduced to national identity? Why could not our ethics be particular rather than general? After all a particular ethics is not to be conflated with the self-interest of the particular will and tends to be as much normative as a universal ethics.

Kant provides the answer. An autonomous individual will must follow a universal law that applies to all human beings and not act upon any laws that hold only for particular groups. Following is Kant's formulation: "Act only according to that maxim by which you can at the same time will that it should become a universal

---

[14] Kant, *'What is Enlightenment?'*, p. 1.

[15] Rousseau, *Of the Social Contract*, p. 49–50.

[16] Rousseau, *Of the Social Contract*, p. 50.

law."[17] Reason cannot come up with a law that only Catholics or Frenchmen, for example, can agree upon. Reason cannot simply express the embedded point of view of some group. Reason requires the universal point of view, the view from nowhere, as Thomas Nagel puts it succinctly, its principles must be based upon justifications that each reasonable being can understand and subscribe to. What sort of reason could it be, if not everyone, at least under ideal circumstances and upon due reflections, can come up with the same conclusion with regard to practical principles? Reason seeks objectivity and truth. An identitarian will risks not only to be contradictory, but above all heteronomous: not the product of reason, but the contingent result of tradition, convenience etc..

The general will is universal in the sense that it is not only independent of any collective identity, but is actually directed *against* identities. The general will represents to some extent the very *emancipation* from identity. Kant continues in his leaflet on Enlightenment: "This immaturity is self-imposed when its cause lies not in lack of understanding, but in lack of resolve and courage to use it without guidance from another. Sapere Aude! 'Have courage to use your own understanding!' – that is the motto of enlightenment."[18]

The opposition between identity and emancipation runs like a red thread through Enlightenment liberalism. It consists not in neutrality with regard to identities as in *modus vivendi* liberalism, but in a harsh and violent attack of identities and efforts to erase them. Today this becomes in particular clear in the attacks liberal thinkers such as Ayaan Hirsi Ali, Paul Berman and Christopher Hitchsen run against Islam as a religion.[19] And as I argue in the introduction, even Rawls, who comes to embrace fully pluralism in *Political Liberalism*, recurs with the requirement of public reason to a transcendental conception of reason and as a consequence conceives emancipation in opposition to identity.

15.3 Final Conclusions

At the outset, according to *modus vivendi* liberalism identity and emancipation are pursued independently from each other. Emancipation takes place in the public sphere and identity is lived out in the private sphere. According to political liberalism, on the other hand, emancipation requires overcoming of at least certain identities and stands in opposition to them. From an identiarian point of view, then, *modus vivendi* liberalism is preferable, since if it does not recognize identities as such, it neither opposes them.

The considerations above come to the conclusion that this distinction between *modus vivendi* liberalism and political liberalism is overdrawn. To some extent, the

---

[17] Kant, *Groundwork for the Metaphysics of Morals*, p. 38.
[18] Kant, *'What is Enlightenment?'*, p. 1.
[19] See for instance, Hirsi Ali, *The Caged Virgin*.

analysis shows that the governance approach and its idea that identities can somehow be neutrally governed is rather an illusion. Any form of governance and liberal neutrality risks to be the result of an identitarian point of view. Why do I still side then with *modus vivendi* liberalism, for the time being?

Although, as I show in the chapter on "Liberal Nationalism" and in the third part of the book on 'Identity politics,' I do not want to defend nationalism or any identitarian project, I believe that the governance approach is eventually politically more justifiable and less dangerous than Kantian liberalism. At least it does not *moralize* the subjugation of minority identities in the name of a higher reason and recognizes quite openly Foucault's point that identity politics is not distinguishable from power politics. It makes clear that the domination of certain identities is the result of a political struggle and not of a moral imperative. This insight does of course not alleviate the grievances of the "wretched of the earth," the victims of racism and colonialism, but it helps to understand that oppression is not about them and their identity, but a 'collateral damage' of power politics.

References

Barry, Brian. 2001. *Culture and Equality. An Egalitarian Critique of Multiculturalism*. Cambridge: Polity Press.
Berdal, Mats, and David M. Malone. 2000. *Greed & Grievance. Economic Agendas in Civil Wars*. Boulder: Lynne Reinner.
Collier, Paul & Anke Hoeffler. 2004. Greed and Grievance in Civil War. *Oxford Economic Papers* 56, pp. 563–595.
Ferarra, Alessandro. 2018. How to Accommodate Modus Vivendi Within Normative Political Theory. In *Biblioteca della libertà* LIII (222), May–August 2018, pp. 1–18.
Gellner, Ernest. 1983. *Nations and Nationalism*. London: Blackwell.
Geuss, Raymond. 2008. *Philosophy and Real Politics*. Princeton: Princeton University Press.
Hirsi Ali, Ayaan. 2015. *The Caged Virigin. An Emancipation Proclamation for Women and Islam*. New York: Atria Books.
Hobbes, Thomas. 1985. In *Leviathan*, ed. C.B. Macpherson. London: Penguin.
Hobsbawm, Eric. 1990. *Nations and Nationalism Since 1780. Programme, Myth, Reality*. Cambridge: Cambridge University Press.
Kaldor, Mary. 2012. *New and Old Wars: Organised Violence in a Global Era*. Cambridge: Polity Press.
Kant, Immanuel. 2002. *Groundwork for the Metaphysics of Morals*. Trans. Ed. Allen Wood. New Haven: Yale University Press.
———. 2009. *An Answer to the Question: 'What is Enlightenment?* London: Penguin.
Kaul, Volker. 2007. Diamantenhandel und der Krieg in Kongo/Zaire. *Afrika Spectrum* 42 (1): 49–71.
———. 2016. Foreword: Contemporary Conflicts, Political Legitimacy and Political Islam. In *Toward New Democratic Imaginaries – Istanbul Seminars on Islam, Culture and Politics*, ed. Seyla Benhabib and Volker Kaul. Basel: Springer.
Kymlicka, Will. 2001. *Politics in the Vernacular: Nationalism, Multiculturalism, and Citizenship*. Oxford University Press.
Maffettone, Sebastiano. 2010. *Rawls: An Introdduction*. Cambridge: Polity Press.
McCabe, David. 2010. *Modus Vivendi Liberalism: Theory and Practice*. Cambridge: Cambridge University Press.

Moller Okin, Susan. 1999. *Is Multiculturalism Bad for Women?* Princeton: Princeton University Press.
Pinker, Steven. 2018. *Enlightenment Now: The Case for Reason, Science, Humanism, and progress.* New York: Viking.
Rawls, John. 1993. *Political Liberalism.* New York: Columbia University Press.
———. 1999. *A Theory of Justice.* Revised ed. Cambridge, MA: Belknap Press.
Rousseau, Jean-Jacques. 1994. *Discourse on the Origin of Inequality. Translated by Franklin Philip.* Oxford: Oxford University Press.
———. 1997. *Of the Social Contract and Other Later Political Writings.* Cambridge: Cambridge University Press.
Salvatore, Ingrid. 2012. Counterfactuals. In *A Companion to Political Philosophy*, ed. Antonella Besussi, 91–100. Farnham: Ashgate.
Smith, Anthony. 2005. Nationalism in Early Modern Europe. *History and Theory* 44 (3): 404–415.
William, Gray. 2000. *Two Faces of Liberalism.* Cambridge: Polity Press.
Williams, Bernard. 2005. *In the Beginning Was the Deed. Realism and Moralism in Political Argument.* Princeton: Princeton University Press.

GPSR Compliance

The European Union's (EU) General Product Safety Regulation (GPSR) is a set of rules that requires consumer products to be safe and our obligations to ensure this.

If you have any concerns about our products, you can contact us on

ProductSafety@springernature.com

In case Publisher is established outside the EU, the EU authorized representative is:

Springer Nature Customer Service Center GmbH
Europaplatz 3
69115 Heidelberg, Germany

www.ingramcontent.com/pod-product-compliance
Ingram Content Group UK Ltd.
Pitfield, Milton Keynes, MK11 3LW, UK
UKHW022130220326
11407UKWH00003B/23